Society, Freedom,
and Conscience

Society, Freedom, and Conscience

The American Revolution in Virginia, Massachusetts, and New York

JACK P. GREENE
RICHARD L. BUSHMAN
MICHAEL KAMMEN

EDITED BY Richard M. Jellison

W · W · NORTON & COMPANY

New York · London

All Rights Reserved
Published simultaneously in Canada
by George J. McLeod Limited, Toronto
Printed in the United States of America
Library of Congress Cataloging in Publication Data
Main entry under title:

Society, freedom, and conscience.

"The McClellan lectures on the American Revolution, Miami
University."
Includes bibliographical references and index.
CONTENTS: Greene, J. P. Society, ideology, and politics.—
Bushman, R. L. Massachusetts farmers and the Revolution.—Kam-
men, M. The American Revolution as a crise de conscience.
    1. Virginia—Politics and government—Revolution, 1775–1783—
Addresses, essays, lectures.   2. Massachusetts—Politics and govern-
ment—Revolution, 1775–1783—Addresses, essays, lectures.   3. New
York State—Politics and government—Revolution, 1775–1783—Ad-
dresses, essays, lectures.   I. Jellison, Richard Marion, 1924–   .
II: Greene, Jack P. Society, ideology, and politics. 1976.   III.
Bushman, Richard L. Massachusetts farmers and the Revolution.
1976.   IV. Kammen, Michael G. The American Revolution as a
crise de conscience. 1976.
E263.V8S58   1976   973.3   76-7432
ISBN 0-393-05582-5
ISBN 0-393-09160-0 pbk.

2 3 4 5 6 7 8 9 0

Contents

[v]

The McClellan Lectures on the American
Revolution, Miami University

Society, Freedom,
and Conscience

Introduction

Richard M. Jellison

HISTORIANS have long been fascinated with the study of revolutions. The attraction is not surprising. Revolutions are the lifeblood of history, a constant in the human experience. Few events are more complex or offer greater variation on a single theme than those internal upheavals which occur in the history of nations with such monotonous regularity. Each revolution is an adventure quite unique, yet hauntingly reminiscent of those which have preceded it. As such, rebellions constitute an exquisite challenge to historians, who must puzzle over and evaluate the self-interests which people cleverly mask under justifiable pretenses during periods of extreme tension. And why do people rebel? Does the "morphology" of revolutions reveal a pattern of precipitating factors common to all? Answers to those interesting questions range from the obvious to the arcane. Revolutions have been contrasted, dissected, quantified, and psychoanalyzed! Recent enquiries probing the nature of rebellions have developed new analytical tools which include J curves and relative deprivation models; strange names, such as ad hoc ideology and the catalytic theory of leadership, are assigned to older concepts.[1] But whatever the orientation of the researcher, the purpose of the investigation is always the same: to pare away the irrelevant, reconstruct the essential, and capture the quintessence of the movement.

The American Revolution is a case in point. First of all,

the crescendo of crisis which culminated in political independence is both the most dramatic and the central happen-
ing in American history. For two centuries Americans have
engaged in a continuing and deliberate glorification of those
extraordinary years. No group is more venerated in our society than the versatile architects of the republic, the
founding fathers. No period looms larger in the national
consciousness than the revolutionary era. The process of
recording and interpreting the break with England began
early, with the publication of David Ramsay's two-volume
work in 1789.[2] A few of Dr. Ramsay's contemporaries wondered if an objective appraisal was possible. John Adams
fretted over the absence of essential documents which were
lost forever and doubted that anyone would ever be able to
write an accurate history of the Revolution. But most did
not share his pessimism. Eventually, he, too, became a little
more hopeful as he suggested that "young men of letters"
might search the records for evidence of the "radical
change" in the sentiment of the people which was the "real
American Revolution."[3] Since that time each successive
generation has attempted to reweave the fabric of those
critical years into a more artful and definitive design, con-
voluting new threads with old.

The ever-shifting focus of monographic studies reflects
both changing individual and societal imperatives. Interpretations have fluctuated between the extremes of moralistic
nationalism and a dispassionate neutrality. The Whig, Imperial, Progressive, Conservative, and other "schools" of
thought, and those carefully researched writings that do not
fit into one of those broad designations, are simply too well
known to need recounting here. It is sufficient to observe
that few aspects of political, economic, social, or intellectual life on either side of the Atlantic during the colonial
era have failed to be singled out and judged in the context
of importance to the turmoil of the late eighteenth century.
The result has given us a lengthy bibliography offering a
plethora of explanations about the Revolution, each a little

[4]

different in emphasis but adding a new facet to our knowledge.

And yet, as our understanding increases, so too does the number of unanswered questions. For example, has the Revolution been adequately investigated in the context of a civil war on both sides of the Atlantic? Although the subject of several special investigations, the Loyalists still remain too poorly defined either individually or as a group for final judgments. What was the relationship between religion and revolution? If religion served as a precipitant to rebellion, in what manner was it changed as a result of that event? Consistent with the current interest in social history is the growing demand to assess the role played by the common people, the "inarticulate masses," who left little or no written record of their thought. What part did this large majority play in the Revolution? Is it possible to reconstruct an accurate account of those crucial years by focusing only on the leadership of the elite? Perhaps the most significant development in recent scholarship is the growing concern with divisive issues that were taking shape a century before the eventful years following 1763. Unquestionably the emphasis on long-range problems alters significantly the importance heretofore assigned to more immediate causes as precipitants to conflict by placing them in a different perspective. The ongoing process, the constant need to recast interpretations in the context of new evidence or conceptual frameworks, stands as mute testimony to the enduring ambiguity, the elusive character, of that period of American history. Certainly John Adams correctly anticipated the difficulty historians would encounter in attempting to reconstruct the true story of the Revolution.

The elaborate projects to celebrate the Bicentennial of the Declaration of Independence currently under way or planned for the future have greatly intensified interest in that critical period. Today, not only the historian but also those with the most casual interest in history are moved by national pride to focus momentarily on those venerable events which culminated in the birth of the nation. Although the festivities have a commercial side which promises to inundate the country with cheap mementos of the occasion, most of the programs fall into a more serious and meaningful category. For Miami University the annual McClellan Lectureship [4] offered an excellent opportunity to participate in the commemoration, contribute to historical scholarship, and renew public consciousness of the American heritage. The colonies of Virginia, Massachusetts, and New York were selected as topics for three McClellan lectures to be delivered in 1973, 1974, and 1975. These colonies were singled out because of their strategic geographical position and the significant leadership roles which they played in achieving independence. To deliver these lectures three scholars were invited who were known for their earlier work in colonial American history and whose current research was centered on one of the designated provinces. No effort was made to select scholars who represented a particular point of view or "school" of thought. Although various themes were considered for the series, in the end a non-structured approach was decided upon to permit the McClellan scholar the greatest possible latitude. Each lecturer was free to investigate and develop a significant aspect of the revolutionary years in the colony which was assigned to him. The interpretive essays which appear in this volume result from the several lectures that each McClellan scholar delivered while at Miami University. The articles offer not only important insights into the Revolution but also reveal the nature and thrust of current research in American colonial history. They are excellent examples of the kinds of questions and issues which remain inadequately explored.

From the founding of Jamestown in 1607 to the adoption of the constitution in 1789, Virginia occupied a position of unique importance in colonial affairs. During that period, Virginians exhibited a style and brilliance in political matters that were virtually unequalled in the English colonies. The frequency with which natural leaders appeared among colonial Virginians and the special features in Virginia society that produced and developed such talent have puzzled historians for decades. Jack Greene, the first McClellan lecturer in the current series, provides answers to these important questions in his penetrating analysis of the relationship between society and politics in that colony.[5]

Greene argues that Virginians were nurtured in a society in which political aptitude and achievement in politics were highly prized. As a consequence, Virginians early accepted a code of political behavior, "rules of the game of politics," which exacted a high degree of integrity and exalted those who performed at that level. This was especially true of the gentry, a broad group of diverse elements cemented together by a common denominator of wealth. But while Virginia life was dominated by the gentry, Greene finds that an "inner" group composed of approximately forty interrelated families devoted primarily to plantation agriculture was especially influential. Never constituting more than 5 percent of the total population, the gentry easily assumed leadership in affairs of the colony, filling virtually all positions at every level of government. Surprisingly, domination by this small minority produced little antagonism among the rest of society because of the widespread belief that government was the responsibility of enlightened and capable men. Out of this concept of stewardship, government by talented men was not merely an ideal; it became "a habit of colonial Virginians."

Once the political system was established in the colony it tended to become self-reinforcing. The sense of duty, the political obligation to society, was passed down from father to son among the gentry. The result found third- and fourth-generation Virginians looking less to the accumulation of wealth and more to public service as the area in which to excel. Politics was a major avenue to distinction. Long after the concept of stewardship broke down elsewhere in the British colonies, it remained valid in Virginia, producing a period of general tranquility during much of the eighteenth century. Few of the disruptions which char-

[7]

acterized other colonies—friction between executive and leg-islature, sectional hostilities—were present in Virginia.

Why did the talented and sophisticated gentry produce so little in the form of theoretical writing about political matters? Greene contends that the Virginia gentry simply placed greater importance upon other kinds of activities. Virginia was essentially an "oral" culture; the gentry admired men of action. Jefferson, Madison, Carter (Landon), and Bland are viewed as exceptions in the peculiar Virginia society. Although political leaders did not speculate, they operated within a loose framework of assumptions which were largely English in origin. They acknowledged the imperfection of human beings, finding them often weak, fallible in judgment, and slaves to vanity. A good, well-ordered society required that government restrain people's weaknesses and evil tendencies. Occasionally government itself became a threat to the people, perhaps dominated by a small group determined to introduce despotic measures. In the unique Virginia scheme of political accommodation, regular elections were expected to restore and maintain the desired equilibrium. In the context of this broad consensus, the most important qualities for political leaders to possess were virtue and an independent posture relative to political parties and loyalties. The consensus about "the rules of the game" was sufficiently loose to permit ample room for political maneuvers about how the game should be played.

By the mid-eighteenth century the concepts of virtue and service were firmly rooted in Virginia society. Yet, leaders fretted over two possible threats to the Virginia way. Externally, the imperial government could always insinuate itself in the affairs of the colony and upset, if not destroy, the workable and viable system. Virginians found an equally serious threat internally in the increasing extravagance, the ostentatious manners, which presaged a moral decay that might easily erode the brilliant leadership. Thus, at the close of the French and Indian War, Virginia faced the future with a curious mixture of quiet confidence and anxiety. Greene concludes that the unusual combination greatly influenced Virginians' responses in the fast approaching crisis.

The importance of Boston as a crucible in which incendiary events were fused into rebellion is well documented. From the time of James Otis' opposition to Writs of Assistance in 1761 through the disturbances which characterized the following years, leaders in that city beat a steady cadence of agitation against England. Thus it is not surprising that Bostonians were among the first to raise the standard of revolt and openly challenge the mother country in response to the coercive legislation of 1774. But much of the population of Massachusetts lived outside Boston and its environs. These were the small dirt farmers, most of whom owned land and resided in rural communities of fewer than five thousand inhabitants. Often unrepresented on the committees which ran their villages, they appeared to have little in common with the influential merchant, busy shopkeeper, and widely traveled seaman who so influenced the coastal region. Certainly the disturbances that rocked Boston had not touched the boundaries of the small towns directly. What, then, did the farmers feel about the drift of events on the eve of revolution? Were they truly attuned to the rhetoric of rebellion? Were they involved in the revolutionary movement because of abstract rights, or motivated by direct issues? Or were they perhaps led to a posture of rebellion by the adroit orchestration of the Boston voices of protest? What did the Revolution really mean to farmers? These important questions stake out the parameters of Richard Busman's penetrating essay tracing the evolution of a revolutionary mentality in rural Massachusetts.[6]

Although the small towns and farm communities in the colony were clearly in support of the patriot cause, Bushman observes that until 1772 farmers were chiefly passive participants in the movement. To that date, agitation was centered in and around Boston. Not until 1774 did farmers shed their passivity and adopt an active role, an event which helped turn Massachusetts into a "tinderbox." Bushman argues that the nature and extent of this change may be accurately judged by the responses of the various towns to the "Boston pamphlet." Prepared by a committee of twenty-one, the pamphlet proclaimed the rights of the colonists against political encroachment and was distributed to the towns of the province for a reaction. As the replies came in, Boston leaders were happy to discover a sophisticated understanding of the constitutional issues involved and broad agreement with the position taken by the authors of the "Boston pamphlet." In this fashion a network of activists was created from the small towns of the colony, harping on revolutionary themes and tied to Boston leaders by fears which they all shared. The replies reveal that farmers were moved not by mere abstractions but by real fears that their way of life, their very freedom, was threatened by imperial policies.

Slavery and tyranny were chief catchwords in the farmers' lexicon that reminded them of similar threats faced by earlier colonists. Certainly New England had received a foretaste of tyranny under Governor Edmund Andros nearly a century before. Accused of bringing strangers to New England who wished to exact a profit from the area and thereby impoverish the people, Andros was thoroughly hated. But the fear was based upon antecedents which extended beyond James II and the Dominion of New England and was perhaps more English than American in origin. Carefully tracing this widespread belief, Bushman finds that out of the deep-seated fear of enslavement evolved a "vernacular sociology" that was understood in all corners of the colony. To speak of enslavement or use words associated with the process instantly triggered a scenario in which guilt was assigned and predetermined roles acted out. The social dynamics of the drama decreed that rulers were greedy and therefore certain to extort both wealth and political rights from the people. If unchecked, enslavement was sure to follow. The outline offered sufficient latitude to include bishops when proposals were made for an Anglican episcopate in Massachusetts. Priests were little different from political rulers and, given the same opportunities, were just as anxious for personal gain. Bushman also finds that the currency problems of the colony fit comfortably into the farmers' programmed view.

Here, then, is an explanation of why Massachusetts farmers fought and what the Revolution meant to them. A recognition of the importance of feudal images—the manner in which the fear of lordship and vassalage functioned as a cohesive agent binding all groups in the colony to a common course of action—is crucial to an understanding of Massachusetts on the eve of revolution. For this reason, Richard Bushman's carefully developed essay adds an important ingredient to our understanding of that event.

The third and final article in the series, written by Michael Kammen,[7] illuminates one of several dimensions of the Revolution which remain largely ignored. Citing problems of contradictory evidence and conflicting interpretations, Kammen reviews recent literature about the Revolution, particularly works by authors stressing the importance of ideology (Bailyn) and those emphasizing political economy (Jensen), and concludes that both groups have been far too selective in examining evidence to establish a fully persuasive case. The primary difficulty with accounts of this nature is that they ignore a large part of the colonial population. Suggesting that the revolutionary historiography has a three-dimensional geometry, Kammen points to the significance of research which emphasizes the vast numbers of Americans who were simply reluctant to commit themselves to either side until the conflict actually touched their lives.

With New York as the locus for his investigation, Kammen acknowledges the importance of recent efforts to clarify the role of the Loyalists. But even these works do not tell the story of the Revolution in terms of the agonizing commitments that the conflict mandated for people who wished to remain loyal to several relationships. How did Americans handle the problem of multiple allegiances? In what manner were priorities established and coordinated for several loyalties to which Americans felt obligated?

How many on the American side were indecisive, or only sometime partisans? Here, one is again confronted with a few of the many countercurrents that characterize the revolutionary epoch and make it one of the most complicated in American history.

Kammen is particularly concerned with the question of involuntary allegiance which often resulted from compulsory oath-taking. Although oath-swearing had become a subject of controversy, oaths were still viewed as a serious matter in the highly charged political atmosphere of the 1760s and 1770s. Indeed the practice was of crucial importance to patriots reluctant to recognize neutrality as an option during the conflict. Inevitably in those trying times religion and politics often complicated the question of conscience. This was certainly the case after 1776, when neutrality was viewed in a pejorative light by an increasing number of New Yorkers. The creation of a committee of enquiry, in September of that year, headed by the energetic John Jay, dramatically signaled the change in attitude. It was precisely at that moment, Kammen argues, that the Revolution became a crisis of conscience. As a consequence, New Yorkers methodically equated non-juring with disloyalty to the colony and the new nation. In other instances refusal to bear arms or having held a Crown-appointed office were assumed to be manifestations of disloyalty. Safety of the province seemed to justify neighbor spying on neighbor. Patriots paid little attention to the fact that, at times, citizens were denied the protection provided by the new constitution prepared by the convention sitting at Kingston. The majority of Americans were, in a sense, placing duty and security above the inviolability of conscience. It was an ominous turn of events. But Kammen is quick to note that New Yorkers did not have a monopoly on restricting conscience. For much the same reason, the British were equally insensitive on this issue.

An understanding of the general problems of allegiance not only isolates and highlights compelling factors that influenced the large body of inhabitants in New York but contributes key pieces, heretofore missing, to a coherent picture of the Revolution. The surprisingly large number of New Yorkers who fought on both sides during the course of the war and the scores who swore not one but several contradictory oaths are indicative of the depth of those issues. The degree to which those practices violated tender consciences and helped to shape the courses of events in the colony and nation is central to Kammen's provoking enquiry.

No doubt the revolutionary era will continue to lure historians so long as new evidence exists or further permutations of those events are possible. Perhaps scholars will always feel a need to rewrite and reinterpret the history of those years, modifying and augmenting to comply with the dictates of contemporary thought. But for most Americans knowledge about the Revolution and the winning of independence serves a reinforcing function, contributing a deeper appreciation of the past and a source from which meaning is extrapolated to the present. It is hoped that this volume will serve readers at both levels. Admittedly, the three essays about Virginia, Massachusetts, and New York are far too brief, too specialized to encompass all of the significant issues in which scholars are interested. And yet, considered as a composite, the book possesses an unexpected symmetry. When colonial America is viewed in the context of problems incident to society, freedom, and conscience, the unique experiences of one colony tend to reflect to a remarkable degree, if not duplicate, issues common to all. In this manner, Greene, Bushman, and Kammen not only make their own unique contributions, but sharpen the focus on works previously published and point the way for researchers in the future.

Certainly they add significant detail to the emerging mosaic of the birth of the nation.

Society, Ideology, and Politics:
An Analysis of the
Political Culture of
Mid-Eighteenth-Century Virginia*

✠

Jack P. Greene

1

OVER the past two centuries, few commentators on the era of the American Revolution have failed to appreciate Virginia's preeminent contribution of political talent to that period, a contribution that has perhaps never been equalled by any other state at any other point in American history. What has been less appreciated, and only imperfectly understood, however, is that this extraordinary flowering of talents was not simply an accident of history and that the high quality of Virginia political leadership derived quite as much from a viable political culture as from the individual talents of its practitioners. The brilliant assemblage of gifted politicians associated with revolutionary Virginia— Patrick Henry and George Washington, George Mason and Thomas Jefferson, James Madison and John Marshall are only the most conspicuous examples—brought much more than their own individual geniuses to the momentous events between 1763 and 1789. Trained in a functional political system that had been tested and refined by a century and a half of experience and coming out of a tradition of superior political leadership that was of more than two generations standing, they brought as well an intimate knowledge of day-to-day politics in a society where politics was an old and laudable pursuit. Perhaps of equal importance, they came with a deep commitment to a code of political behavior and a political ideology that was peculiarly well suited to meet the demands of a revolutionary situation. That commitment governed their relationships with one another and with leaders from other places and determined to a remarkable extent the nature of their responses to the successive problems of their generation. To identify the code and the ideology to which they were committed—the rules of the game of politics as it had come to be played in mid-eighteenth-century Virginia—and to elaborate the social circumstances and political conditions that underlay them are necessary first steps toward understanding Virginia's extraordinary contribution to the foundation of the American nation.

II

The key to any comprehension of the politics of colonial Virginia is that unusual group referred to by contemporaries as the "Virginia gentry." In its largest meaning, the term *gentry* referred to a broad and miscellaneous category of people: old families and new, those of great and only modest wealth, mannered gentlefolk and crude social upstarts, the learned and the ignorant. As the dissenter James Reid, an obscure but effective social satirist, said of the gentry of King William County in the 1760s, any person who had "Money, Negroes and Land enough" was automatically considered a gentleman so that even a person "looked upon as . . . unworthy of a Gentleman's notice because he had no Land and Negroes" could, if "by some means or other, [he] acquired both," become "a Gentleman all of a sudden." What Reid's remarks underline is that the only common denominator among all of the members of the broad *social category* of gentry was possession of more than ordinary wealth. Within that broad category, however, was a much smaller, cohesive, and self-conscious *social group*, at the core of which were about forty interrelated families that had successfully competed with other immigrants for wealth and power through the middle decades of the seventeenth century and consolidated their position between 1680 and 1730. Initially, their fortunes had been derived from a wide variety of sources—planting, shipping, commerce, land development, public office, the law—but by the early decades of the eighteenth century, plantation agriculture—specifically, tobacco culture—had become the most prestigious economic pursuit. Members of this inner gentry continued to engage in a variety of subsidiary or auxiliary enterprises, and some even spent more of their energies in commerce or at the bar than in managing their estates. But almost all of them were heavily involved in planting, and, although by the 1740s and 1750s antiquity of family was also becoming of some consequence, possession of large holdings of land and slaves was perhaps the most visible symbol of membership of the group. Because wealth in a rapidly expanding economy was available to most enterprising men and, especially after 1730, to the lawyers who were needed in large numbers to handle an ever-increasing volume of land and business transactions, the inner gentry was continuously replenished from below and without, and the social structure remained open throughout the colonial and revolutionary periods. There was always room for the ambitious, talented, and successful from among both new immigrants and scions of the older yeomanry, and frequent marriages between families with new wealth and those of the older gentry meant that assimilation was quick and easy.[1]

The gentry dominated virtually every phase of life in the colony. Its members created with the use of slaves and large units of production a disproportionate amount of the colony's wealth, frequently served as entrepreneurs for smaller producers in their immediate areas, and stimulated the growth of the colony by their activities in land development. In politics, they early assumed leadership, filling almost all posts of responsibility at every level of government from the governor's Council and the elective House of Burgesses down to the county courts and the parish vestries. In social and intellectual life, they were the unquestioned leaders, defining the preferred social roles and the dominant values, setting the style of life to which all ambitious Virginians aspired, providing, as the young New Jersey tutor Philip Fithian observed in 1773, "the pattern of all behaviour." [2]

Although the gentry was preeminent in Virginia life and was probably, as the English traveler J. F. D. Smyth noted in the 1780s, more numerous than its equivalents in other colonies, it never constituted more than a small percentage of the total population. If the category is defined as the larger plantation owners and their families—a definition that would include all of the larger merchants and the wealthier and more important lawyers—it probably did not comprise much over 2 to 5 percent of the total white inhabitants, with the inner gentry group comprising no more than a fraction, perhaps a fifth, of the whole category. Beneath the gentry was a numerous miscellany of people that contemporaries customarily divided into two ranks—a very large middle rank consisting of the less affluent planters, independent yeoman farmers, and rural artisans and tradesmen, who together with their families seem to have comprised the bulk of the white population in every Virginia county; and an apparently smaller lower rank, landless overseers and agricultural laborers, many of them young or just out of their indentures, who, according to travelers, were seldom miserable and were fewer "in number, in proportion to the rest of the inhabitants, than perhaps [in] any other country in the universe." [3]

If there was little real poverty among white people in colonial Virginia, there were nonetheless great extremes in wealth, and traveler after traveler was impressed, as was Smyth, by the "greater distinction supported between the different classes of life" in Virginia than in most of the other colonies. Just how this distinction affected the inner dynamics of Virginia society, the relations between the various social groups, is not an easy matter to determine. Smyth thought that that "spirit of equality, and levelling principle" which pervaded "the greatest part of America" did not "prevail to such an extent in Virginia," and Fithian testified in the early 1770s that the "amazing property" of the gentry so tended to blow "up the owners to an imagination, which is visible in all, but in various degrees according to their respective virtue, that they are exalted as much above other Men in worth & precedency, as blind stupid fortune has made a difference in their property." [4] To many outsiders Virginia seemed to be patently aristocratic. The Massachusetts lawyer Josiah Quincy, Jr., found that Virginia in 1773 was diffused with an "aristocratical spirit and principle," and the Marquis de Chastellux, an officer in the French forces during the War for Independence, was convinced that "the national character [of], the very spirit of government" in, Virginia was and would "always be aristocratic." [5]

Though members of the gentry seem neither to have described nor to have thought of themselves as aristocrats—a word they held in the utmost abhorrence because of its pejorative connotations of rule by a small, legally privileged group for their own private ends—there is no lack of evidence that they consciously asserted their social superiority over and marked themselves off from the rest of society by their fine dress, splendid "equipages," stately houses, "polish'd conversation," genteel bearing, and, increasingly, sumptuous life style. The gentry invariably "rode in Coaches, or Chariots, or on fine horses," and only "the very elevated sort" wore finery imported from London or "Perukes." Virginians of all classes might take pride in their celebrated hospitality to friends and strangers. But only the wealthy could afford the "lavish entertainments, often lasting for days" to which the gentry turned for diversion.[6] Moreover, frequent references to the lower rank as the "vulgar herd," "common herd," or "ignorant Vulgar" suggest that the gentry shared the traditional disregard for the abilities and worth of the poorer segments of society that was so universal among western European elites before and even after the elevation of "the people" by the French Revolution. Although they might not all have approved his characteristically intemperate choice of language, few of his equals in Virginia or elsewhere would probably have disagreed with the judgment of Colonel Landon Carter of Sabine Hall, one of the leading members of one of the largest and most respected Virginia families, that there was little about the generality of mankind to be admired and that some of them were "but Idiots." [7]

Whether this attitude was matched at the other end of society by that envy of the rich that modern social analysts have come to expect from the poor is less easy to establish. The lower sort, quite obviously, left few records of their aspirations and resentments, but there was at least some suspicion among the gentry that, as Landon Carter phrased it in response to a poetic election attack on him, there was "something in a good Estate, which those who don't enjoy, will ever hate." There were also some poorer sorts like the Reverend Devereux Jarratt, a carpenter's son, who remembered in his old age that as a small boy he had regarded the "*gentle folks*, as beings of a superior order" and "kept off at a humble distance." Still others who, like the growing group of dissenting Baptists after 1760, found the life style of the more crude and dissolute segments of the gentry thoroughly reprehensible, reviled the gentry as "men brought up in ignorance, nourished in pride, encouraged in luxury, taught inhumanity and self conceit, tutored in debauchery, squandering youth either in idleness, or in acquiring knowledge which ought to be forgot, illiterate, untinctured by sentiment, untouched by virtues of humanity." [8] Most remaining evidence, however, indicates that deference and respect, not envy and resentment or fear and obsequiousness, were the conventional attitudes of the rest of Virginia society toward the gentry. How many people shared the pride in the gentry exhibited by the York County blacksmith—and erstwhile poet—Charles Hansford is not clear. "Who can but love the place that hath brought forth/ Such men of virtue, merit, honor, worth?" rhymed Hansford in 1752:

> The gentry of Virginia, I dare say,
> For honor vie with all America.
> Had I great Camden's skill, how freely I
> Would celebrate our worthy gentry."[9]

Economic inequality does not, however, seem to have resulted in any deep or widespread social or political antagonisms toward the gentry, at least not before the 1760s. A remarkably wide franchise that extended even to tenants who rented the requisite amount of land;[10] a fluid social structure with a vital upper stratum that not only was always eager to receive but also was constantly searching out new talents and new abilities; the scattering of tenants, yeomen, small planters, and gentlemen amongst one another in every section of the colony; and frequent interchanges among people of all social classes at church, court days, horse races, cockfights, militia musters, and elections—all seem both to have precluded the development of a rigidly stratified social system and to have promoted free and easy intercourse among all groups in the society. Moreover, the fact that tobacco was the lifeblood of the entire economy and every segment of society meant that disparity of economic interests among people of various social categories was rare. Richard Bland, perhaps the most impressive political thinker in mid-eighteenth-century Virginia and also member of an old gentry family, accurately characterized the situation when he wrote in 1745 that he would "always act to the utmost of my capacity for the good of my electors, whose interest and my own, in great measure, are inseparable."[11]

The traditional portrait of colonial Virginia as dominated by a small body of privileged aristocrats who ruled by overawing and closely controlling the rest of society derives, one suspects, less from the society itself than from the romantic writings of later historians like Edmund Randolph and, especially, William Wirt. Committed to a post-1789 Jeffersonian view of the American Revolution that had borrowed its language and symbolism from the French, rather than the American, Revolution, they felt compelled to show that their Revolution had been revolutionary too, that, like the French Revolution, it had unleashed the people by breaking the hold of a privileged aristocracy.[12] But even while Randolph and Wirt were writing there were older Virginians who recognized the inaccuracy of their characterization. One of these was Judge St. George Tucker, who had immigrated to Virginia from Bermuda in the early 1770s and had become a leading figure at the bar. He objected vigorously in 1815 to Wirt's "exaggerated" portrait of colonial Virginia society, denying that there was any "such thing as Dependence" of the rest of society upon the gentry "except in the case of overseers" and declaring that he had never found any "expression of *Jealousy* towards the rich" among "what is called the *yeomanry*." Rather, he observed, the "rich . . . never failed to pull off their hats to a poor man whom they met, and generally, appear'd to me to shake hands with every man in a Court-yard, or a Church-yard, and as far as I could judge the planter who own'd half a dozen negroes felt himself perfectly upon a level with his rich neighbor that own'd an hundred." If the Virginia gentry were aristocrats, he emphasized, they were certainly "*harmless aristocrats*" in no sense "*embodied*" and without any "Inclination, to do any political Injury." [13] Tucker's observations accord with the impressions of most contemporary travelers, who, even when, like Chastellux, they were impressed with the aristocratic character of Virginia, never remarked upon either any explicit conflict among the several social categories or the "dependence" of the middle and lower ranks upon the gentry. Chastellux, in fact, found the freedom and independence of the ordinary white property-owning Virginian one of the most striking features of the society. "A Virginian," he noted, "never resembles a European peasant: he is always a free man, who has a share in the government, and the command of a few Negroes." By thus uniting "in himself the two distinct qualities of citizen and master," the Virginian, Chastellux thought, enjoyed a place in society far above that of the bulk of men throughout the rest of the world and closely resembled those "individuals who formed what were called *the people* in the ancient republics." Unlike their equivalents in the old world, the vast majority of adult white males in Virginia and, for that matter, all of British colonial America, were neither burdened with poverty nor deprived of a right to participate in government. [14]

III

Some of the cement of this relatively harmonious relationship between the gentry and the rest of society was supplied by the related concepts of stewardship and order. Frequent observations by travelers and Virginians alike on the indolence of the lesser gentry and the middle and lower ranks in the colony with their fondness for society and their addiction to pleasure suggest that apathy may have been the primary reason why men from those ranks failed to play a more prominent role in political life.[15] But a factor of enormous importance was the widespread belief among Virginians at all levels of society that government should be reserved for and was the responsibility of enlightened and capable men. "The happiness of mankind," Reverend David Griffith, Anglican rector of Shelburne Parish, declared in a sermon before the Virginia Convention in 1776, "depends, in a great measure, on the well ordering of society," while order, in turn, depended upon a necessary "subordination in society." However complex the economic and social divisions in colonial Virginia, there were only two orders in politics. All society was divided between the rulers and the ruled, and, although the line of separation was neither very sharply nor very rigidly drawn, the habit of equating the rulers with "Gentlemen of Ability and Fortune" had the sanction of a long tradition that stretched back well beyond the original settlement of the colonies to Antiquity. Although the gentry never pretended to have an "exclusive title to common sense, wisdom or integrity" and insisted upon the "right" of all "orders of men" to "assume the character of politicians," men of "High Birth and Fortune," as one anonymous writer, perhaps the Reverend Jonathan Boucher, pointed out in 1774, did have "the solid and splendid advantages of education and accomplishments; extensive influence, and incitement to glory." Because they also had "a greater Stake in the Country" and enjoyed a "larger Property," the Reverend William Stith of the College of William and Mary declared in a sermon before the House of Burgesses in 1752, they were naturally "bound . . . to be more studious of that Country's Good." The conclusion followed almost irresistibly that they were, therefore, the proper persons to entrust with the political leadership of the country.[16]

On the other hand, those in the middle and lower ranks, who, it was assumed, lacked the talent, wisdom, training, time, or interest for politics, were expected, as Lieutenant Governor William Gooch put it in the early 1730s, to live as honest men, mind their own business, fear God, honor the King, make good tobacco, shun those "given to Noise and Violence," and "Submit . . . to every Law." The liberty of the governed depended, in fact, declared Reverend James Horrocks, also of the College, in 1763, upon "a dutiful Obedience to the Laws of our Country, and those [of] our Superiors, who have the Care of them." The alternative, he suggested, was no less than complete licentiousness, a state in which those handmaidens of the happy state—"Liberty and public Safety"—actually became enemies instead of allies to each other. There was, then, in society no antagonism but, as David Griffith observed, *a mutual obligation . . . between the governed and their rulers.* That obligation consisted in a reciprocal promise, a kind of covenant, to which all free white inhabitants were a party by which the rulers—those "virtuous and enlightened citizens" whose numbers were small in every community—were to provide good government and the governed were to obey them.[17]

Government by the "virtuous and enlightened" was not only the ideal but also, to a remarkable degree, the habit of colonial Virginians. Members of the native gentry occupied almost all important appointive posts. Right up to 1776, the Crown regularly chose them for all Crown offices except the governorship and lieutenant governorship as well as for its twelve-man Council, which throughout the middle decades of the eighteenth century was for the most part "composed of some very respectable characters." Similarly, governors invariably selected the gentry for justices of the peace, sheriffs, militia officers, and other positions in county government. Within the counties, the critical areas where the values of the community were enforced, the gentlemen justices of the peace had complete authority to administer the laws and dispense justice. Particular status and responsibility attached to membership in the *quorum*, that inner circle of justices designated by the governor from among the most esteemed men in the county whose presence was required in all "Matters of Importance." Charged with the heavy responsibility of doing "equal Right to all Manner of People, Great and Small, High and Low, Rich and Poor, according to Equity, and good Conscience, and the Laws and Usages of . . . Virginia, without Favour, Affection, or Partiality," all magistrates, and especially members of the quorum, said the handbook which described and directed them in the execution of their responsibilities, were supposed to be:

> . . . Men of Substance and Ability of Body and Estate; of the best Reputation, good Governance, and Courage for the Truth; Men fearing God, not seeking the Place for Honour or Conveniency, but endeavouring to preserve the Peace and good Government of their Country, wherein they ought to be resident; Lovers of Justice, judging the People equaly and impartially at all Seasons, using Diligence in hearing and de-

termining Causes, and not neglecting the Public Service for private Emploiment, or Ease; of known Loialty to the King, not respecting Persons, but the Cause; and they ought to be Men of competent Knowledge in the Laws of their Country, to enable them to execute their Office and Authority to the Advancement of Justice, the Benefit of the People, and without Reproach to themselves."

Moreover, the freeholders regularly exercised their liberty of choice to select gentrymen to represent them in Williamsburg in the elective House of Burgesses, the only institution of government elected by the voters in Virginia and by the 1750s certainly more powerful and perhaps more prestigious even than the royal Council.[18]

Because the small size of the Council excluded all but a few from a seat in it, the pinnacle of success for most of the politically ambitious among the gentry was a position of leadership in the House of Burgesses. To reach such a position a man had to go through a process of rigorous selection. First, he had to have the approval and the backing of the leading local gentry. Individuals without such approval often sought and occasionally won election, but because of the long and vital tradition of gentry leadership the sanction of community leaders was usually a decisive advantage. Moreover, the gentry tended to select from among its numbers not the gamesters or the spendthrifts, not those whom the Reverend John Camm, the contentious Anglican rector of Yorkhampton Parish, derisively referred to as "decayed gentry" or James Reid cruelly lampooned as "Assqueers," but the men they most admired; and those they most admired were those who most successfully adhered to the most cherished—the most deeply held—values of the group. The man who was "best esteemed and most applauded," Fithian found, was the one who attended "to his business . . . with the greatest diligence," and it was not only diligence but a whole congeries of related qualities—honesty and generosity, "probity and great Integrity," moderation and humility, courage and impartiality, learning and judgment, "Circumspection & frugality"—that recom-

[25]

mended a man to his neighborhood peers.[19]

The broad body of freeholders, the next hurdle on the path to political preferment, seem routinely to have looked for the same qualities. Of course, few candidates, no matter how impressive their other qualities, could expect to secure election if they were personally disagreeable to the voters. Only the most secure candidate did not find it necessary "to lower himself a little" to secure election. "Swilling the planters with bumbo," "Barbecues," and other forms of "treating" paid for by the "friends" of the candidates—for candidates themselves were strictly prohibited by law from engaging openly in such activities—were common practices at elections. "At an election," said one caustic observer, "the merits of a Candidate are always measured by the number of his treats; his constituents assemble, eat upon him, and lend their applause, not to his integrity or sense, but [to] the quantities of his beef and brandy." But character and distinction rather than "Bribery" or a willingness to "cajole, fawn, and wheedle" before the populace seem to have been the characteristics that most frequently recommended men to the electorate. The freeholders understood, as a popular handbook for justices of the peace put it, both that the House of Burgesses was "one of the main Fundamentals of our Constitution, and the chief Support of the Liberty and Property of the Subject" and that, "considering the great Trust reposed in every Representative of the People in General Assembly," "every Freeholder" should "give his vote for Persons of Knowledge, Integrity, Courage, Probity, Loialty, and Experience, without Regard to Personal Inclination or Prejudice." Enjoined by the election law to choose "Two of the most fit and able Men" among them for their representatives, the freeholders regularly returned the same men whom the leading gentry also found most suitable.[20]

Perhaps the best contemporary analysis of the "Humours of a Virginia Election," of voting behavior and voter preferences, is *The Candidates*, a didactic farce written in 1770 by Robert Munford, himself a burgess for Mecklenburg

County. In this play there are five candidates. The freeholders initially seem to be most favorably disposed toward
the three who themselves most "love[d] diversion": Sir John
Toddy, a likable sot and a vivid example of Camm's "decayed gentry," as well as Strutabout and Smallhopes, a pair
of ignorant and ostentatious social upstarts who seek to secure votes by keeping "the liquor . . . running." When all
of the votes are tallied, however, the freeholders have
chosen the two obviously superior candidates: Worthy, a
gentleman of unquestionable distinction, and Wou'dbe, a
"man of sense, and . . . larning." Worthy is clearly one of
those men celebrated by Charles Hansford

> . . . whose genius seems design'd
> For legislators and to keep mankind
> Within the bounds of reason and justice.
> This is a province which is very nice
> And difficult, yet of the greatest use;
> For men too often liberty abuse.
> Bounds must be set to mankind, or else they
> From justice and morality will stray.
> 'Tis difficult to make such laws, be sure
> That vice be punish'd, liberty secure.
> But yet Virginia yieldeth some of these
> Whose penetrating judgment searches, sees
> As far as human prudence will extend,
> Good laws to make, and people's morals mend.

Not every county had a Worthy to send to Williamsburg,
but all had sober and sensible gentrymen of good parts like
Wou'dbe. Of course, *The Candidates* was clearly inspired
by instances in which the freeholders had not behaved in
the prescribed manner and was intended to recall them to a
proper sense of their responsibilities. Most of the time, however, Virginia freeholders, like Munford's imaginary ones,
seem to have borne out the judgment of the Scottish philosopher David Hume that the "lower sort of people and small
proprietors are good judges enough of one not very distant
from them" and would, therefore, in local elections "probably chuse the best, or nearly the best representative." By

one means or another, lesser men might occasionally win election. But only men of unusual merit and responsibility could expect to continue to enjoy the support of their constituents in the long run.[21]

But even after a man had obtained election he still had to undergo an even more exacting scrutiny within the House of Burgesses. Of the many called to that body, only a few were chosen for leadership. In the Burgesses, as in most large assemblies or societies, a few men, as the German traveler Johann David Schoepf found in the 1780s, led the debate and thought and spoke for the rest. The Burgesses was the theater for political talents, and only those who turned in superb performances could expect to secure a leading role. Men with special qualities or skills that set them off from their fellows had a decided advantage, and it was usually those with thorough legal training, good education and clear and refined ideas, an impressive command of language, a brilliant oratorical style, a capacity for business, unusual personal charm, or some combination of these characteristics who played the most active and influential roles, who were singled out by their fellows, the demands of the institution, and their own qualities for the pinnacle of Virginia political life.[22]

The very ideal of government by extraordinary men imposed an enormous obligation upon the ruling group in colonial Virginia. Acceptance of the office of burgess—of the designation as one of the "ablest" in the community meant, for instance, that one accepted the responsibility not only to represent his constituents but also to work, as Munford put it in *The Candidates*, "for wholesome laws" and his "country's cause." To be sure, there were men who sought office simply to gratify their ambition—which in the eighteenth century generally connoted an insatiable thirst for wealth and power. Like the unnamed object of attack in the anonymous Virginia political tract *A Defense of Injur'd Merit Unmasked*, they were "swayed by avarice, and spurr'd on in" their "ambitious views to obtain a place of profit, whereby to gratify that insatiable passion . . .

avarice." Even the most devoted public servants could scarcely be expected not to consider the direct economic and social benefits in the form of access to public lands, special business or professional advantages, lucrative public offices, or higher social status that might be the incidental by-products of political office. But the point is that they were incidental and by the mid-eighteenth century were becoming increasingly so. However important such consideration may have been in the gentry's formative period from 1660 to 1730, most of the older gentry families were so well established by 1740 that they could have obtained whatever economic benefits they sought through social and family connections without taking on what Munford's character Wou'dbe correctly described as the "troublesome and expensive employment" of public office. And it was the older families that set the pattern of behavior for the rest of the gentry. Clearly, one has to look elsewhere for the primary motives that impelled the gentry into politics in the late colonial and revolutionary periods.[23]

Perhaps the most important element in the gentry's assumption of political leadership was the commitment to the notion built into the concept of stewardship that it was not merely the right but the duty of the social and economic leaders of society to exercise the responsibilities of government. In the best tradition of the English country gentlemen, the Virginia gentry labored tirelessly at the routine and tedious business of governing in the county courts, the parish vestries, the House of Burgesses, and various local offices—offices that were "Attended with a certain Expense and trouble without the least prospect of gain"—not primarily to secure the relatively small tangible economic rewards they derived from their efforts but rather to fulfill the deep sense of public responsibility thrust upon them by their position in society. That all good men should concern themselves with the welfare of their country lay at the very center of the value structure of the gentry, and when George Washington expressed his strong "Sense of Obligations to the People" to do everything in his "power for the

Hon'r and Welfare of the Country" upon his first election to the House of Burgesses from Frederick County in 1758, he was merely subscribing to a time-honored belief. "It *surely* is the duty of every man who has abilities," observe Wou'dbe in *The Candidates*, "to serve his country, to take up the burden, and bear it with patience." [24]

Nor were the gentry's burdens limited to the chores of government. Upon them fell the task of providing social models and moral leadership for their respective communities. As the magistrates for the counties, the gentry was obligated, Governor Gooch declared, to give the rest of the people "all the Light they" could "into the Intent and Meaning" of the laws, which were "the Peoples Direction in moral Actions." As "Gentlemen and Persons of Dictinction" they were expected, William Stith declared in a sermon against gaming in 1752, "by their Example to lead" the "lower people . . . on to every thing, that is virtuous and honest, and with the utmost Severity of the Law to restrain and punish" vice and dishonesty. Nothing would ever affect "the Generality of the People," he added, if it were "contradicted by the Lives and Conversations . . . of their rich and powerful Neighbors." Landon Carter agreed that it was the obligation of the "polite and more considerable part" of society to set "Patterns and examples" for and give "Prudent advice and assistance to" the rest of the community, and he was convinced that there was nothing more commendable than "to let men see our good works that they may take example by them in their conduct to each other and to the happiness and safety of their Country." Charles Hansford underlined the importance and spelled out the nature of this obligation in verse in the early 1750s:

> A gentleman is placed so that he
> In his example cannot neuter be:
> He's always doing good or doing harm.
> And should not this a thinking man alarm?
> If he lives ill, the vulgar will him trace;
> They fancy his example theirs will grace.
> Many are fond to imitate a man
> That is above their class; their little span

Of knowledge they consult not. In the way
Their betters walk, they think they safely may.
Thus, both are wrong but may, perhaps, be lost,
And all God's goodness disappointed, cross'd.
For, sure, His goodness always should be prais'd
By those He hath above the vulgar rais'd.
'Tis most ungrateful not to bless that hand
By which we are plac'd above the crowd to stand.

Contrariwise, when gentry do live well,
Their bright example is a kind of spell
Which does insensibly attract the crowd
To follow them in virtue's pleasant road.
In such a way who would not take delight
To see gentry and commons both unite?
This would true honor to our gentry bring,
And happiness to all would flow and spring.
We find example is of greater force
Than the most famous clergyman's discourse.
None will deny the assertion to be true:
Example always precept will outdo.

How widely diffused and generally accepted these notions were is indicated by the remarks of the Presbyterian divine Samuel Davies, the most influential dissenting minister in Virginia in the 1750s and himself only on the fringes of the colony's establishment, to the Hanover volunteers during the Seven Years' War. Emphasizing the obligation of the gentleman-officers to "enforce Religion and good Morals by your Example and Authority" and to "suppress the Contrary," he argued that "Such a Conduct" would render them "popular among the Wise and Good" and would bring them no other censure than "the senseless Contempt of Fools." [25]

Among the gentry, fathers sought to instill this strong sense of social duty—this powerful commitment to public service—in their sons from a very young age. They took deliberate care to transmit the political values, ideals, and attitudes of the group and to nurture that devotion to the public good that was the mark of all gentlemen of distinction. One of the most important elements in the education of young gentlemen was the constant exposure to the inner workings of governmental institutions and their early involvement in discussions of political and judicial affairs. Their study was purposely oriented towards politics and the law. Because laws, one writer said in the *Virginia Gazette* in 1745, were "the Ties of harmonious Society, and Defence of Life, Liberty, and Property against arbitrary Power, Tyranny, and Oppression," they were obviously worth intensive study. The gentry, wrote one unfriendly observer, "diligently search the Scriptures; but the Scriptures which they search are the Laws of Virginia: for though you may find innumerable families in which there is no Bible, yet you will not find one without a Law-book." "Bring [up] any Subject from Mercer's abridgement [of the laws of Virginia], and the youngest in Company will immediately tell you how far a grin is actionable." Thus did fathers encourage their sons to prepare themselves for their public responsibilities. Landon Carter urged his son Robert Wormeley to study the laws of the colony so that he might ready himself for the day when he would be "in a Capacity to lend a hand towards their improvement or support." By the time they had reached manhood, sons of the gentry had an intimate knowledge of the Virginia political process and thorough preparation for the tasks of government and community leadership, and the politically ambitious among them looked forward with eagerness to the time when they could assume their duties. "It is in our Power, if we be not wanting to ourselves," declared William Leigh exhuberantly in a student oration at the College of William and Mary in 1771, "to support with Dignity the Cause of Religion, to sustain with Firmness the Rights of Society, and to interpret with Precision the Laws of our Country." Each of his classmates, he remarked, had it in his power to make of himself "an Honor to this Temple of Science, a Blessing to the State, and an Ornament to Humanity." [26]

These were aspirations of the highest order, and they suggest still another motive for gentry participation in politics —the opportunities for diversion and distinction in public life. The give and take of politics was the most exciting and challenging activity in the life of rural Virginia, and the gentry enjoyed it thoroughly. Even if they proved unequal to the challenge it presented, politics still offered an escape from the isolated and sometimes enervating life of the large plantations. For the most part, gentry families were widely dispersed among the counties, and neighboring with equals was neither easy nor frequent. Even men of a bookish turn, like Landon Carter or Richard Bland, longed for the conversation and company of people with similar interests and aspirations. "In Virginia," Landon Carter complained in his diary in 1762, "a man dyes a month sooner in a fit of any disorders because he can't have one soul to talk to." [27] Yet it was not so much the possibility for diversion that pulled them into politics as the desire to excel. Their fathers and grandfathers—the men who had between 1640 and 1740 established and consolidated the position of the gentry in Virginia life—had fulfilled themselves by acquiring landed estates, enhancing the family name, and obtaining status and wealth in the community. But their extraordinary success in realizing these ambitions meant that members of the third generation, who were just coming into manhood in the 1720s and 1730s, had to look elsewhere to find a proper outlet for their talents. Whereas the desire of the older generations to outdistance their fellows had led them primarily into the pursuit of wealth and status and only incidentally into politics, the third generation found that their desire to excel could best be realized in the public sphere; hence they entered into politics with the same avidity and the same devotion that their ancestors had shown in carving out a place for their families in the new world environment. Increasingly in the decades after 1725 politics became the chief road to individual distinction. It was in the public arena that men could test their mettle in discussion and debate, employ their talents for the benefit of the community as they had been taught they were supposed to, perhaps even attain real praiseworthiness, that elusive and rare quality that set extraordinary men off from the rest of mankind

and obtained for them the respect and admiration of society. It was perhaps because the stakes were so high that
the gentry learned to play the game so well.

At least in part because of the gentry's devotion to politics and because of the relatively high quality of government it provided through the middle decades of the
eighteenth century, the concept of stewardship retained its
vitality and meaning in Virginia long after it apparently
had begun to break down elsewhere in the British colonies.
In Virginia it was not just an anachronistic tradition, an
empty ideal that no longer conformed to reality; it was a
fact of life. The result was a harmonious political relationship between the gentry and the rest of society, the central
feature of which was the willing acquiescence of the middle
and lower ranks in gentry government. "From the experience of nearly sixty years in public life," the politically
powerful Edmund Pendleton, one of the foremost lawyers
in Virginia, wrote in 1798, "I have been taught to . . . respect this my native country for the decent, peaceable, and
orderly behaviour of its inhabitants; justice has been, and is
duly and diligently administered—the laws obeyed—the
constituted authorities respected, and we have lived in the
happy intercourse of private harmony and good will. At the
same time by a free communication between those of more
information on political subjects, and the classes who have
not otherwise an opportunity of acquiring that knowledge,
all were instructed in their *rights* and *duties* as freeman,
and taught to respect them." How strong this relationship
between the gentry and the rest of society was is perhaps
nowhere better illustrated than in the story told to Chastellux by Benjamin Harrison of Brandon. On Harrison's departure for the First Continental Congress in the early fall
on 1774 "a number of respectable but uninformed inhabitants" waited upon him and said: "You assert that there is a
fixed intention to invade our rights and privileges; we own
we do not see this clearly, but since you assure us that it is
so, we believe it. We are about to take a very dangerous
step, but we have confidence in you and will do anything

you think proper." It was just such an extraordinary confidence of the governed in their governors, repeatedly demonstrated in day-to-day political relationship, at elections, and at points of crisis throughout the era of the American Revolution, that was the distinguishing feature of the Virginia political system. What the Anglican minister Jonathan Boucher said of Virginia's delegates to that first Congress might well have been said, albeit in somewhat more moderate language, of the leadership at large: that "the general opinion of your knowledge, abilities, and virtues" caused the colony to "look upon you as the oracles of our country; your opinions . . . have the effect of laws, on the mind of the people." [28]

IV

This impressive harmony was symptomatic of the general tranquility of Virginia public life through the middle decades of the eighteenth century. None of the disruptive forces—sectional hostility, religious conflict, factional strife, institutional rivalry between executive and legislature—that disturbed other colonies were present to a sufficient degree in Virginia to overturn established patterns of politics. There was no wide social, economic, or political gulf between the Tidewater and the Piedmont. The latter was in general simply an extension of the former. Many younger sons of old Tidewater inhabitants settled there, and it always had close ties with the eastern region and almost precisely the same economic, social, and political structure. Only after 1750, when the Appalachian and transmontane regions began to fill up with the Scotch-Irish and German immigrants who were spilling south from Pennsylvania, was a heterogeneous element introduced into the colony. Eschewing the plantation system and Negro slavery for the smaller family farm, the new immigrants established a society that was markedly different from that in the older regions. But economic bonds with the east were strong, representation in the House of Burgesses was not seriously disproportionate, and sectional tensions never developed during the colonial and revolutionary periods.[29]

The same situation prevailed in the colony's religious life. Prior to the late 1740s Virginians were overwhelmingly Anglican, the Church of England being the established church. Not only was Anglicanism—"equally distant," said the Reverend William Dawson of the College of William and Mary, "from Superstition on the one Hand, and Enthusiasm on the other"—in general moderate in its traditions, but the Anglican laity in Virginia had long been notorious for its lack of interest in theology and its mildness in religious matters. "As they have little or no Religion," said James Reid, "they have no religious quarrels." Moreover, the Anglican tradition of outward conformity not only encouraged individual dissent in theology but contributed to an easy toleration of religious diversity. As was the case in Britain, "Positive statutes," as Edmund Randolph later wrote, "were still scourges to the preaching and assembling of dissenters," small in number though they were, "but a spirit of mildness was an antidote to the licensed severity of laws." Long before the Great Awakening and the migrations from Pennsylvania had begun to add perceptibly to the dissenting elements in the colony during the 1740s, liberty of conscience, at least for Protestants, had become a convention of Virginia society, with the result that the great increase in Presbyterians and other dissenters after 1750, though it thoroughly alarmed the Anglican clergy and even some of the more devout members of the laity, and produced demands from the dissenters for more precise legal guarantees of toleration, initially neither upset most of the Anglican laity nor created serious political discord. With virtually no support among the leading gentry, the Presbyterians, who had in any case adopted an extremely conciliatory posture towards the existing religious establishment, simply did not appear to represent a formidable political challenge. Only after 1765 did religious issues intrude deeply into the public realm, as the more militant Baptists began to make significant inroads in the Virginia countryside. By their visibly different life style, their vigorous condemnations of the Anglican establishment, their appeals to slaves as well as freemen, and their seemingly uncontrolled enthusiasm, they clearly challenged in fundamental ways many traditional social mores; by their belligerent demands for full toleration and separation of church and state, moreover, they thrust religion into the political arena, where it remained an issue of substance for over two decades.[30]

Equally impressive was the absence of significant political tensions; Virginia political leaders managed to maintain a remarkable degree of unanimity both among themselves and with royal administrators. There was some competition between rival speculating groups over western lands after 1745, and temporary cliques occasionally formed around the leading men in the House of Burgesses over specific issues, but there was never any issue of sufficient force to create deep or lasting political divisions. As a result, colonial Virginia was largely free from "party spirit," as St. George Tucker later remarked, and such divisions as there were arose merely from "differences of opinion" which "different men, coming from different parts of" an "extensive Country might well be expected to entertain." Even the rivalry between Council and lower house that was so characteristic of politics in some other colonies failed to materialize in Virginia, where the Council and the House of Burgesses were bound by close family and social ties.[31]

Nor were there the traditional antagonisms between the Burgesses and the royal lieutenant governors. The failure of a vigorous attempt by Lieutenant Governor Alexander Spotswood (1710–22) to lessen the powers of the Virginia Council and the enormous amount of discord and animosity it provoked taught him an important lesson about Virginia politics: success and tranquility depended in large measure upon the governor's reaching an accord with the native gentry. By following this course during his last years, Spotswood finally succeeded in putting a stop to the strife and discord that had characterized the colony's political life for most of its existence.[32] This lesson was not lost on either of Spotswood's immediate successors, Hugh Drysdale (1722–26) and Sir William Gooch (1727–49). During his long twenty-two-year tenure, Gooch, in fact, became the principal architect of a system of political stability that remained essentially intact for the rest of the colonial period. Like his contemporary English model, Sir Robert Walpole, Gooch was a pragmatic and judicious politician who emphasized the virtues of conciliation, harmony, and compromise in the public arena. Carefully avoiding transgressing local interests and cherished customs and traditions, he in effect made himself the prime minister of the local gentry. With the cooperation of three powerful and immensely popular speakers of the House of Burgesses—John Holloway (1720–34), Sir John Randolph (1734–38), and John Robinson (1738–66)—Gooch managed largely through the force of his own scrupulous moral leadership—with almost none of the patronage that had provided the principal cement for Walpole's comparable achievement in Britain—to establish a *modus vivendi* with the gentry in which the vast majority of legislators routinely supported the administration and thereby, in one of the very few such instances in the whole of the Anglo-American colonial experience, actually exhibited habits of obedience to the Crown similar to those displayed by the "average, uncorrupted or little corrupted M.P." in Britain, whose normal posture was one of support for the administration.[33] "By discountenancing Public Animosities," Gooch also "extirpated all Factions," something even the great Walpole was never able to do. The result, as Speaker Randolph told the Burgesses in 1734, was a "Happiness, which seems almost peculiar to our selves, of being under none of the Perturbations which we see every where else arising from the different Views and Designs of Factions and Parties." As an aspiring poet put it in the *Virginia Gazette* two years later,

> Now Wars and Tumults wholly cease,
> And all the Land enjoys sweet Peace.

Just Order holds its curbing Reins,
And wild Licentiousness restrains.
Vice out of Countenance is fled,
And Virtue rises in its Stead,
With Pleasure, Honour'd Sir, we view
Our Country flurish under You.
And whilst You with Impartial Hand,
Distribute Justice through the Land:
No private Broils shall Feuds create,
No Civil Wars disturb the State.[34]

In achieving this extraordinarily stable political situation, Gooch was, of course, aided by a new concern among imperial authorities under Walpole to achieve peace and order in the colonies, no matter what the cost, and by the fact that, in contrast to the situation in earlier years, Virginia was no longer tied so closely into the British patronage system. He was helped as well by a fortunate set of social circumstances within Virginia, some of which have been referred to earlier and all of which discouraged sharp or enduring political divisions: a generally favorable long-term economic situation beginning in the 1730s; a homogeneity of economic and social interests among the free population, which was increasingly feeling pressures to unite in the face of a rising tide of alien black African slaves; a high degree of social and religious integration; and a community of political leaders so large as to make it virtually impossible for a single small group to monopolize political power. Within Virginia, however, Gooch reaped most of the credit for the new political tranquility. Widely heralded for his "disinterested and unprejudic'd PATRIOTISM," he was compared favorably to George I and Augustus. His "love and good will to the people of this Country, and . . . readiness" to "exert it upon all occasions" had, as Speaker Randolph told Gooch in August 1736, "given universal satisfaction to the people under your government." By refusing to be "intoxicated with . . . power," Gooch had shown himself to be "a faithful trustee of the public good" and had convinced Virginians that he had learned the "art of governing well"—the "most abstruse, as well as the usefullest science in the world"—"to some degree of perfection." John Markland expressed the prevailing sentiment in 1730 in an ode extolling Gooch for his role in bringing printing to Virginia:

> He came, He saw, and was belov'd;
>   Like Lightning, quick but strong,
> An universal Gladness mov'd
>   Throughout th' admiring Throng.
>   No sooner was He seen,
>   His calm, yet awful Look,
>   Majestic, yet serene,
> The very Pow'r of Prejudice remov'd,
>   And ev'n His *Silence* spoke.
>   But when His graceful *Tongue*,
>   Copious of reason, did display
> To Happiness, or nearest, surest Way,
>   Ev'n Party-Rancour dy'd away,
>   And private Spleen.
>   We found whence *Britain* is so blest,
>   Which had so much our Envy bore,
> We found—and griev'd we found it not before—
>   We found, that when by Love and Peace,
>   A Prince has fix'd his Throne
>   In ev'ry Subject's loial Breast,
> No wonder Factions end, and Murmurs cease,—
> Since now, what GEORGE is there, GOOCH here has amply
>   shewn.[35]

To be sure, Gooch purchased this "universal satisfaction" at a price that was somewhat more than imperial officials ideally would have liked to pay, a price that included acceptance by the Crown's chief official of strong local institutions with sufficient power even to counterbalance royal authority in the colony. In the bargain, however, he gained enormous personal influence in legislation. Thus, he managed in the mid-1730s, in a great individual triumph, to secure an effective tobacco inspection law for the first time in the colony's history, and against much opposition from rank-and-file planters. Equally important, his conciliatory and judicious behavior helped to mitigate that deep

suspicion of executive authority traditionally exhibited by
colonial legislators and was essential in gaining acceptance
within the Virginia legislature of the ideal of institutional
cooperation in pursuit of the common good. Indeed, the
Burgesses even took pride, as Speaker Randolph noted in
the speech just quoted above, in not pretending to be any
"more than the Representative Body of a Colony, naturally
and justly dependent upon the Mother Kingdom, whose
Power is circumscribed by very narrow Bounds, and whose
Influence is of small extent. All we pretend to, is to be of
some Importance to those who send us hither, and to have
some Share in their Protection, and the Security of their
Lives, Liberties, and Properties." What a sharp contrast to
the lower houses in most other colonies, where insistence
upon a rigid adherence to imperial claims for an overblown
prerogative and patently self-interested behavior by governors caused legislators to become suspicious of all executive authority and to regard it as their solemn duty to
undermine gubernatorial power wherever possible.[36] That
the Burgesses' actual power was far greater than Randolph's
remarks would suggest and that the Burgesses were willing
to pretend to less authority at the very time when most of
its counterparts were doing precisely the opposite are a
striking indication of the success of Gooch's policy of
pragmatic compromise and institutional cooperation. "But
oh! much more extended is the Pow'r," said Markland in
the poem quoted earlier,

> Than o'er the Length of boundless Land,
> Or o'er the Sea's remotest Strand,
> Where Goodness and paternal Care
> The Sovereign's native Vertues are,
> And Subjects Hearts with Loialty run o'er:
>   Where envious Thoughts abortive die,
>   Nor Malice rowls her low'ring Eye:
>   Where, with contending Zeal,
>   The *Prince* and *People* strive,
>   The *Prince* to make his *People* thrive,
>   Their Grievances to heal;

And all good and adverse Fortune shares;
They, in Return to *Him*,
Pay mutual Rev'rence and Esteem,
And all his Pow'r his Honour, Happiness, is theirs.[37]

Moreover, this same policy seems to have been in considerable part responsible for Virginia's intense British patriotism and loyalty to the Crown through the middle decades of the eighteenth century. Probably no other colony had so high a regard for things English as Britain's "eldest Foreign Care." "Every political sentiment, every fashion in Virginia," wrote Edmund Randolph later, "appeared to be imperfect unless it bore a resemblance to some precedent in England," and this "almost idolatrous deference to the mother country" made Virginians willing even to bear serious violations of their rights by the metropolis "upon a mere reluctance to quarrel with the mother country." Virginians delighted in conceiving of the colony as "the most dutiful and loyal" of the Crown's overseas dominions, "the happy retreat," as Reverend Hugh Jones phrased it, "of true Britons." [38]

Though it provoked a violent political hassle, pushed the Burgesses into that grasping posture it had not openly assumed since the middle years of Spotswood's administration, and ultimately resulted in a concerted and successful drive by the Burgesses to establish its political supremacy within the colony, not even the ill-conceived attempt in 1753–54 by Robert Dinwiddie (1752–58) to charge without the Burgesses' consent a fee of a pistole for signing and sealing patents for land could lessen the good will toward the Crown that Gooch had so carefully cultivated. In fact, Dinwiddie's experience only reaffirmed the wisdom of his predecessor, and he tried thereafter to steer a similar course. The antagonisms created by the pistole fee incident were so strong that he never overcame them during the remaining four years of his administration. But his two successors, Francis Fauquier (1758–68) and Norbone Berkeley, Baron de Botetourt (1768–70), cast themselves in the Gooch mold and won the esteem of Virginia political leaders. With governors like Gooch and Fauquier—patriot governors who, as James Horrocks said of Fauquier, were friends to liberty, protectors of the constitution, and promoters of the colony's welfare—it was no wonder the Virginia governors at the close of the Seven Years' War had, as various commentators noted, more extensive powers and were more independent of the lower house than governors of other colonies, that the colony was and had been for over thirty years a model of dutiful and affectionate loyalty.[39]

V

That a group so devoted to politics should have produced so little theoretical writing on political matters has puzzled many later historians. But the imperatives of Virginia political life as well as the values of the gentry dictated that other qualities would be more admired than the speculative. In Virginia, as elsewhere in the English colonies, politics had already assumed that functional and pragmatic character that has been so predominant a feature of subsequent American politics, and Virginians were wary, as Jonathan Boucher noted, of "the false refinements of speculative men, who amuse themselves and the world with visionary ideas of perfection, which never were, nor ever will be found, either in public or in private life." It was the man of action, the man with a capacity for business who addressed himself directly to problems at hand, rather than the philosopher, that Virginians most admired. Many of the older gentry families and many of the new professional men, especially among the lawyers, had large libraries and seem to have read widely. One English traveler reported in the 1740s that many of the gentlemen were "a most agreeable Set of Companions, and possess a pretty deal of improving Knowledge; nay, I know some of the better sort, whose Share of Learning and Reading, would really surprize you, considering their Educations." But the Reverend Hugh Jones's characterization of Virginians as "more inclinable to read men by business and conversation, than to dive into books" seems to describe the vast majority of the gentry, who, Jones reported, were "generally diverted by business or inclination from profound study, and prying into the depths of things." Virginia's was essentially an oral culture whose predominant orientation was toward action. The gentry valued "mental acquirements" and paid "particular Respect to Men of Learning," but they appreciated other traits, including industry, polish, good character, and affability, even more, and preferred that men demonstrate their "clear and penetrating powers of mind" in their deeds or in conversation and speaking rather than in writing. Men with a strong scholarly or speculative bent, such as Landon Carter and Richard Bland, or, in a later generation, Thomas Jefferson and James Madison, were not quite the "biological sports" one writer has suggested, but they were the exception rather than the rule among the leading Virginia politicians.[40]

Lack of concern for political theory and speculation did not mean, however, that Virginians did not operate within a clear, if nowhere systematically articulated, framework of assumptions and perceptions about politics and society. This framework was wholly conventional and almost entirely English, albeit it contained a heavy infusion of ideas from the classics. It was drawn from a wide variety of English sources: the Anglican literature of piety such as Richard Allestree's *The Whole Duty of Man;* popular works of civility, including Henry Peacham's *Compleat Gentleman*, Richard Braithwaite's *English Gentleman*, and Allestree's *Gentleman's Calling*; mainstream English political thought, especially as expressed in contemporary English periodicals which quickly found their way to Virginia and were frequently pirated by the editors of the *Virginia Gazettes;* English legal theorists, particularly Coke and, later, Blackstone; seventeenth-century Whig opposition writers like Milton, Harrington, Sydney, and Locke; Tory Augustan or "country" opposition writers, most heavily Addison, Pope, Swift, and Bolingbroke; and—to a much lesser extent—

[44]

radical Whig thinkers such as Trenchard and Gordon.[41] However derivative in origin and however commonplace in content, this framework of political and social ideas played a powerful role in Virginia politics. It underlay and informed virtually all political behavior. It was, moreover, above debate. No important Virginia politician rose to challenge it at any point between 1720 and 1790, and this consensus was an important factor in both the absence of speculative political philosophy and Virginia's unanimity in the face of the repeated political crises between 1760 and 1789.

At the heart of that framework was the conventional belief in the imperfection of man. Man was not depraved or innately sinful, but he was weak, shortsighted, fallible in his judgments, perpetually self-deluded, prone to favor his own errors, and a slave to his vanity, interests, prejudices, and passions. *"Humanum est errare"* (to be human is to err) was Reverend David Griffith's succinct expression of this belief, and the most frequent source of man's errors, he noted in a sermon in 1775, was his "Selfishness and ambition." The pursuit of self was behind man's "insatiable passion of . . . avarice" and his "Fondness for Power incontroulable," and it was his inability to resist those desires, which, as Landon Carter observed in his diary in 1770, "increased like a dropsical thirst . . . the more they are indulged," that led him into corruption and ultimately into that state of complete depravity where "power and self aggrandizement" became the sole "object of . . . pursuit," ambition and passion ruled unrestrained, and, as Richard Bland put it in 1764, a man would "trudge, with Might and Main, through Dirt and Mire, to gain his Ends." The natural weakness of men and the conscious malevolence of some meant that they could never be left entirely to their own devices or to the mercy of one another, for it was virtually certain, as Landon Carter pointed out, that sooner or later some of them would "fall into such Depravations of Mind, as to become more cruel than the most savage Beast of Prey." The good of every individual and of society in general demanded, therefore, that man's weak and evil tendencies be restrained; and it was the function of government to protect man from himself and his fellows, to neutralize his passions by checking them against those of other men, to "restrain vice and cherish virtue," and to promote order and happiness by securing the life, liberty, and property of every individual.[42]

This was a large order. Because they were necessarily composed of imperfect men, all governments, no matter how benevolent the intentions of the rulers, could be expected to be fallible, to be continually, if usually inadvertently, inflicting injustice and injury upon the very society they were trying to serve. It was in the very "nature of men in authority," it seemed to Richard Henry Lee, "rather to commit two errors than to retract one." An even greater difficulty arose from the probability that there would always be some among the rulers who would be unable to resist their grosser passions. It was a lamentable fact of history, David Griffith noted, that "more determinations of government have proceeded from selfishness and ambitions, than from disinterested and benevolent measures," and the paramount danger to any state was man's unquenchable thirst for power. Virginia politicians were wary of the possibility that some one or some group might eventually acquire what Richard Bland called a "Leviathon of Power" and introduce the worst sort of arbitrary and despotic polity. Clearly, the governed had to be protected from the baser tendencies of their governors, and the main instrument for their protection was the constitution.[43]

To the Virginia gentry *constitution* was the most hallowed term in their political vocabulary. The constitution was the guarantor of their rights, liberties, and property. The "most valuable Part of our Birthright as Englishmen," Richard Bland asserted, was the "vital Principle in the Constitution" that "all men" were "only subject to Laws made with their own Consent." It was that principle that provided the primary security for the "liberty and Property for every Person," that placed them beyond the reach of the "highest EXECUTIVE Power in the State" as long as they lived in "Obedience to its Laws," and that insured that they would live under a government of impartial laws rather than partial men; for, although laws made by fallible legislators could never be entirely satisfactory to everyone in society, they were infinitely preferable to the "voluntary Mercy" or "charitable Disposition" of men.[44] Every branch of government was bound by this principle, but the House of Burgesses, as the predominant force in the legislative process and as the agency through which the governed gave their consent to laws, was the "natural" guardian of their rights. It had a special obligation to keep a sharp eye out for any transgressions of the law and to oppose every measure that had "the least tendency to break through the legal Forms of government" because, as Bland argued, "a small spark if not extinguished in the beginning will soon gain ground and at last blaze out into an irresistible Flame." The rule of law had to be absolute. "LIBERTY & PROPERTY" were "like those previous Vessels whose soundness is destroyed by the least flaw and whose use is lost by the smallest hole."[45]

The House of Burgesses itself, of course, was a potential threat to the liberty, property, and basic rights of its constituents. The House, said Edwin Conway, a representative from Northumberland County, in 1737, was like "the *Lion*, in the Fable who are stronger in Power than any single Subject in the Colony." Precisely because of this great power, both the constituency and the members of the house had to be ever watchful lest a conspiracy of evil or misguided men capture the House and seek to subvert or destroy the rule of law. One protection against such a development was the customary prohibition within the Anglophone world of legislative tinkering with those traditional and fundamental rights of individuals—such as trial by jury and the right to a writ of habeas corpus—that were firmly rooted in English common law and had been guaranteed by the Revolutionary Settlement of 1688. Another check against the legislature, of course, was the requirement of periodic elections. Although there was no law in Virginia requiring elections at stated intervals, eighteenth-century governors followed English practice and never tried to keep a legislature in existence beyond the seven-year limit. No matter how often the elections, however, it was always possible that the representatives could by deliberately deceiving and playing upon the emotions of their constituents secure their support for the worst species of legislative tyranny. "In all free governments, and in all ages," Jonathan Boucher observed in 1774, there would always be "Crafty, designing knaves, turbulent demogogues, quacks in politics, and imposters in patriotism" who sought to overturn the constitution while pretending to defend it. The ultimate safeguard against such a threat was a balanced constitution, that "ingenious" contrivance that most of the eighteenth-century British world regarded as the secret of a successful polity. By mixing the various elements of the polity together in such a way as to keep them in a constant state of equilibrium, so that each would serve as a countervailing force against the others and harmful tendencies would thereby be checked or neutralized, a balanced constitution was the device through which imperfect men could live together in a state of relative harmony. Exactly what was balanced by the constitution—whether the governors were balanced against the governed, the gentlemen against the commoners, the prerogative against local interests, or each of the three branches of government—the legislative, judicial, and executive—against one another—was nowhere spelled out precisely by any Virginian prior to the 1770s. But Virginians were thoroughly persuaded that "in every state" it was absolutely "necessary for the publick weal that as just an equilibrium as possible should be preserved." It was an article of faith, as Robert Carter Nicholas declared in 1774, that the preservation of the whole polity depended upon maintaining a proper balance and a distinct separation of functions between its several parts, and the failure of the House of Burgesses, even after it had gained the ascendency in Virginia politics in the mid-1750s, to attempt a significant extension of its authority over executive affairs after the fashion of its counterparts elsewhere in the colonies is in part a testimony to the continuing devotion of Virginia politicians to the ideal of a well-balanced constitution.[46]

This ideal with its emphasis upon the subordination of the several parts of society to the interests of the whole was closely related to another "fundamental . . . Rule of the *English* Constitution": the doctrine of *salus populi est suprema lex*. Landon Carter and Richard Bland employed that doctrine extensively between 1759 and 1764 as a defense first of Virginia's wartime paper money emissions against the opposition of British merchants and then of the Two-Penny Acts—which enabled people to pay their public obligations in money instead of tobacco in two years of extremely short crops—against the attacks of the clergy, the prime victims of the acts. As defined by Carter and Bland, the doctrine meant simply that anything that was "absolutely necessary for the Good of the Community," for the corporate welfare of the society, was "therefore just in itself," some other rule of the constitution or individual interests to the contrary notwithstanding. Not the disadvantages to a few individuals but "the Advantages . . . to the People in general" was the "principal Consideration with legislatures in forming Laws," Richard Bland asserted in defending the Two-Penny Acts, and Landon Carter thought it was a "great Absurdity" to suggest that the interests of any man or group of men were more important than the preservation of the "community, which they compose." Even the King's prerogative, great and powerful as it was, Bland had argued against the Crown's disallowance of laws the Virginia legislature had thought necessary for the welfare of the colony, could "only be exerted . . . for the Good of his People, and not for their Destruction," and Carter contended that the constitution itself, which in normal circumstances should be kept "as sacred as possible," might have to be "aided, extended or qualified . . . to support and preserve the Community." Everything had to give way before the public good.[47]

To make sure that the welfare of the entire community

would always be its central concern, government, Virginians felt strongly, had to be especially careful not to grant any group within it—and particularly no group among the rulers—any special status, privileges, exemptions, or benefits. However salutary such a grant might appear at the time it was given and however virtuous the men to whom it was given might be, "Ambition and lust of power above the laws" were, as Jonathan Boucher asserted, "such predominant passions in the Breasts of most men, even of men who escape the infection of other vices," that they could never be trusted not to try to turn it to their own selfish ends, perhaps even to attempt the establishment of a despotism or what Landon Carter disapprovingly called "a mere Aristocratic power," that "Arbitrary and Oppressive" form in which men governed for their own private ends rather than for the common good. So pronounced was the tendency of a few to try to extend their power in any state that the legislature had to be constantly on the alert, Landon Carter declared, to protect the "greater Number of Individuals against an almost certain Oppression from the lesser Number," and the only certain way to prevent the polity from degenerating into an aristocracy was to preserve the absolute equality of all freeman within it. It was, therefore, a first principle with Virginia political leaders that "Subjects have no Pretence to Immunities, one more than another." [48]

The evils of an excessively popular government were similar. The people, as young James Madison, cousin of the fourth president and later bishop of the Episcopal Church in Virginia, said in a Phi Beta Kappa oration at the College of William and Mary in 1772, were "the original Springs of Government." But they donated at each election part of their liberty to the men they chose for representatives, thereby giving them a large measure of independence and freeing them from the necessity to cater to the whims or act according to the sentiments of their constituents. Except in cases that "related particularly to the interest of the Constituents alone" and on which he had the "express Instructions of . . . his Constituents" a representative had to

[50]

"be Governed" not by the collective "sentiments of his Constituents" but by "his own Reason and Conscience," so that, in consultation with his fellow legislators, he could act on behalf of the good of the colony as a whole and not simply in the narrow interest of a particular constituency. The alternative, that a representative was bound by the wishes of his constituents in all cases, was unacceptable largely because it placed responsibilities on the people at large that they had neither the breadth of perspective nor the capacity to bear and perhaps even paved the way for their inevitable domination and manipulation by a small band of demagogues who could be expected to play upon the "credulity of the well-meaning, deluded multitude" for their own selfish ends and to introduce, under the guise of democracy, "an Aristocratic Power." The electorate was simply too restricted in its vision and too prone to be misled by men who could appeal to the passions of humors of the moment to be trusted to act in the best interests of the community at large.[49]

To prevent the degeneration of the polity into either aristocracy or democracy and to preserve the constitution in its "due Poise," Virginians depended upon the stewardship of the "real Patriot." A patriot could never be a man who was indolent, "ambitious of power," "proficient in the arts of dissimulation," or governed by "self and gain alone." Rather, he had to be an impartial and disinterested man whose "first principle"—his "Ruling Passion"—was his "love of . . . Country"—a determination "to act under all appointments relative to the Public" and for no "Interest less than that of a whole Country." He had to be a man who would always "view the whole ground and persevere to the last" and one who would constantly adhere rigidly to the commands of the Burgesses' oath and upon "all Things proposed . . . deliver" his "Opinion faithfully, justly, and honestly, according to" his "best Understanding and Conscience, for the general Good, and Prosperity of this Colony, and every Member thereof; and to do" his best "endeavours to prosecute That, without mingling therewith, the

particular Interest of any Person or Persons whatsoever."
He could not "value" himself upon "Titles and Honors"
or other "empty Things . . . of no intrinsic Worth" or
"exchange his Duty and Integrity for Civilities" or other
blandishments from the hand of power. He had to be, as
the epitaph of William Byrd II of Westover declared he
was, "the constant enemy of all exorbitant power, and
hearty friend to the liberties of his country," an "honest
Man" chosen, as an anonymous writer said in the *Virginia
Gazette*, "to represent his County, or Borough, from the
Knowledge his Constituents have of his Worth. He believes
no Party can ever be in the Right, or always in the Wrong:
He votes and speaks as he judges best for the Service of his
Country, and when the Session ends, returns, like *Cincin-
natus*, to the Plough." He could not attach himself to any
party because parties, Virginians were convinced, were the
instruments of partial men whose devotion to factional ends
necessarily robbed them of their independence of judgment
and prevented them from considering the welfare of the entire country impartially. And he had to concern himself primarily with keeping "Society moving on its proper Hinges"
and to be willing to justify unpopular "public Measures
when he thinks them necessary," to renounce the "people
when he thinks them wrong" and to "call the first Con-
nexions to an Account" whenever they acted unjustly or
injuriously to the public.[50]

The two most essential qualities for the patriot and
ideally for all men were virtue and independence. Virtue
required a devotion to truth, honesty, moderation, reason,
a "Behavior . . . above every Appearance of Evil" and a determination both to guard against one's weaknesses by a
constant exercise in self-control—a virtuous man could
never be "a Slave to his own Ill-nature"—and to attempt to
ennoble one's life by "real Goodness." "Whoever does not
take care to govern his Passions, they will soon govern him,"
wrote James Reid, "and lead him into labyrinths of vice,
error, prejudices, and immoralities from whence he will
find it very difficult to extricate himself; for in time he will

become fortified and impregnable against common sense and the dictates of right reason." "Virtue," Reverend William Stith asserted, was the "grand Fountain of publick Honour and Felicity," and no man, as Robert Carter Nicholas once remarked, could "be safely trusted" with public office who did "not act upon *solid, virtuous* Principles," who would not "sacrifice every sinister, selfish Consideration" for the "True Interest" of "his Country." Only men who were "conscious of the Uprightness and Integrity of their Actions" and who were therefore "not easily dismayed," Richard Bland explained, could be expected to "stand firm and unshaken" against the imperfection of themselves and other men; and Landon Carter was convinced that chaos could frequently be reduced to "order and comfort" by "the appearance only of some good man." Nor was independence any less important than virtue. Perhaps in part because their constant exposure to black slavery impressed upon them how miserable and abject slavery could be, Virginians took great pride, as Wou'dbe inferred in *The Candidates,* in thinking that a spirit of personal independence was particularly strong among them. In Virginia, Edmund Randolph later remarked, "a high sense of personal independence was universal": "disdaining an abridgment of personal independence," he declared, was one of the most essential "manners which belonged to the real Virginian planter and which were his Ornament!" Foreign travelers and internal social critics alike were repeatedly impressed with this strong sense of independence among Virginians. A Virginia gentleman, said James Reid, had such overweening pride as to regard anything that seemed to deprive "him of his free agency" as "an imposition which is not to be put up with in a land of Liberty. It would be making him a piece of Clock work, a mere lump of mechanism, and a cypher of no value. It would be changing one who was born a Gentleman into a vile slave, and depriving him of that freedom which nature has vested him with." For the aspiring patriot, independence was especially important. It was, as Landon Carter wrote in 1769, the "base or footstool on which Liberty can alone be protected," and without liberty, without complete freedom to act impartially and independently, no man could fulfill the obligations of the patriotic public servant. [51]

VI

Within this broad consensus of working political assumptions there was considerable room for maneuver, and what divided the political leadership within the House of Burgesses was a disagreement not over the rules of the game but rather over how the game should be played. By the 1740s and 1750s, and perhaps even earlier, there had emerged two poorly delineated but recognizable postures or style of leadership. One style may best be described as responsible. The conspicuous minority who assumed this posture insisted upon a strict adherence to the traditional ideals of politics. They were the disinterested patriots par excellence, the ideologues of virtue and independence. They prided themselves upon their personal virtue, their willingness to sacrifice even friendship for truth and justice, and their elevation above the clamour of the multitude. It was not praise they sought but praiseworthiness; it was not enough for them just to *seem*—they had to *be*—men of distinction. Like Worthy in *The Candidates*, they professed to have "little inclination to the service" and an "aversion to public life." Far from ever courting the favor of their constituents, they had the "troublesome office" of burgess thrust upon them. Rather than part with an ounce of their virtue, they preferred to withdraw from public life. They were fond of quoting Cato's lines from Joseph Addison's play *Cato:* "When vice prevails and impious men bear sway/ The post of honour is a private station." Epitomized by such men as Landon Carter, Richard Henry Lee, George Washington, and George Mason, the responsible men were often more rigid in their professions than in their practice. But they were the consciences of Virginia politics, the idealists who were devoted to the goal of impersonal and impartial government, the visionaries who insisted that man should strive to be perfect in spite of his imperfections and in the face of almost certain failure. They were the vigorous public servants who stood for activity, energy, and resolution in times of crisis.[52]

The second style was more representative—more flexible —in its orientation. Those who exhibited it showed no disposition to oppose the conventional ideals of politics, but they were willing to interpret them more loosely than the men of the more responsible style and to deviate from them somewhat if there was no obvious danger in doing so. They were the pragmatic politicians whose primary emphasis was upon accommodation, moderation, deliberation, and control, and whose most fundamental commitment was to the continuing stability of the polity. Although they were careful never to "fawn or cringe" before the freeholders and did not violate the gentleman-candidate's rule not to solicit votes openly, they believed, like Wou'dbe in *The Candidates*, that "the Prudent candidate who hopes to rise,/ Ne'er deigns to hide it, in a mean disguise." They had few scruples about courting the freeholders and, though they often found it distasteful, were not too proud to mingle with the voters in order to reinforce through ties of affection the relationship between themselves and their constituents. Within the House of Burgesses they were the amiable and assiduous men of business with "sound political Knowledge" who were ever willing to arrange a compromise in order to avoid a convulsive struggle among contending interests. Inclined to be more concerned with the wishes of the electorate than with the preservation of their own unsullied virtue, they were—in the interests of preserving control and maintaining stability—willing to tailor their behavior and even to employ what Landon Carter derisively called a "low popular argument" to suit the "humour of the Plebians." They were the realists of Virginia politics who took politics on its own terms. They accepted man's limitations and the fact that he would often err, and were not disposed to fret if the political system became somewhat personal and partial as long as no gross evils seemed to result. Exemplified by Sir John Randolph and John Robinson, the latter the very "Darling of the Country" for twenty-eight years during his tenure as speaker of the Burgesses between 1738 and 1766, Peyton Randolph, Edmund Pendleton, Archibald Cary, and Benjamin Harrison, the men of the representative style provided the responsive and practical element in Virginia politics.[53]

The existence of the two styles and the measure of difference between them were revealed in two important debates during the 1750s. The first, lasting only a few hours and recorded only in Landon Carter's private minutes of the session, concerned the nature of representation and the function of a representative. Men of the representative style—the "favourers of Popularity"—headed by Speaker John Robinson, argued that a representative was "to Collect the sentiments of his Constituents and whatever that Majority willed ought to be the rule of his Vote,"—that he was, in fact, "obliged to follow the direction of his Constituents" even "against his own Reason and Conscience." Men of the responsible style—those who considered themselves "Admirers of Reason and Liberty of Conscience"—took the position that "reason and Good Conscience should direct" except in cases "where the matter related particularly to the interest of the Constituents alone."[54] The second and more important debate concerned the extent and nature of Virginia's contribution to the Seven Years' War and seems to have lasted throughout the period from 1754 until the demands on Virginia became lighter after the war took a turn for the better in 1757. Although the evidence is sketchy and the details of motivation by no means certain, it is clear that one of the main issues was whether the House of Burgesses, as Landon Carter and Richard Bland insisted, should "give, freely and liberally, such Supplies, as will enable the Government, to act with Spirit and Resolution" or follow the more popular course, advocated primarily by Robinson and his friends, of making less of an effort and thereby pleasing an apparently large segment of the public which was grumbling about paying such heavy taxes.[55]

The importance of these divergent styles in the day-to-day politics of Virginia should not be overemphasized. Their existence seems to have been only dimly perceived by contemporaries, who had neither defined their character nor identified their tendencies clearly. Perhaps no politician fitted precisely or wholly into either of the models just described. Responsible men like George Washington, Landon Carter, and Richard Henry Lee could resort to treating at a crucial election or to acting the *"Babbling Dog"* and *"the angry Man in the Lobby"* if they thought it necessary to win public support for a measure they favored. Similarly, representative types like Peyton Randolph and Edmund Pendleton by no means ignored their consciences in the blind pursuit of the whims of their constituents and could upon occasion insist on the strictest devotion to the rules of the game, especially in the face of an external challenge.[56] But the push and pull between these two orientations within a large framework of consent provided still another element of balance within the Virginia political system and supplied much of the energy that made it function so effectively. It insured that there would usually be both responsibility and responsiveness, wisdom and practicality, strength and adaptability, a concern for virtue and talent among the rulers and for the liberty and sentiments of the constituents. This concern for both virtue and liberty prevented the political system from becoming a closed corporation and gave it both an amazing capacity for assimilating new men and a strength, effectiveness, and responsiveness to the electorate that won for it the confidence of the public at large.

VII

These several qualities were revealed most clearly during crises, and they became especially manifest in the decade immediately preceding the debate with Great Britain over Parliament's right to tax the colonies and the nature of constitutional relationships within the Empire. Between 1752 and 1763 the Virginia political system had not only to meet the heavy demands of the Seven Years' War but also to cope with its first serious challenges since the frontal assault of Alexander Spotswood four decades earlier. The contests over the pistole fee, the legal-tender status of wartime paper money issues, and the Two-Penny Acts put the system to a series of demanding tests. In each case, it proved its essential viability, as it demonstrated an ability to cope with political crises while at the same time both preserving overall political stability in the colony and a high degree of unanimity among its leaders and retaining the support of the electorate at large—all testimonies to the caliber of its leadership, the strength of the relationship between the leadership and the constituency, and the vitality of its traditional political ideals. In addition, the three crises vividly underlined for Virginia political leaders the necessity for a vigorous and jealous cultivation of those ideals.

In all three controversies, the central issue was the same: some individual or group was trying to extend its power or gain some private advantage at the expense of the good of the whole community. Dinwiddie's behavior in the pistole fee incident left no doubt that he was "an avaritious and designing Delegate" who was attempting by "illegal and arbitrary" means to introduce a "branch of Power" not sanctioned by law that would lead straight to "that Hydra Oppression." The complaining British merchants were obviously "men of low and selfish Notions," "very *inhumane Principles*," "governed . . . wholly by Avarice" and "no otherwise *interested* in the Country, than in the dirty Demands" they had "against it." The opposing clergymen were clearly "avaritious, merciless" men without a grain of patriotism "who, in Defiance of the Truth, stick at no Artifice to bring their evil Machinations to Perfection." [57] Such behavior provided ample confirmation of the validity of the Virginians' traditional conception of human nature and of their conviction that the general good required that all men be placed under strict legal and constitutional restraints. Reverend William Stith's ringing toast, "*Liberty & Property and no Pistole,*" dramatically reaffirmed for Virginians what could never have been very far from the thoughts of men in a society where the possession of land was so important, that there was an intimate connection between liberty and property and that the chief security for both was the rule of law as guarded over by the elective House of Burgesses. Each contest, in fact, only convinced Virginia political leaders that the Burgesses was the only body that could be trusted to act in the best interests of the colony.[58] What continued to bother those leaders, however, what became distressingly clear during these three crises, was that there was one very important defect in the Virginia political system: no matter what kind of workable balance of power might be attained within the colony, they could never, because of their colonial status and the vague constitutional arrangements that prevailed at the time, be sure that the imperial government would not upset it.

Not that these fears inhibited Virginia political leaders to any significant degree. In each crisis the House of Burgesses acted with extreme boldness, branding anyone who paid Dinwiddie his pistole "a Betrayer of the Rights and Privileges of the People," refusing to comply with a royal order to remove the legal tender requirement from its paper money on the grounds that it "would be an Act of Injustice" to its constituents, and arguing with imperial authorities over portions of their ruling in the hassle over the Two-Penny Acts. Moreover, the House never once had to back down completely in the face of imperial power. Crown officials upheld the constitutionality of the pistole fee, but they also made important concessions to the House, exempting certain land patents from the fee and requiring Dinwiddie to reappoint Peyton Randolph, agent for the House against Dinwiddie in London, to the attorney generalship from which Dinwiddie had removed him. The Burgesses' stand on the paper money question was one of the chief considerations in prompting imperial officials to obtain Parliamentary prohibition of legal-tender paper money in the Currency Act of 1764, but again the Burgesses was pleased that the act only prohibited future issues and required the prompt retirement of old emissions at the times stipulated in the issuing acts and did not alter the legaltender status of old bills. Finally, although the Crown disallowed the Two-Penny Acts, it did not yield to the clergy's demand that the acts be declared null and void from their first passage, so that the disallowance had no practical effect because both laws had long since expired. That the Burgesses achieved some degree of victory in each of these contests did not mean, however, that house leaders regarded the resolution of any one of them as ideal.[59]

The primary cause for their anxiety was the potential threat to the colony from two potent weapons in the royal arsenal: legislative review and the royal instructions. By the first, imperial authorities could disallow colonial laws. By the second, they could, by forbidding the governor to pass certain kinds of measures, prevent the Burgesses from legislating in those areas, no matter how pressing the need, and thus actually exercise legislative power in the colony without the consent of the people's representatives in the Burgesses. Virginia leaders did not fear that the Crown under ordinary circumstances would use these weapons deliberately to oppress the colony, but they were concerned lest it unintentionally injure the colony because it had taken the wrong advice. When it came to Virginia affairs at least, the Burgesses was in full agreement with Dinwiddie's sarcastic comment during the pistole fee contest that it thought itself "more Wise than any other Body of People upon the Face of the Earth," and the House regarded it as preposterous that Dinwiddie, British merchants, or a few of the Virginia clergy should presume to set their judgment against that of the Burgesses, the representatives of the entire colony. For imperial officials to listen to such "selfish and interested" parties and to make decisions even partly in accord with their demands was a source of considerable discomfort. Initially, to prevent such developments the Burgesses sought to secure the right to keep an agent of its own choosing in London to explain its position on any questions that might come up. But even that safeguard, which the Burgesses obtained in 1759, would not be sufficient if the direction of imperial affairs fell into the hands of evil men. As long as "An Act of Assembly" was such "a trifling thing," both legislative review and the royal instructions could, as Landon Carter bitterly remarked in 1752 when he heard of the Crown's disallowance of ten laws from the revisal of 1749, be employed "in a Clandestine manner" to introduce "All imaginable Bribery." [60] Fear of precisely just such a development as well as the desire to establish the Burgesses' competence in local legislation and to remedy what Virginian leaders considered a glaring flaw in the Virginia constitution led the Burgesses, especially Richard Bland and Landon Carter, to seek, during the controversy over the Two-Penny Acts, some precise constitutional arrangement that would limit the Crown's use of these two powers while at the same time providing Virginia permanent protection against the unlimited might of the parent state.

Specifically, this search was prompted by the Privy Council's 1759 instruction to Governor Fauquier threatening him with recall if he did not obey the royal instruction forbidding him to assent either to acts of less than two years' duration or to acts that repealed laws already confirmed by the King unless they contained a clause suspending them until the royal pleasure should be known. The potential dangers of that instruction were spelled out by Landon Carter's brother Charles Carter of Cleve, next to Speaker John Robinson the most powerful member of the House of Burgesses, in a letter to a correspondent in England. "By a late revival of an old Instruction," he wrote, "we cannot alter or amend any Law before Application is made to his Majesty, which has taken away our Constitution." Unless the London agent could "get an Alteration," he predicted, "we in all Probability may be ruined, as no body of men is infallible, and all Laws are found by Experience deficient." In an opening round of pamphlets in 1759–60, Landon Carter and Bland argued that by preventing the enactment of laws that were "absolutely necessary" for the preservation of the colony such a "Rule strictly adhered to must, sooner or later, prove the Destruction of the . . . State." Obviously, no instruction could be permitted to operate in such a way as to "destroy the Country," and Bland insisted that it was a "clear and fundamental . . . Rule of the *English Constitution*" that any "pressing Necessity" justified "any Person for infringing them," for deviating from them "with Impunity." "The Royal Prerogative," Bland argued, could "only be exerted while in the Hands of the best and most benign Sovereign, for the Good of his People, and not for their Destruction," and it was "impossible that any Instruction to a Governour" could "be construed so contrary to the first Principles of *Justice* and *Equity*, as to prevent his Assent to a Law for relieving a Colony in a Case of . . . general Distress and Calamity." [61]

Although Carter had argued that "instructions" were "neither Laws of publick Authority, nor Rules of Constitution," the 1759–60 tracts in general tended to question the wisdom rather than the constitutionality of the instruction; but the refusal of imperial officials to take seriously a formal protest against the instruction in question from the House of Burgesses demonstrated just how frail such arguments were as a protection against the preponderant power of the imperial government. A rigid observance of that instruction, the Burgesses had pleaded, parroting the contentions of Bland and Carter, would "involve the Colony in the most insuperable Difficulties." The necessity for some clearly defined constitutional restraints upon imperial use of instructions was now more obvious than ever, and Richard Bland attempted to work out what such restraints ought to be in *The Colonel Dismounted*, published in late 1764 at the end of the Two-Penny Acts controversy. "Under an *English* Government," Bland argued, all men were born free and were "only subject to Laws made with their own Consent." Because Virginians had not lost the "Rights of Englishmen" by their removal to America, they were protected by the same rule, which required that Virginia have "a legal Constitution, that is, a Legislature, composed, in Part, of the Representatives of the People," without whose consent no "Laws for the INTERNAL Government of the Colony" could be made. Drawn up by people at a distance with insufficient knowledge of conditions in the colony and kept secret from the colonial political community, instructions could therefore, be only "Guides and Directions for the Conduct of Governors" and never law because the people had not consented to them through their representatives. To make them law, said Bland, would be "at once, to strip us of all the Rights and Privileges of *British* Subjects, and to put us under the despotick Power of a *French* or *Turkish* Government." "Submission, even to the supreme Magistrate," he argued, "is not the whole Duty of a Citizen . . . Something is likewise due to the Rights of our Country, and to the Liberties of Mankind." [62]

The difficulty with such constitutional speculations, of course, was that they were foredoomed to failure by the very problem they were contrived to solve. There was absolutely no way for Virginians to force imperial authorities to observe them; voluntary action by the imperial government was the only hope for acceptance. But the imperial government was clearly not even interested in them, much less willing to accept them, and the resulting anxiety at their inability to achieve some precise limitations upon imperial authority, to repair such a glaring deficiency in their political system, haunted Virginia political leaders through the early years of the 1760s and fed a rising suspicion of imperial intentions and a fear that they would be unable to preserve themselves and their constituents against an unintentional or corrupt exertion of the unlimited power of the home government.

Despite this anxiety, many of the leading Virginia political leaders exhibited a curious smugness in the early 1760s. Having found, averred a satiric poet, probably the Stafford County lawyer John Mercer,

> . . . this loyal land in peace
> nor striving nor contending
> than how to prove 'its loves increase
> tow'rds one of George's sending,

Dinwiddie had raised the spectre of arbitrary royal power in the colony for the first time in over thirty years and had inaugurated a long series of controversies through which "Virginians hitherto distinguished for their Loyalty" seemed to be repeatedly and "shamefully traduced, were Oppressed, Insulted, & treated like rebells, by the very persons from whom they" had been so "long taught to Expect Succour." But the luxuriant British patriotism so carefully nurtured by Gooch and then, after Dinwiddie, by Fauquier was too strong to be quickly stunted. Imperial behavior in the disputes of the 1750s and early 1760s weakened but by no means destroyed Virginia affection for the parent state. Jubilant over the great British victory over the French and Spanish in the Seven Years' War and the Treaty of Paris in 1763, they were proud of the rather conspicuous part they had acted in defending the frontiers of the Empire and looked forward to a grand new era of expansion and liberty under the "admirable Constitution" of Great Britain, a constitution, as James Horrocks observed, that Britons had "Preserv'd . . . pure and uncorrupted thro' all the Struggles of Ambition and the most dangerous Attacks of Power." Indeed, Virginians virtually wallowed in professions of affection to the King and mother country. "Our Dependence upon Great Britain," the House of Burgesses told Lieutenant Governor Fauquier upon hearing of the peace, "we acknowledge and glory in, as our greatest Happiness and only Security." It was ironic perhaps that the source of their greatest happiness was also the cause of their deepest political frustration. But as long as that frustration was assuaged by the mildness of Crown officials, as long as it arose from an anticipated rather than from a felt danger, they could easily push it to the backs of their minds. Besides, over the past decade, they had succeeded, if not in defeating, at least in checking, the malignant designs, in turn, of a "mercenary" and corrupt governor, an influential group of selfish merchants, and a small knot of scheming clergymen while simultaneously making a major contribution towards the destruction of a powerful union of blood-thirsty savages and cunning papists, and the concessions they had won from the imperial government in these several disputes helped to perpetuate their belief in the essential justice of the mother country and its basic good will towards Virginia. Moreover, they had the satisfaction of knowing that they had behaved throughout these disputes with a "loyalty debased by no servile compliance and . . . a patriotic watchfulness never degenerating into the mere petulance of complaint." Hopefully, as Edmund Randolph later phrased it, "to know when to complain with truth and how to complain with dignity was . . . ample for the only end which could then be projected" within a beneficent political system such as the first British Empire.[63]

VIII

The most pressing, perhaps, but not all, or ultimately even the most important, sources of anxiety to the Virginia political community were external, however. Throughout the middle decades of the eighteenth century, the internal state of Virginia society was a source of persistent concern. Part of this concern was endemic to a largely one-crop economy and derived from the enduring fear that if the bottom ever fell out of the world tobacco market Virginia's prosperity would quickly go down the drain. Thus, the *Virginia Gazette* might celebrate the virtues of tobacco by equating it with the rural virtues of peace, ease and freedom:

Sing, ye Muses, Tobacco, the Blessing of Peace,
Was ever a Nation so blessed as this?

.   .   .   .

Let foreign Climes the Vine and Orange boast,
While wastes of war deform the teeming Coast;
Britannia, distant from each hostile Sound,
Enjoys a Pipe, with Ease and Freedom crown'd;
E'en restless Faction finds itself most free,
Or if a Slave, a Slave to Liberty.

.   .   .   .

Tell, if ever you have seen
Realms so quiet and serene.

But the limited success of repeated attempts to encourage agricultural diversification through legislation rendered the colony's economy especially vulnerable to sudden fluctuations in the demand for tobacco. Through most of the period between 1725 and 1775, the world tobacco market was expanding, almost even bullish, the result to a great extent of a growing tobacco market in France. But a major economic downturn at the end of the Seven Years' War vividly reminded Virginians of the disadvantages of too heavy a concentration upon a single crop. Tobacco prices were low and falling, and credit was especially tight. Invariably, in such periods of contraction the normal indebtedness of the planters—in flush times a major economic resource—seemed to be an overwhelming burden. Also with a large public debt arising out of the heavy military expenditure made by the colony during the war and a contracting money supply caused by the successful offensive of British merchants against the colony's fund of paper currency, the economic picture by 1763 seemed especially bleak. As Arthur Lee wrote to his brother Philip Ludwell Lee from Britain in November 1763, Virginia was "a country overburdened with debts," both private and public, "threatened with the horrors of a [renewal of] savage War [brought on by Pontiac's uprising in the west]: her produce sinking universally in its value; without funds, trade or Men"—a "truly miserable" situation that required "the utmost Exertions, of the few able & patriotic Men among you, to save the state from sinking." The causes of this seemingly desperate—but ultimately only short-term—situation were numerous, but Lee thought a major part of the problem traceable to the colony's excessive dependence upon tobacco. "Tobacco, your present Staple," he declared, "seems to be [a] very precarious commodity; its culture appears to be falling continually & shoud the same consumption continue, yet as the Colony becomes more populated, the produce must of course overstock the Markets & reduce its value." It was "therefore incumbent" on Virginians to develop a diversified agricultural economy. Nor was the excessive vulnerability of a one-crop economy the only evil attributable to "that baneful weed tobacco." It had, said Edmund Randolph, "riveted two evils in the heart of Virginia, the declension of that agriculture which is the most safe and most honorable [i.e., mixed agriculture], and the encouragement of slavery, the most base of human conditions." Furthermore, as was becoming increasingly clear by the 1750s, tobacco was also exhausting "the fertility of our soil" and swallowing "up in its large plantations vast territories, which if distributed into portions were best adapted to favor population." [64]

As Randolph's recitation of the malicious effects of the race for tobacco profits suggests, black slavery, which had expanded so dramatically as a result of increasingly heavy importations of new slaves after 1720, was a second internal source of social unease among white Virginians. Every state has "an internal Weakness, or Distemper," said an anonymous writer in the *Virginia Gazette* in April 1752: "I take the *Slavery* established here to be . . . a greater Fund of Imbecility to the State, than the old English *Villainage*, or the late *Clanship* of Scotland," a "poison," said another writer, which had diffused itself "in a variety of destructive shapes." The mad "Rage" for these "innumerable black Creatures" not only "swallow'd up" all the liquid resources, the rich "Treasure" bestowed upon the colony by nature and industry, declared an anonymous correspondent in a trenchant allegory in the *Virginia Gazette* in 1738, but it also introduced a powerful internal enemy of incalculable danger. "Having no Enemy from without," said the allegorist, "this simple People are madly fond of securing one in their own Bowels," an enemy, another writer pointed out, who might, if a constant vigilance were not maintained, at any time rise in "conspiracy" and wind up cutting our T[hroa]ts." Along with the "propitious" natural environment which was too "luxuriant" to "generate the noble art of living upon little," slavery had also discouraged, other observers lamented, art, industry, and a respect for labor. Nor was the diminution of the industry of whites the only "ill Effect" slavery had "upon the Morals & Manners of our People." It also gave rise to such "Habits of Pride, and Cruelty in . . . Owners" as to make it unclear whether, as James Reid remarked, a "vicious, rich" slaveowner differed in any respect from "his . . . vicious, poor Negro, but in the colour of his skin, and in his being the greater blac[k]-guard of the two" and to raise the question of whether every such master would not in justice "be punished in hell by his own slaves." Tobacco and the excessive avarice it had generated had thus "stained the country with all the pollutions and cruelties of slavery," and it was almost universally known, as George Mason, the learned Fairfax County planter and future author of the Virginia Declaration of Rights, pointed out in 1765, that "one of the first Signs of the Decay, & perhaps the primary Cause of the Destruction of the most flourishing Government that ever existed was the Introduction of great Numbers of Slaves—an Evil very pathetically described by the Roman historians." Some observers still hoped that the evils of slavery might be mitigated if further importations of slaves were prohibited by high duties and "proper Encouragement" were offered "to white persons to settle the Country." "The Policy of encouraging the Importation of free People & discouraging that of Slaves has never been duly considered in the Colony," Mason complained, "or we shou'd not at this Day see one Half of our best Lands in most parts of the

Country remain unsetled, & the other cultivated with Slaves." But the "blessings" to be expected from such a policy, another writer had bitterly remarked in the mid-1750s, were probably "too great" either "for the consent of a British Mother, or for the Option of a people already Infatuated & Abandoned." [65]

The fear that Virginians were indeed growing increasingly "Infatuated & Abandoned" was still a third—and infinitely the most powerful—internal source of social anxiety. Beginning in the late 1730s, a growing number of Virginians complained about the decline of the old values of industry, thrift, and sobriety, certain signs, they predicted, of the moral declension of Virginia society. Particularly disturbing was the exorbitant growth of luxury. Increasingly, after 1740, travelers and thoughtful members of the gentry alike remarked upon the "extravagance, ostentation, and . . . disregard for economy" in the colony, particularly among the wealthy, and Lieutenant Governor Francis Fauquier expressed alarm in 1762 at the planters' rising indebtedness to British merchants, which he attributed to the planters' unwillingness to "quit any one Article of Luxury." Certain it was that a growing number of gentlemen planters, including William Byrd III, Benjamin Grymes, and other scions of old gentry families, were rapidly bringing "ruin upon themselves by their extravagance" and were able to "screen themselves from ignominy only by the ostentation and allurements of fashionable life," which they were able to keep up only by plunging themselves ever further into debt. The ultimate consequences of this rising addiction to luxury were well known. "There are two pernicious Things in the Government of a Nation, which are scarce ever remedied," warned Mentor in the *Virginia Gazette* in 1752: "the first is an unjust and too violent Authority in Kings: the other is Luxury, which vitiates the Morals of the People." Of the two, luxury was most to be dreaded. Whereas "too great an Authority [only] intoxicates and poisons Kings," "Luxury poisons a whole Nation," as it

[69]

habitates itself to look upon the most superfluous Things, as the Necessaries of Life; and thus every day brings forth some new Necessity of the same Kind, and Men can no longer live without Things, which but thirty years ago were utterly unknown to them. This Luxury is called fine Taste, the Perfection of Arts, and the Politeness of a Nation. This Vice which carries in its Womb an infinite Number of others, is commended as a Virtue; it spreads its Contagion from the Great down to the very Dregs of the People: The Lowest Rank of Men would pass for greater than they are; and every one lives above his Condition, some for Ostentation, and to make a Shew of their Wealth; others through a mistaken Shame, and to cloak their Poverty. Even those who are so wise as to condemn so great a Disorder, are not so wise as to dare, to be the first to stem the Tide, or to set contrary Examples. Thus, a whole Nation falls to Ruin; all Conditions and Ranks of Men are confounded; an eager Desire of acquiring Wealth to support a vain Expence corrupts the purest minds; and when Poverty is accounted infamous, nothing is minded but how to grow rich . . . Even those who have no Fortune, will appear and spend as if they had, and so they fall to borrowing, cheating, and using a Thousand mean Arts to get Money. But who shall remedy these Evils? The Relish and Customs of a whole Nation must be changed; new Laws must be given them. And who shall attempt this unless the Great Men should prove to be so much of Philosophers, as to set an Example of Moderation themselves, and so, to put out of Countenance all those, who love a pompous Expence, and at the same Time, encourage the Wise, who will be glad to be authorized in a virtuous Frugality.

In his sermon on the peace in 1763, James Horrocks warned his listeners against too "great a Tendency amongst us to Extravagance and Luxury" and admonished them to eschew the "insignificant Pride of Dress, the empty Ambition of gaudy Furniture, or a splendid Equipage . . . which must undoubtedly serve more for Ostentation and Parade, than any real Use or valuable Purpose." [66]

But luxury was not the only sign of moral decay in mid-eighteenth-century Virginia: drunkenness and swearing seemed to be increasing at an alarming rate, and, beginning in the 1740s, a rampant "spirit of gaming" had broken "forth . . . in ways [equally] destructive of morals and estates." By the early 1750s gaming had become so "very fashionable among the young Men" of the colony that William Stith preached a sermon before the House of Burgesses on *The Sinfulness of Gaming,* and the pages of the *Virginia Gazette* contained numerous warnings on its evil effects. Charles Hansford spelled out the magnitude of the problem in verse in the early 1750s.

> For, oh, my country, it would not be right
> Nor just for me only to show thy bright
> And shining side! I fear thou hast a dark
> And gloomy one. Attend thee! Do but hark!
> The dice-box rattles; cards on tables flow.
> I well remember, fifty years ago
> This wretched practice scarcely then was known.
> Then if a gentleman had lost a crown
> At gleek or at backgammon, 'twere a wonder,
> And rumbled through the neighborhood like thunder.
> But many now do win and lose pistoles
> By fifties—nay, by hundreds. In what shoals
> Our gentry to the gaming tables run!
> Scoundrels and sharpers—nay, the very scum
> Of mankind—joins our gentry, wins their cash.
> O countrymen! This surely would abash
> Our sleeping sires! Should one of them arise,
> How would it shock *him!* How would it surprise
> An honorable shade to see his boy
> His honor, time, and money thus employ!

"What a damned situation our Country is in," complained James Mercer in 1754. "No money to be got but at Horce-races & Gaming Tables & that not sufficient to open the Eyes of the People who frequent those places & are worse than selling their Wives & Children." But it was not just that the rage for gambling, as Hansford put it, did "much harm/ To some estates; 'tis like a spell or charm"; it also had devastating effects upon the character of the gamesters. The "prevailing Passion and Taste for Gaming . . . Racing,

Cards, Dice and all other such Diversions," warned James Horrocks, carried with them a "fatal Tendency" that ate away at the very foundations of Virginia society. Said Hansford,

> Honor, it stabs! religion it disgraces;
> It hurts our trade, and honesty defaces.
> But, what is worse, it so much guilt does bring,
> That many times distraction thence does spring.[67]

What was infinitely more frightening, however, was the increasing possibility that Virginians were already too far abandoned even to feel any guilt, that they had already proceeded too far along the road to corruption travelled by Rome to avoid the inner decay and destruction that were the ultimate Fate of that once mighty empire. Indeed, so prevalent was the addiction to luxury and pleasure that the very character of Virginia society seemed to be changing. "I have observed," wrote "A Gentleman" to the *Virginia Gazette* in 1751, "that the Majority of those that claim" the "term GENTLEMAN . . . have abandoned themselves to such trifling or vicious Practices, and glory in them as their peculiar Badge and Characteristic, that I am afraid the unfashionable Minority who sustain the same Denomination, will not be able to preserve it in its original Reputation, especially since their Number and Influence seem [to be] daily declining. I am already," he added, "somewhat uneasy, when I am complimented with the Character; and indeed could not bear it, did I not take the Liberty to abstract from it the modern Ideas crowded under it, and assure the Company I am not a *Gamester*, *Cock-Fighter*, or *Horse-Racer* by Trade; that I speak *English*, not *Blasphemy*; that I drink to quench my Thirst, not to quench my *Reason*; &c. &c. &c." In the new scheme of things, "Learning and good sense; religion and refined morals; charity and benevolence" seemed to have "nothing to do in the composition" of a gentleman. To be sure, there were still a "discerning few" among the gentry in every county in whom "good sense abounds." Such men were truly "an honour to humanity, a glory to the Colony, and the luminaries of the County." But could this "unfashionable Remnant of Gentlemen of the antique Stamp" possibly stem the tide of fashion, the corrosive "degeneracy in morals which is so conspicuous all around us" and had already struck deep roots in Virginia society? For that degeneracy, various observers noted, proceeded from the very conditions of life in Virginia, from the ease, and affluence, and indulgence, and the lax—some said, vicious—"manner of Education" they promoted. "For the Youth" of Virginia, observed one English traveler, "partake pretty much of the *Petit Maitre* Kind, and are pamper'd much more in Softness and Ease than their Neighbours more Northward," with the result that, "young Fellows" were "not much burden'd with Study" and, in sharp contrast to their fathers, learned to spend more of their "Time and Money in modish Recreations than in furnishing" their libraries "with valuable Collections, in charitable Distributions, or intellectual Improvements." Complained James Reid:

> Before a boy knows his right hand from his left, can discern black from white, good from evil, or knows who made him, or how he exists, he is a Gentleman. Before he is capable to be his own master, he is told that he is Master of others; and he begins to command without ever having learned to obey. As a Gentleman therefore it would derogate greatly from his character, to learn a trade; or to put his hand to any servile employment. His dog & horse are his favourite companions, and a negro about his own age, stature & mental qualifications, whom he abuses and kicks for every trifle, is his satelite. He learns to dance a minuet, that is, to walk slowly up and down a room with his hat on, and look wondrous grave, which is an affectation of the body to hide the defects of the mind. He is taught too how to skip and caper when ever he hears a few horse hairs rubbed with rozin, scraped across the guts of a cat, and he procures a competent skill in racing and cock-fighting. With these accomplishments, and a small knowledge in cards and dice, he becomes a gentleman of finished education, of consummate politeness, that is impudence & ignorance, consequently he is fit to enter into gay company, and to be a

companion, humble admirer, & favourite of the fair-Sex. There is no matter whether he can read or not, such a thing has nothing to do in the composition. He has money, land and negroes, that's enough. These things procure him every honour, every favour, every title of respect.

How could men thus "brought up" possibly reverse the precipitous moral decline that seemed to have seized the colony? For Virginians, in common with all western Europeans, had been taught—most vividly by the example of Rome—that "revolutions of life" were inexorable: "Obscurity and indigence are the Parents of vigilance & economy; vigilance and economy of riches and honour; riches and honour of pride and luxury; pride & luxury of impurity and idleness; and impurity and idleness again produce indigence and obscurity." Were Virginians really on the downward turn in this irreversible wheel of fortune? "We need only to open our eyes," wrote James Reid, "to behold this in the most glaring colours. The father toils his body, vexes his mind, hurts his soul, & ruins his health to procure riches for his son, who not knowing the trouble of acquiring them, spends them without prudence, and sinks into his original obscurity with contempt, disgrace and mortification." [68]

Clergymen of all persuasions seconded Reid's opinion. During the Seven Years' War, the Presbyterian Samuel Davies developed at great length in a series of blistering sermons the proposition that the war was God's punishment for the colony's sins. The roots of Virginia's troubles, he announced, were its "Riches." Excessive wealth had produced so great a "deluge of Luxury and Pleasure" that wherever one looked he found not virtue but a surfeit of drunkenness, swearing, avarice, craft, oppression, prodigality, vanity, sensuality, gaming, and disobedience to superiors: the catalogue of Virginia's sins was endless. "O VIRGINIA! a Country happy in Situation, improved by Art, and hitherto blessed of Heaven," he cried in 1756, "but now undermined and tottering by thy *own sins*," sins so great that it could be said of the "Men of *Virginia*, as well as those of *Sodom, They are wicked, and Sinners before the Lord exceedingly.*" Anglican clergymen from James Blair in the late 1730s to William Stith in the early 1750s and James Horrocks in the early 1760s echoed these sentiments, albeit in the more moderate and less impassioned tones befitting their religious persuasion. "The Vice and Wickedness of a Nation," Stith had counseled the Burgesses in 1752, "are the certain Forerunners and Cause of its Disgrace and Destruction," and both Davies and Horrocks agreed that all signs suggested that the destruction of Virginia was eminent. Davies believed that the situation called for nothing less than "A THOROUGH NATIONAL REFORMATION" marked with "Repentance, Reformation and Prayer," and Horrocks, that a permanent return to the solid virtues of their forefathers was needed. In such an enterprise, responsibility fell heavily on those men of solid virtuous principles, that increasingly "unfashionable Remnant," which still in the early 1760s dominated both the House of Burgesses and the other major political institutions of the colony. How or even whether they could fulfill that responsibility was a question of crucial importance to Virginia society that would soon have to be confronted.[69]

IX

In the early 1760s—on the eve of the great political and emotional crisis that preceded the American Revolution—the Virginia political community thus faced the future with an uncertain blend of anxiety and confidence. It was anxious over the unhealthy state of the tobacco market, the pernicious effects of black slavery upon white society, the disturbing crisis in moral behavior, and, more than at any time since the very first decade of the century, the colony's constitutional security within an empire whose leaders were showing disturbing signs of a growing disregard for the political welfare of its peripheral members. But it was also confident in the basic stability, responsiveness, effectiveness, and virtue of the Virginia political system and in the colony's long-term future within an empire that enjoyed so great a blessing, so great a security to liberty and property, as the British constitution. Over the next quarter of a century, this peculiar combination of anxiety and confidence would in considerable measure shape the responses of the Virginia political community to a series of political challenges of a magnitude undreamed of in 1763.

Massachusetts Farmers and
the Revolution

⊹⊹⊹

Richard L. Bushman

In the winter cold of December 1772, on the last day of the
year save one, the people of Hubbardston, Massachusetts,
met to hear read a letter from the town of Boston. The
meeting chose a committee of nine to frame a reply and
agreed to meet on January 20 next at the house of John
Ames, innholder. On the appointed day, the people dutifully listened twice to the committee's draft, "the vote was
called for and passed in the afermitive." The meeting instructed the clerk to record the committee's report in the
Town Book and transmit a copy to Boston.[1]

The reply began with a fundamental principle of government:

> We are of opinion that Rulers first Derive their Power from
> the Ruled by Certain Laws and Ruls agreed upon by Ruler
> and Ruled, and when a Ruler Breaks over Such Laws and
> Rules as agreed to by Ruler and Ruled, and makes new ones
> that then the Ruled have a Right to Refuse Such new Laws
> and that the Ruled have a Right to Judge for themselves when
> Rulers Transgress.

Moving to grievances, the committee declared that taxation by "Parliment," making the governor "independent of
the people by appointing him a Salary from home," and
especially paying judges of the Superior Court "appears to

us so big with Slavery that we think it enough to arouse Every Individual (that has any Ideas of arbitrary Power above the Brutal Creation) to use his utmost indeavors in a lawfull way to Seek Redress for our Injured Rights and Priveleges." The committee urged resistance "in the most firm, but most peaceable manner." "The Cause of liberty is a cause of too much dignity to be Sullied by Turbulence and Tumult. It ought to be maintained in a manner suitable to her Nature; those who ingage in it should breathe a Sedate yet Fervent spirit animating us to actions of Justice and Bravery. . . ." [2]

Boston had formed its committee to correspond with the towns in a meeting on November 2, 1772. A month earlier Governor Thomas Hutchinson had refused the town's request for a special session of the Assembly to discuss the recently announced royal salaries for justices of the Supreme Court of Judicature. In the absence of an Assembly to protest this threat to the independence of the judiciary, the town appointed a committee of twenty-one persons "to state the Rights of the Colonists and of this Province in particular, as Men, as Christians, and as Subjects; to communicate and publish the same to the several Towns in this Province . . . requesting of each Town a free communication of their Sentiments on this Subject." Boston unanimously approved the work of Josiah Quincy, James Otis, Samuel Adams, Joseph Warren, and their associates and authorized the printing of six hundred copies of *The Votes and Proceedings of the Town of Boston*, or the "Boston Pamphlet," as it came to be called. On November 30 the committee prepared lists of persons who could be "best intrusted" to distribute the pamphlet to leaders of the some 260 towns and districts of the province. By the middle of December, Samuel Adams reported in the *Boston Gazette*, the "Votes and Proceedings" had been "forwarded to four fifths of the Gentlemen Selectmen in the Country, the Representatives of the several Towns, the Members of his Majesty's Council and others of Note." Hubbardston was one of more than 144 towns to reply to Boston in 1773. Replies arrived from Becket, a tiny mountain town in Berkshire County, from Lancaster and Concord, market towns in Worcester and Middlesex, from Newburyport and Duxbury, port towns along the coast. In a subsequent letter, the Boston committee expressed appreciation for the interest of "so large a Majority of the Towns." Nearly half of the responding towns set up standing committees to correspond with Boston.[3]

The collection of replies is of great interest because it gives us a cross-section of backcountry opinion on the eve of the Revolution. From the time of the Stamp Act crisis, the bulk of the revolutionary agitation took place in Boston and along the seaboard. Mobs attacked the stamp distributors and customs officials in the coastal towns where they were assigned. Most of the pamphlets came off Boston presses. Most of the province's newspapers were printed in Boston. And yet the bulk of the population lived in small rural towns with populations under five thousand. Most adult men were not carters, shopkeepers, or seamen, but farmers. In Concord in 1771, eight out of ten heads of household owned land.[4] These people were poorly represented in the crowds that tore down Andrew Oliver's warehouse in 1765 or heard James Otis in the Boston town meeting. They did not have the benefit of the annual Boston Massacre oration. It is clear enough that sentiment in the towns was behind Boston and the American cause. Representatives to the Assembly had consistently voted against Britain on imperial issues by lopsided votes like 85 to 19 or 101 to 5. But the towns themselves had not spoken out before and the strength of their feeling was unknown. The replies to the Boston committee are the first broad sample of opinion from large areas of the Province which heretofore were silent.[5]

The town committees, of course, were not composed of plain dirt farmers. They were selectmen and treasurers, physicians and larger farmers, who had customarily held positions of leadership. Six of the nine Hubbardston committee members had been selectmen before their appointment, and two others were subsequently elected. Before and after 1772 they were chosen as assessors, clerks, and treasurers. The Boston committee had aimed at precisely this group, the "most respectable inhabitants." They were the men who shaped opinion. In a few towns, incipient Tories raised objections to the patriots' statements, and in still fewer the Tories carried the day. Usually, however, the committees' reports were adopted unanimously. Even in towns divided on local issues, the populace as a whole closed ranks on their statements of rights and grievances. If plain farmers thought otherwise than the town leaders, nothing was said in town meeting.[6]

Two aspects of the replies impressed the Boston patriots. One was the high level of political understanding dispersed throughout the Province. The fluency in eighteenth-century political language is impressive even today. In the smallest town there was at least one individual who could discourse on the British constitution even if he could not spell. A member of the Boston committee observed that "we seem to have a Solon or Lycurgus in every second or third town and district." Tactfully the Boston committee commented to Westborough that "the knowledge of the true Spirit of our Constitution, which has spread even to the remotest parts of the Province, must astonish those who represented us as ignorant, as savages." [7]

The other surprising and pleasing quality of the replies was their consistency with the Boston Pamphlet. The replies differed slightly in the grievances listed, in the formulation of principles, in emphasis and tone. Each local committee had taken pains to compose a statement that was truly its own. But the general principles were the same. The town replies were less polished versions of essays that might have appeared in the *Boston Gazette*, including standard complaints about Customs commissioners, a standing army, and judges independent of the people. The Boston Committee of Correspondence jubilantly expressed its "unspeakable satisfaction, . . . that their [the towns'] sentiments so nearly accord with ours." [8]

Taken as a whole, the responses from the towns are evidence of a network of political activists stretching from Boston to the remote corners of the Province. Only about three hundred souls, men, women, and children, occupied Hubbardston when its committee wrote on the mutual obligations of "Ruler and Ruled." [9] The network was not Boston's creation nor its tool. The Boston Committee of Correspondence was happily surprised to discover its existence. The patriot spokesmen in each town were independently committed and informed, probably taking their origin from traditions and models much older than the revolutionary agitation. But Boston could transmit manifestoes along the network in the confidence that the messages would be delivered in much the same form as they were sent. The network of activists meant that revolutionary language by 1773 was sounding in virtually every adult ear in Massachusetts, and that there was a fluid continuum of discourse joining the Boston press and town meeting and the talk in meetings and taverns throughout the Province.

Until 1774 most farmers passively participated in the revolutionary movement. They listened in town meeting and assented to the reports of the town committees. Perhaps they put their names to a boycott agreement. That changed in 1774. Through the summer and fall activity replaced passivity. In September, for example, General Thomas Gage aroused the Province when he confiscated arms and powder stored in Charlestown. Though it was neatly done without firing a shot, the rumor spread of armed conflict. Before the true story could be told and the men turned back, as many as sixty thousand, it is estimated, sprang to arms. An eyewitness reported that he had never seen "such a Scene before—all along were armed Men rushing forward some on foot some on horseback, at every house Women and Children making Cartridges, running Bullets, making Wallets, baking Biscuit, crying and bemoaning and at the same time animating their Husbands and Sons to fight for their Liberties, tho' not knowing whether they should ever see them again." [10] General Gage wrote to London that the people were "numerous, worked up to a Fury and not a Boston Rabble but the Freeholders and Farmers of the Country." [11] By then it was clear that the Province was a tinderbox. For the sake of liberties which earlier had been words, they were now ready to face the fire of the British line.

What did the Revolution mean to farmers and their families? Did they fight purely for the abstract legal rights of their declarations, or did the political language connect with their everyday lives? The town declarations intimated that much more than political abstractions were at issue. Chatham urged Boston to take action "to save from Impending Ruin this Distressed People." Andover opposed the "unnatural" ministerial scheme "which they justly apprehended to be big with their own Destruction." Words like "destruction," "ruin," "miseries," "fatal evils" dot the declarations. "We are deeply impressed," wrote the committee from Ashby, "with a Sence of the miseries we and this People are under and are likely to be Reduced to. . . ." [12] The single most commonly used word was "slavery." Acton said the various violations of charter rights had a direct tendency to break the constitution "and bring us into a State of abject Slavery." Hubbardston had said British measures were "big with Slavery." [13] Had the farmers not resisted the British at Concord and the colonists' supplies been confiscated, were the British troops free to roam the countryside and dominate the cities, if every Parliamentary statue and tax could be enforced and American rights violated at will, then the Massachusetts countryside would be on the way to slavery.

What would the life of an enslaved farmer be like? The concrete meaning often went unexplained. Sheffield wrote that the violation of rights could have "the most obvious and fatal Consequences to the good people of this province." [14] Whatever doom lay on the other side of a violated constitution was so obvious that the committee needed say no more. But despite the assumption of common understanding, the publicists did give glimpses of what slavery would mean and of the fate of New England if the farmers failed to resist. From the writings created for the purpose of mobilizing the farmers we can get an idea of what lay in the minds of farmers as they marched off to Concord in April of 1775.

Words like "slavery" and "tyranny" were all the more powerful because they were not newly introduced into political usage. Sixty years earlier, John Wise, the Ipswich pastor who bravely spoke out for New England rights during the Andros regime and later argued on behalf of democratic congregationalism, touched the key point when he said a tyranny was a state "where the chief end of Government is the Inriching and Greatness of its Ministers," meaning rulers. Hovering over all of the talk of rights and ruin was the image of the avaricious official. The *Independent Reflector* in New York City stated the point concisely: When a people's ruler "found his Happiness in the Prosperity of his People, they enjoyed the Sweets of Liberty; but no sooner did his Views center in the Pursuit of his own Interest, and the Gratification of his private Passions, than they were reduced to the wretched Condition of Slaves." [15]

New England had firsthand experience with slavery under Governor Edmund Andros. James II had invested the appointed governor and council under the Dominion of New England with authority to pass laws and levy taxes without any form of popular consent. A representative assembly was never called. The response in Massachusetts was revealing because the Dominion was in many respects a foretaste of Parliament's threat to representative government later on. After the Glorious Revolution, with James and Andros discredited, New England could speak freely about what it feared from the loss of political rights. The crux was that the absence of a legislature and independent judiciary gave license to official avarice. Cotton Mather reported in the *Magnalia* that Andros gathered about him a group of strangers with no interest in New England's welfare who "laid their designs to make an unreasonable profit of the poor people." Joseph Emerson in 1766, with the

[83]

Stamp Act freshly in mind, saw the parallels and quoted the *Magnalia* on the nature of official extortion. Without check of legislature or judiciary, "these harpies" whenever they "were a little out of money" imprisoned "the best men in the country" and put them to "intolerable expenses." The victims were helpless in the hands of "these greedy oppressors" because stripped of their rights.[16]

The principle of course went back further than Mather and was as much English as American. Charles I in his answer to the Nineteen Propositions in 1642 had stipulated that the reason the Commons was entrusted with the proposal of money bills was to prevent the prince from making use of "the name of public necessity for the gain of his private favourites and followers." Over a century later the town of Athol spoke out of the same tradition when it saw danger "rushing in upon us like a flood from the artful devices of a Corrupt and Designing ministry" who aimed to "put in Execution their avoritious Schums for enriching and agrandizing themselves and their favour rights although it be at the expence of Enslaving a free and Loyal People." Not that any one measure brought slavery, but so simple a matter as the privileges granted to the East India Company "was artfully projected to open the gate for the Admission of Tyranny and oppression with all their rapacious Followers to Stalk at large and uncontrouled to ravage our fair and dear bought Possessions. . . ." [17]

Tradition had created in the images of enslavement what amounted to a vernacular sociology. All who used the words associated with slavery, whether in Boston or Hubbardston, implicitly subscribed to that sociology, and they assumed that the plain people who listened also understood. Enslavement for those who spoke and heard was a process in which stock figures acted out predetermined roles. Once they were given the stage, the plot moved inexorably forward. The greedy ruler played a leading part. His designs on power and wealth were assumed to be incessant and undeviating. Equally important was the social organizations rulers constructed among their "rapacious followers" with the wealth extorted from the people. Favorites enjoyed the benefits of pensions, lesser offices, bribes, and fees, all within the ruler's disposal. In their eagerness to share in the spoils, the beneficiaries of the ruler's largesse became his lackeys. They cravenly subjected themselves to his will and thus became his tools in further political adventures.

In an obvious swipe at the British ministry, a 1775 sermon sketched the circle of dependents which the notorious Old Testament tyrant Haman the Premier gathered around himself.

> Haman the Premier, and his junto of court Favourites, flatterers, and dependants in the royal city, together with governors of provinces, counsellors, boards of trade, commissioners and their creatures, officers and collectors of Revenue, sollicitors, assistants, searchers and inspectors, down to tide-waiters, and their scribes, and the good Lord knows whom, and how many of them, together with the coach-men and servants of the whole made a formidable number through that great empire, all dependant upon the breath of Haman the court favourite, and with him breathing the same spirit, and expecting to share with him some part of the spoil.[18]

The entire structure, called an "establishment" in the eighteenth century, was much more than a system for dividing the spoils. It was a certain kind of society bound by fixed obligations. The ruler was the patron of the lesser men, their protector and giver of gifts. Bound by duty, gratitude, and interest to yield and obey, they became his clients and dependents. His object was to create power. All were "dependant upon the breath" of the ruler. Lust for the spoils and the moral obligation of having accepted protection compelled each person in the lower niches to yield to the will of those above. In the social dynamics of enslavement, the loss of political rights led inexorably to the ruler's unconstrained governance of a host of dependents. Motives were constant, the forms of social bonding familiar and powerful. Once the ruler collected taxes without the consent of the people nothing could stop him from assembling establishments and generating arbitrary power.

The publicists could assume an understanding of these processes because Massachusetts politicians had always known about the ligaments binding clients to their patron and assiduously watched for alliances and conspiracies forming to circumvent the limits on avarice. Joseph Dudley, governor from 1702 to 1714, like Edmund Andros before him, was believed to have his tools and creatures. Virtually every governor was subject to the same suspicion. Collections of power of any kind, even apart from politics, were potentially dangerous. John Wise in 1713 had warned against the scheme for the formation of clerical associations above the congregational level on the just "Prejudice or Presumption of Corruption in the Clergy." Given the opportunity, priests would use their office for personal gain as readily as rulers.

> Simony we know began almost as early as the Christian Church, and has prevailed amongst Clergy-men to a Prodigy. The Sacred things of Gods House have been a Trade and Merchandize, which has beggared Churches, and filled the Clergy in some Kingdoms with a Sacriligious and Exorbitant Pile of Wealth, and the World with a flood of Debauchees.

"That Government which sensibly Clogs Tyranny, and Preserves the Subject free from Slavery, under the ambition of men of great Fortune and Trust, is the only Government in the State to advance mens temporal Happiness," Wise believed, and by the same token "such a Constitution in Church Government," designed to clog ecclesiastical tyranny, was the only way to advance man's eternal happiness." [19]

Proposals for an Anglican episcopate in Boston after mid-century disturbed the province because episcopacy posed a threat to congregational dominance in Massachusetts; but a bishop was particularly detestable because, like the avaricious ruler, he surrounded himself with dependents living off tithes. When the Society for the Propagation of the Gospel constructed a large house on the slope overlooking the Charles River in Cambridge, opponents assumed it to be a prospective bishop's palace. It seemed the perfect symbol of the luxury and power the Anglican clergy intended to enjoy. Jonathan Mayhew, the vitriolic Boston clergyman who struck out at episcopacy, reminded his readers that the Church of England was far removed from the simplicity of the Gospel in apostolic times. The Church had erected an "enormous hierarchy" which ascended "by various gradations from the dirt to the skies." Once it was established, all of Massachusetts would "be taxed for the support of bishops and their underlings." [20]

When the introduction of customs commissioners and payment of gubernatorial and judicial salaries from royal revenues established in Massachusetts a number of officials dependent on the ministry and eager to do its bidding for a larger share of the spoils, the danger was widely recognized. It did not require extensive political education to instruct the backcountry in the consequences. The activists in every town were well acquainted with the sociology of enslavement and understood Samuel Adams when he warned that tax revenues extorted from Massachusetts would eventually be used for a host of malignant purposes: "standing armies and ships of war; episcopates and their numerous ecclesiastical retinue; pensioners, placemen, and other jobbers, for an abandon'd and shameless ministry; hirelings, pimps, parasites, panders, prostitutes and whores." [21] Townsmen knew how that host of dependents could range themselves under a corrupt ministry, feasting on the bread dispensed from the top, and servilely yielding to the arbitrary wishes of their masters.

The lure of wealth and power emanating from the ministry ultimately could reach to the remotest corner of the empire. With sufficient revenues at its command, rulers could extend their web of influence almost indefinitely. The colonists themselves would be drawn in (Hutchinson and Oliver, of course, had long since sold out) and turned into lackeys of the ministry. John Adams saw behind the schemes for an American revenue no concern for national or provincial prosperity. "All that will or can be raised," he cautioned his audience, will be applied "to corrupt the sons of America, and create a faction to destroy its interest and happiness."

> Corruption, like a cancer . . . eats faster and faster every hour. The revenue creates pensioners, and the pensioners urge for more revenue. The people grow less steady, spirited, and virtuous, the seekers more numerous and more corrupt, and every day increases the circles of their dependents and expectants, until virtue, integrity, public spirit, simplicity, and frugality, become the objects of ridicule and scorn, and vanity, luxury, foppery, selfishness, meanness, and downright venality swallow up the whole society.

In the farthest corner of the state, Berkshire county magnates, appointees of the royal governor to military and judicial posts, were astonished to find themselves represented "as seeking our own private emolument only at the expense of the interest of the people." By 1775 Pittsfield radicals believed that was precisely the truth. By means of the governor's powers, "a secret poison" had been "spread thro'out all our Towns and great Multitudes have been secured for the corrupt Designs of an abandoned Administration." "At this Door all Manner of Disorders have been introduced into our Constitution till it has become an Engine of Oppression and deep Corruption and would finally, had it been continued, have brought upon us an eternal Destruction." [22]

Slavery, to summarize, was extorted taxes, greedy rulers, tools and creatures, and a web of influence that entangled leaders in every town. What did it all mean for a farmer? How did the "Engine of Oppression" touch him? In a word, it meant impoverishment. Those webs of influence were costly, ever voracious of wealth, and possessed of the means of obtaining it. "Chicanery and craft, will be played backward, and forward, by designing and ambitious men, for places of profit and honour, until the wealth of a kingdom is exhausted, until its strength is at first weakened, then destroyed, as with a deluge. . . ." The association of tyranny and poverty was for this reason a fixed principle. "Liberty and Property" were polar opposites to "Slavery, Wooden

Shoes and Beggary." The English act for abolishing king-
ship in 1649 candidly stated the animosity long felt: "for
the most part use hath been made of the regal power and
prerogative to oppress and impoverish and enslave the subject. . . ." Petersham saw parliamentary taxation in the self-
same vein as "Draining this People of the Fruits of their
Toil." That was the heart of the matter: under slavery the
tyrant prevented people from enjoying what they had
earned. Should the colonies fail to resist tyranny, William
Gordon declared, "we may have the honor of burning under the heats of summer and freezing under the colds of
winter in providing for the luxurious entertainment of
lazy, proud, worthless pensioners and placemen." "Minions,
and court parasites, those blood-suckers of the constitution" would gluttonously devour the wealth of the people,
and in the declining nation, "poverty and misery come upon
its honest industrious inhabitants, like the breaking in of
mighty waters." [23]

Perhaps that is enough to explain the farmers' willingness
to fight, but the literature itself does not stop there. More
was said, and though usually briefly, there is sufficient to
suggest a still larger framework. Glancing comments, coming at critical junctures, give us a glimpse of even more
devastating social consequences following on unchecked
taxation. Taxation by avaricious officials, it would seem,
threatened not only the farmers' modest prosperity but the
entire order of society and impelled regression to an older,
oppressive, and degrading life.

Daniel Leonard, the wealthy Boston attorney and mem-
ber of the Royal Council who gave aid and comfort to the
Tories in the fall and winter of 1774 with his Massachu-
settensis articles in the *Massachusetts Gazette and Boston
Post-Boy*, provided a clue to the colonists' apprehensions.
One of Leonard's aims was to deflate radical propaganda.
He credited the whigs with expertly playing on the pas-
sions: "They were intimately acquainted with the feelings
of man, and knew all the avenues to the human heart. . . ."
They exhibited "Effigies, paintings, and other imagery,"

celebrated the anniversary of the mobbing of Andrew Oliver, delivered orations on the day of the Boston Massacre, and published "lists of imaginary grievances." What were the grievances? "The people were told weekly that the ministry had formed a plan to inslave them; that the duty upon tea was only a prelude to a window tax, hearth-tax, land-tax, and poll-tax; and these were only paving the way for reducing the country to lordships. . . ." [24] The notion of tax added upon tax is of course familiar, but the final outcome, "reducing the country to lordships," is a new theme in the rhetoric of enslavement. Lordships referred to feudal landlords who owned or controlled all the land, while the populace were tenants, obligated to them for feudal dues of money and service. Without saying how this was supposed to come about, Leonard had the Whig propagandists connecting taxes and lordships. Presumably heavy taxes could eventually bring a farmer's property to the auction block where local magnates could add it to their holdings. The farmer would have no choice but to become a tenant. The details apparently did not matter. Leonard assumed that his audience understood how the reduction to lordships took place.

John Adams returned from the Continental Congress in the winter of 1775–76 to find Massachusettensis "shining like a moon among the lesser stars" and set about at once to frame a reply. His essays over the pseudonym Novanglus began appearing in the *Boston Gazette* on January 23, 1775, and answered Leonard point by point. When Adams came to Leonard's summary of Whig grievances, he did not deny any of them or claim Leonard had exaggerated in the business of lordships. Quite the contrary. The people "were certainly rightly told, then, that the ministry and their governors together had formed a design to enslave them, and that when once this was done, they had the highest reason to expect window-taxes, hearth-taxes, land-taxes, and all others; and that these were only paving the way for reducing the country to lordships. Were the people mistaken in these suspicions? It is not now certain, that Governor

Bernard, in 1764, had formed a design of this sort?" [25]

In the light of the Leonard-Adams exchange, is it fair to say that in Massachusetts parliamentary taxes ultimately meant loss of land and, in the last stages of enslavement, a return to feudalism—great lords overshadowing the countryside and independent farmers reduced to tenants and laborers? The theme recurs in that portion of the Boston committee's letter to the towns prepared by James Otis, Josiah Quincy, and Samuel Adams and called "The Rights of the Colonists and of this Province in Particular." The Boston town meeting's two previous tracts were written for English merchants and politicians and sought redress from the administration. "The Rights of the Colonists" was for the people of Massachusetts and aimed to enroll them in the resistance. At the end, to drive the point home, the authors summarized the injustice of parliamentary taxation and sketched a scenario for Massachusetts if taxed by a body which had "no natural care for their interest."

> Hitherto many of the Colonists have been free from Quit Rents; but if the breath of a british house of commons can originate an act for taking away all our money, our lands will go next or be subject to rack rents from haughty and relentless landlords who will ride at ease, while we are trodden in the dirt.

The striking thing about the committee's statement is how little they felt required to say about the process of reduction to lordships. Like Leonard, they moved in one sentence from taxation by the British House of Commons to "haughty and relentless landlords who will ride at ease, while we are trodden in the dirt," assuming the selectmen in Hubbardston would understand. [26]

The explanation for the committee's confidence may lie in an observation of John Adams in the Novanglus essays. Following his comment on taxes "paving the way for reducing the country to lordships," Daniel Leonard had said that "this last bait was the more easily swallowed, as there seems to be an apprehension of that kind hereditary to the

[91]

people of New-England. . . ." In his rejoinder, Adams enlarged on the point. "It is true," he said, "that the people of this country in general, and of this province in special, have a hereditary apprehension of and aversion to lordships, temporal and spiritual," referring of course to the ecclesiastical lords whom Mayhew opposed in his anti-episcopate campaign, as well as to manor lords. What was meant by "hereditary apprehension"? It began, Adams went on, even before the founding of Massachusetts Bay. Their ancestors "fled to this wilderness to avoid [lordships]; they suffered sufficiently under them in England. And there are few of the present generation who have not been warned of the danger of them by their fathers or grandfathers, and enjoined to oppose them. And neither Bernard nor Oliver ever dared to avow before them, the designs which they had certainly formed to introduce them." Though abbreviated, the passage is intriguing, for in it Adams laid out a usable past for revolutionary New England. At the center was a traumatic conflict with lordships in England, both bishops and manor lords. The antagonism drove the first settlers from England and beyond that created a New England tradition of hostility. Fathers told sons who told their sons. Each generation admonished the next to resist lordships. So strong was this folk tradition that neither Bernard nor Oliver dared speak of them aloud. "Nor does Massachusettensis dare to avow his opinion in their favour," Adams concluded, intimating that every Tory had ambitions for a manor.[27]

Although Adams was in touch with currents of enlightenment thought unknown to the Hubbardston selectmen, he could not have been far ahead of backcountry opinion in these assertions. He was not an isolated Boston intellectual. He had apprenticed himself to the law in Worcester, mixed in Braintree politics, and ridden the circuit of county courts. He knew what he could count on in a broad audience, and it was a popular audience he addressed in the Novanglus essays. He was not aiming to impress London Whigs, but to make true Whigs of his own people. More-

over, he could not befuddle them with erudition or modish
London ideas on this particular point, because he was tell-
ing them what they had learned from their own fathers and
grandfathers.

Adams, of course, was also an intellectual with high pre-
tensions to enlightenment. In his mind, the farmers' vague
fear of an oppressive feudal past was more fully articulated
than his brief observation in 1775. During the Stamp Act
crisis ten years earlier he had written at length on feudal
law. In January of 1765, a few months before the Stamp Act
was passed, Jeremiah Gridley, dean of Boston students of
the law, had invited Adams and two other young attorneys
to join him in a detailed inquiry into feudal law, the better
to detect feudal vestiges in the English common law. As the
fruit of his investigations with Gridley's sodality, Adams'
Dissertation on the Canon and Feudal Law was published
serially in the *Boston Gazette* in the midst of the furor
caused by the stamps. This essay was doubtlessly more advanced and elaborate than the views of the average town se-
lectman. It can be taken as a guide to the current beliefs of
Boston's radical publicists. Thomas Hollis, the American
radicals' London tutor in libertarianism, immediately appreciated the essay's merits and reprinted it in the *London
Chronicle*. In Boston it was attributed to Gridley himself,
who, as the town's intellectual leader, enjoyed a "great and
deserved character for learning." [28] More exhortatory than
scholarly, the *Dissertation* sharpened and applied to the issues of the day modish enlightenment conceptions of the
feudal order and can be used to illuminate the intellectual
underpinnings of ideas which were abbreviated in appeals
to the backcountry.

At the core of the *Dissertation on the Cannon and Feudal
Law* was a description of the "wicked confederacy" between "two systems of tyranny." The first, represented by
the canon law, "was framed by the Romish clergy for the
aggrandizement of their own order." They were "enabled
to spread and rivet among the people" belief in priestly possession of "the keys of heaven, whose gates they might open

and close at pleasure." By their reducing the minds of men "to a state of sordid ignorance and staring timidity," human nature was "chained fast for ages in a cruel, shameful, and deplorable servitude" to the Bishop of Rome and "his subordinate tyrants." [29]

The feudal law, the other branch of tyranny, originated as a code for a "vast army in a perpetual encampment," formed for "the necessary defense of a barbarous people against the inroads and invasions of her neighboring nations." Although once necessary to organize the populace of Europe, it was "for the same purposes of tyranny, cruelty, and lust, which had dictated the canon law." The "general" of this army derived his powers from being "invested with the sovereign propriety of all the lands within the territory." No one held his property free and clear. "Of him, as his servants and vassals, the first rank of his great officers held the lands," and so on down to the bottom of society. "In the same manner the other subordinate officers held of them; and all ranks and degrees held their lands by a variety of duties and services, all tending to bind the chains the faster on every order of mankind." The system of land ownership made slavish servants of the people. "The common people were held together in herds and clans in a state of servile dependence on their lords, bound, even by the tenure of their lands, to follow them. . . ." [30]

It was the wicked confederacy between the two systems of tyranny that was "still more calamitous to human liberty." The temporal grandees used the sword of civil power to "maintain the ascendancy of the priesthood," and the "spiritual grandees" in turn used "their ascendancy over the consciences of the people" to require "blind, implicit, obedience to civil magistracy." Ignorance was the foundation of the confederacy, and the spread of knowledge in Europe, beginning at the Reformation, marked the beginning of its downfall. "The people grew more and more sensible of the wrong that was done them by these systems, more and more impatient under it, "till at last under the execrable race of the Stuarts, the struggle between the people and the confederacy aforesaid of temporal and spiritual tyranny became formidable, violent, and bloody." [31]

That bloody resistance to Stuart tyranny was the critical moment for New England and the New World, for "it was this great struggle that peopled America." Not religion alone, but "a love of universal liberty, and a hatred . . . of the infernal confederacy before described . . . accomplished the settlement of America." The Puritans, "more intelligent and better read" and also "vexed and tortured" by power, "resolved to fly to the wilderness for refuge from the temporal and spiritual principalities" of England. They were, then, the advance edge of the European movement for liberty (not merely of the Reformation, as Cotton Mather would have it), and they formed both ecclesiastical and civil governments "in direct opposition to the canon and the feudal system." One principle was paramount. "They saw clearly, that popular powers must be placed as a guard, a control, a balance, to the powers of the monarch and the priest, in every government, or else it would soon become the man of sin, the whore of Babylon, the mystery of iniquity, a great and detestable system of fraud, violence, and usurpation." In ecclesiastical government, moreover, they demolished diocesan episcopacy, that is, a bishop governing a diocese full of lesser priests. Puritan pastors ministered to one congregation, thus dismantling the "scale of subordination, from a pope down to priests and friars and confessors,—necessarily and essentially a sordid, stupid, and wretched herd." [32]

In civil government the first adventurers "detested all the base services and servile dependencies of the feudal system." "Slavish subordinations" were "inconsistent with the constitution of human nature." To give each man his independence, they had to break up the feudal system of graded ranks of property holding with each man dependent on the one above. "To have holden their lands allodially," however, with no obligation to a superior "would have constituted a government too nearly like a commonwealth." They were contented with the next best. They held their lands of the king, but with no intermediate "mesne or subordinate lords." New England was to be free of lordships. Each individual was lord and proprietor under the overarching lordships of the king. All the baser feudal services were wiped out. "In all this they were so strenuous, that they have even transmitted to their posterity a very general contempt and detestation of holdings by quitrents. . . ." [33]

New England thus sped the dissolution of the feudal order by flattening the social landscape: bishops were brought down and manor lords excluded, permitting pastors to lead single parishes only, and setting up farmers as lords of their own lands. Without lordships spiritual or temporal to exploit the people, New England from the beginning enjoyed greater liberty than England, until the "ardor for liberty" became "hereditary." Adams did not believe, however, that because New England had escaped the toils of the canon and the feudal law, progress would inevitably continue. "The canon and feudal systems, though greatly mutilated in England, are not yet destroyed. Like the temples and palaces in which the great contrivers of them once worshipped and inhabited, they exist in ruins; and much of the domineering spirit of them still remains." America was at that very moment in danger of being "driven blindfolded to irretrievable destruction." "There seems to be a direct and formal design on foot to enslave all America." Both kinds of lordships were contemplated. "A certain society" conspired to introduce a bishop, Adams said in a broad reference to the Society for the Propagation of the Gospel; and the Stamp Act, besides taxing the means of disseminating knowledge of English rights, "introduced the inequalities and dependencies of the feudal system, by taking from the poorer sort of people all their little subsistence, and conferring it on a set of stamp officers, distributors, and their deputies." America was threatened with "an entire subversion of the whole system of our fathers by the introduction of the canon and feudal law into America." The Stamp Act led the colonies backward into the feudal condition from

which their ancestors had heroically extricated themselves.[34]

Adams wrote under the influence of a number of historians for whom the central theme in English history was
the struggle to rid the nation of feudalism. It was a question
of pressing historiographical and political importance from
the seventeenth century on. Harrington had constructed
his view of English development around the issue of free
tenure of land for citizen soldiers who would therefore be
loyal to the nation rather than the lord who granted tenure,
and there were many variations. A number of Europeans
of John Adams' own time—Obadiah Hulme, Jean Louis de
Lolme, Catherine MacCaulay, William Robertson—treated
the same question. Jeremiah Gridley's sodality embarked on
a classic investigation when it chose to study the feudal
remnants in Coke. Because of its topicality, the *Dissertation
on the Canon and Feudal Law*, while published in the *Boston Gazette*, was probably intended for an English audience
as much as an American one. Adams was delighted when it
was recommended for English publication and Thomas
Hollis obliged. It was Adams the aspiring provincial with
eye fixed on the metropolis who wrote the *Dissertation*.[35]

Provincial farmers, of course, lacked even a sketchy
knowledge of the authors from whom Adams borrowed.
But his work may not have been so remote from the colonists as it would seem. Adams himself suggested that hostility to lordships was kept alive in folk tradition. When he
spoke about feudal law and lordships, he believed that he
connected with popular sentiments which had descended
along a route of their own. If so, the traditional aversion to
lordships was a link between high political culture and vernacular sentiments. The revolutionary polemicists could
tap this popular source of indignation whenever they
wished to mobilize resistance.

How accurate was Adams' interpretation of New England folk culture? Are we to believe in the actuality of an
underground stream of protest against the remnants of a

feudal order in England, a stream that ultimately flowed into the Revolution? While farmers were much less vocal before the revolutionary movement began than after, there were occasions when the active dislike of lordships surfaced and we have an opportunity to test the truth of Adams' views. To begin with, the assertion that the first settlers arrived with a dislike for the burdens of feudal tenures and a partiality for clear and independent title is probably accurate. The chafing burdens of the various derivatives of feudal tenure in sixteenth- and seventeenth-century England caused perplexity and despair among a large proportion of the English rural population. The trouble with most English tenures under the remnants of feudalism was that the landlord's claim on the land gave him rights that were incredibly expensive for the tenant. Tenants who had the right by custom to pass on land to their heirs or to sell portions as they chose were required to pay fines at such junctures of four or five times the annual rent, or in some cases as much as twenty or thirty times the rent. Under other tenures, the land reverted to the lord entirely after a certain number of generations in one family. One of the most annoying and costly of the landlords' privileges under a tenure called knight service was the right to take all the profits of a minor heir until he came of age. John Winthrop served at the London Court of Wards, where the king's wardships were administered. The court let out management of the minor's lands to the highest bidder, who then had every incentive to return the farm depleted and run down. Wardships were particularly hard on the great families of the realm, which were most likely to hold by knight service and which the King sometimes wished to chasten for insubordination. "Families were often at mercy, and were used according to their behaviour." Wardships "became then a most exacting oppression, by which several families were ruined." The Long Parliament ended wardships and the Restoration Parliament upheld the measure in 1660.[36]

While great families suffered at the King's Court of

Wards, ordinary people complained of the loss of common lands, where their animals grazed, and of wastes, the sources of firewood. Gerrard Winstanley appealed to the House of Commons in 1649 to "let the gentry have their enclosures free from all Norman enslaving entanglements whatsoever, and let the common people have their commons and waste lands set free to them, from all Norman enslaving lords of manors. . . ." [37] All of these manipulations, encroachments, and fines were possible because of the complex system of tenures in which no one owned the land outright. Always a superior had some claim, and in the intricacies of a given plot's history there was often a basis for a superior wresting control of the land from its customary user.

The pressure on landlords to encroach on customary privileges during the fifteenth and early sixteenth centuries stemmed from the fivefold rise in food prices. As prices rose, various expedients were adopted to increase the landlord's returns instead of all the benefits accruing to tenants with their fixed customary rents. Landlords found ways to deprive villagers of the strips they farmed jointly in open fields, then to enclose the fields with hedges and work the land as a single private farm. Manor lords had their lawyers scrutinize tenants' titles in search of pretexts for engrossing the land. Efforts were also made to interrupt tenures with fixed customary rents, which left the profits from rising prices to the tenant, and switch to leases with their chance to raise rents at each renewal. Rack-renting, as this practice was called, sometimes compelled the tenant to forfeit his lands altogether and become a laborer on acreage he had once called his own.[38]

The improving food market impartially benefited everyone with products to sell, and therefore yeoman farmers were as quick to grab land as lords of the manor. But because the lords had greater claims and at the same time were thought to be obligated to protect the poor, landlords were blamed for the suffering. Clerics and reformers from Hugh Latimer in the reign of Henry VIII to William Laud under

Charles I attacked greedy landlords and sought, though vainly, to stop the tide of enclosures and engrossments. Frustrated by parliaments composed almost entirely of landlords, the reformers brought little relief, and peasant wants went unattended. Throughout the sixteenth century, abused villagers threw down enclosures. In 1536, in the Northern Rebellion, hundreds of men rioted across two counties. In 1621 a play by a Lancashire schoolmaster was performed at Kendal Castle to protest the landlords' abuse of their tenants. In the play two tenants look into hell and see what appear to be ravens feeding on sheep. Ravens? No, says one. "Its false landlords makes all that croaking there, and those sheepe wee poore men, whose right these by their skill, would take awaie, and make us tenants at will, and when our ancient liberties are gone theile puke and poole, and peele us to the bare bone." [39]

A number of Englishmen saw in America an opportunity to erect manors and renew in the colonies the profitable and satisfying hierarchy of lord and tenant. Sir Ferdinando Gorges dreamed for decades of a great feudal proprietary in New England. Even after Puritan settlement, Gorges, with the aid of Sir Henry Spelman, the eminent student of feudal institutions, sought a patent that would make the settlers in Massachusetts Bay his vassals and tenants. Gorges even considered binding each tenant like a serf by not allowing him to "depart from the place where he is once planted, without lycence from his Land Lord." [40]

But with the hardships of such tenures so notorious in England, the counterforces in America were too strong. There were among the sponsors of colonies men like Edwin Sandys, active in the Virginia Company, who had opposed feudal tenures in England and was not of a mind to perpetuate them here. Ordinary men who came with their families were even less willing in America to bow to the yoke that had galled them in England. A Maine settler declared that "he would be a tenant to never a man in New England." The colonists boasted to their friends in England: "We are all freeholders, the rent day does not trouble us." Right through to the eighteenth century, officials explaining the peculiar nature of the New World to their superiors noted the intolerance of tenancies. Cadwallader Colden in 1732 complained that people were abandoning New York to escape the Hudson River manor lords. "People will not become their Vassals or Tenants for one great reason as peoples (the better sort especially) leaving their native country, was to avoid the dependence on landlords, and to enjoy in fee to descend to their posterity that their children may reap the benefit of their labor and industry." [41]

In virtually all of the colonies land was held in free and common socage, the most free of feudal tenures which required only a modest quit-rent to sustain the tie to the lord proprietor. In New England the break with the feudal past was still more complete. Land was held of the King by charter but with no fees or obligations except allegiance. The Massachusetts Bay charter authorized the court to impose quit-rents as in other colonies, but except for a few large grants to individuals, the General Court yielded that right. The towns and the people who received lots from the towns held their land by simple absolute tenures that secured their property against any legal assaults from a superior in the hierarchy of tenures. The tenure in effect was not feudal at all but allodial. Except for the faint shadow of the King's symbolic hold, the settlers of Massachusetts possessed the land in their own right as sovereign lords of their own holdings. It was only to bar a door already shut and locked that the Body of Liberties of 1641 declared that all land should be held free of feudal incidents such as wardships, liveries, escheats and forfeitures.[42]

By conscious design the legal foundations for lordships were never laid in New England. The General Court chose not to collect quit-rents and it forbade by law all feudal incidents. The moral foundations were similarly weak. Puritans honored and valued the sympathetic English lords whose support advanced the cause, but the colony was less than cordial when a group of them proposed to migrate. Lord Saye and Sele, who was prominent in the settlement of New Haven Colony, speaking on behalf of a number of noblemen, laid down the conditions under which settlement in Massachusetts Bay would be agreeable. John Cotton, who answered for the Puritan hierarchy, accepted without question the basic condition that society consist of "two distinct ranks of men," gentlemen and freeholders. But Saye and Sele further demanded that he and Lord Brooke be the first admitted to the ranks of gentlemen and they be empowered to admit others in the first round. Subsequently the legislature would designate gentlemen. Moreover, these gentlemen and their heirs were automatically to have seats in the upper house of the legislature. In response Cotton politely demurred. The ranks of the gentlemen, he reported, were more open in Massachusetts Bay. The colony acknowledged "not only all such eminent persons as themselves and the gentlemen they speak of, but others of meaner estate, so be it is of some eminency, to be for them and their heirs, gentlemen of the country." As for political position, the lords would have to qualify like everyone else —by gaining admission to a church and standing for election. "Hereditary honors both nature and scripture doth acknowledge," but hereditary authority was another matter. "Where God blesseth any branch of any noble or generous family, with a spirit and gifts fit for government," it would be wrong to neglect them in public election. But where He does not so furnish their posterity, the colony could not properly "call them forth, when God doth not." Men of high rank were welcome in New England, Cotton was at pains to say, and particularly these friends of Puritanism. But in fact they would have to stand for election to office, live without the benefit of manors, and leave their ranks open to men "of meaner estate." [43]

Cotton could not tactfully repudiate the idea of a class of noblemen, nor would he wish to under any circumstances, but he so restricted their privileges that life in New England was not inviting to the lords. Saye and Sele and friends did not migrate, nor did any other peers. The Puritan leaders for whom Cotton spoke were apparently sensitive to the dangers and rather than compromise were willing to do without the entire class of men who in England were accorded an essential place in the constitution. New England villages were thus distinguished in the North Atlantic by the total absence of lords and the dominance of the freeholding farmer. Titles to the land were free of those feudal remnants in their structure that permitted landlords to attack the rights of the occupants of the land. Enclosures and engrossment accelerated in England in the eighteenth century and comprised a large category of court business. None of that occurred in New England. No landholder had legal grounds for absorbing the property of another.

Even so, New England's freeholders were not permitted to lapse into complacent security. The strains on the English (and European) peasantry which the founders had experienced firsthand did not fade entirely from the memories of their children. There was reason for the sons to heed the warnings of their fathers about lordships as Adams hypothesized. The source of the colony's anxiety was the modest but persistent effort of the Stuart bureaucracy after 1660 to reassert a measure of control over royal possessions neglected during the turmoil of the Civil War. Commissioners were sent to Massachusetts Bay in 1664 to investigate the temper of His Majesty's subjects and to hear complaints about the asperity of Puritan rule. In 1676 Edward Randolph, invariably impertinent in his zeal for the King's service, arrived as a royal commissioner on a second round of investigations and in 1679 returned as the collector of customs. An unusually venal royal governor, Edward Cranfield, was appointed in neighboring New Hampshire in 1679. This handful of officeholders started suspicions that were never laid to rest. Looking back in 1691 a friend of New England expressed the view that these "Publicans" as he called them (in contrast to New England's supposed republicanism) were a surplus from the government patronage lists in the last years of Charles II when "the Craft was almost worn Thred-bare." "Therefore some of the weaker Brethren began to look out for Imployment, and to think of Transporting themselves somewhere else." After making inquiry they discovered that "the People of New-England were grown exceeding Rich, and that, without doubt, they had been so imploy'd in improving themselves, as to have little or no leisure to study Court-Juggles, and little Tricks; And therefore like to be the easier purchase for a parcel of poor hungry Publicans." Their first move on arrival was to wring all they could from "money, Ships, Goods, Merchandizes" by subjecting the people to the "utmost Severities of Law. . . . And when Moveables began to fail them they fell upon the poor Innocent Houses and Lands. . . ." This writer and many like him chose to interpret the reassertion of royal power as a facade for profiteering by avaricious officials under the guise of service to the King.[44]

Lands became an issue because of that one slight remnant of feudal control in Massachusetts titles—the King's overlordship. The colony had made two technical errors in dispersing the land granted by Charles I. In grants to individuals, the government had neglected to affix the seal in many instances, a requirement in the charter. In grants to towns there was that problem plus the fact that the towns were not proper legal entities. To hold land and disperse it the towns should have been incorporated. They were not and could not be without charter from the King or Parliament. The old dicta held: a corporation (which Massachusetts Bay was) could not create another corporation. As Massachusetts heard over and over again, their towns were mere villages and did not exist in law. Where did that leave the towns' land? It would have reverted to the colony, except that in 1684 Massachusetts lost its charter. The complaints of Edward Randolph and others about official recalcitrance, blatant disregard of the Navigation Acts, and refusal to allow the appeal of court decisions to England resulted in the dissolution of the Massachusetts Bay Company as chartered in 1629, and the formation of a royal dominion including Rhode Island, Connecticut, New Hampshire, and New York. With the company dissolved, all ungranted lands, all lands whose ownership was in dispute, and all the land dispersed in town meeting or without the seal reverted to the Crown, the ultimate owner. Very little else was left.[45]

Andros knew that he risked revolution in announcing the weakness in Massachusetts titles. The essence of the legal truth was that the colonists did not own the lands they had labored on for as long as fifty years. The King could grant their holdings to anyone he chose. Andros' aim was not to reclaim all the land but to reconfirm the questionable titles (for a fee) and assess a quit-rent. Even that appalled the colonists. The Lords of Trade had contemplated foregoing the quit-rents for fear of the colonial reaction, until at the last minute it was decided that the rent was a necessary reminder of the King's ultimate ownership. Rather than confront the population directly, Andros leaked a rumor and then let members of the Council tell the people in their locales. He asked the Council to set the example by petitioning for confirmation of titles. When even some great men hung back, he entered writs of intrusion against five of the largest landholders and forced the holdouts into court. Samuel Sewall, after refusing as long as he dared, petitioned for confirmation and felt the sting of popular disapproval. "The generality of People are very averse from complying with any thing that may alter the Tenure of their Lands," he noted, "and look upon me very sorrowfully that I have given way." [46]

The severity of the colony's situation struck home when Andros' friends began petitioning for land within the towns. Andros had no intention of wresting farms from individual landholders, but the town's undivided common lands were another matter. These titles were held by the invalid town corporations and hence reverted to the King. Edward Randolph brazenly asked for seven hundred acres of such land in Cambridge between Spy Pond and Saunders Brook. Cambridge objected that the tract of unimproved land provided firewood, lumber, and pasture for eighty families who would be ruined without it. When reminded of the flaws in their titles, the town implicitly acknowledged that "the formality of the Law" had not been exactly observed in all respects. "Nor doe wee judge it can rationally be expected from a people circumstanced as the first Planters were, by whome those matters were acted in the Infancy of those Plantations, They not haveing Council in the Law to repaire unto, nor would the imergencies that then inevitably happened admitt thereof." [47] There was a gross injustice in faulting the people who had cleared plots in the wilderness for minor legal failings. The court paid no heed to Cambridge's plea and awarded the land to Randolph. Objections to grants within the bounds of other towns—Charlestown, Lynn, and Newport and Portsmouth in Rhode Island—met a similar fate.

In mid-April 1689, rumors of the overthrow of James II and the landing of William of Orange sharpened the colony's outrage. On the morning of April 18, the inhabitants of Boston turned out to the beat of drums and formed themselves into militia companies. By sunset, Andros was in prison along with about twenty-five friends. The Dominion government was non-operative, and a committee of gentlemen with Governor Simon Bradstreet at the head governed the Colony. The uprising was not solely Boston's doing. By mid-afternoon more than a thousand armed colonists marched in Boston's streets, and more were pouring in from Charlestown every minute. The country towns responded with the same alacrity as on the more famous April morning eighty-six years later. A Charlestown merchant's diary entry said that the adjacent towns along with Boston "did this day rise as one man." The committee reported "the strangely unanimous inclination which our Countrymen by extreamest necessities are driven unto." The country people were the ones who could not tolerate regard for Andros' comfort. In "rage and heat" they demanded that he be removed in chains from Councillor John Usher's house and delivered to the fort. The towns quickly complied with the request for a convention of delegates, and the representatives by a large majority voted to commit the government to the governor, magistrates, and deputies chosen before the Dominion. The population far and wide hated the Andros government and were quick to reconstruct a government under which their property was secure.[48]

The conceptual framework in which all of these events took place was explicated in a series of pamphlets and declarations published in defense of the rebellion. With land titles in jeopardy and a "Crew of abject Persons fetched from New York" preparing to cut out estates for themselves, it is a little surprising that some reference was not made to the feudal law. Andros had governed without the aid of an elected legislature. The governor and his appointed council levied taxes and enacted laws. The combination of circumstances could well have evoked comments about the Norman yoke (feudal government and land tenure) in New England in 1689 as similar conditions had provoked such allusions under Charles I. Lordships, and feudal law, however, are not in the manifestoes. The closest allusion is to the French system, but no details are given and popery and monarchial tyranny are as likely referents as manors and tenancies.[49]

The picture drawn by the Boston committee in the declaration read before the army of insurgents on April 18 was much simpler than Adams' complex description of interlocking ecclesiastical and political hierarchies in the *Dissertation on the Canon and Feudal Law*. The colony's specific grievances are set in the frame of a popish plot to eradicate Protestantism, to which the presence of the French, James' Catholic sympathies, and New England's commitment to reformed worship lent credibility. But the nature of the conspiracy and the sociology of the conspirators' designs are left to the imagination. The French plot hovered vaguely in the background. The heart of the colonists' complaint was simply the free rein given "strangers to and haters of the People" when Massachusetts had its "*Charter* Vacated, and the hedge which kept us from the wild Beasts of the field, effectually broken down." Andros' friends, these "Tools of the Adversary," had preferments loaded upon them, and extorted fees "from every one upon all occasions, without any Rules but those of their own insatiable Avarice and Beggary." "Nor could a small Volume contain the other Illegalities done by these Horse-leeches in the two or three Years that they have been sucking of us." "Because these Things could not make us miserable fast enough" these wretches went against the colonists' land. Under pretext of flaws in title, "the Governor caused the Lands pertaining to these and those particular Men, to be measured out for his Creatures to take possession of" and thus to "impoverish a Land already Peeled, Meeted out and Trodden down." The assault on New England's farms was merely one more outburst of official greed, not the prelude to the introduction of a feudal social order. The colonists were obsessed with a venal bureaucracy, not the return of lordships.[50]

The effect, nonetheless, was to jeopardize Massachusetts land titles as many English titles were endangered during the century of inflation. "Several Towns in the Country had their Commons begg'd." In England manor lords had turned pastures into sheep runs. Andros challenged every farmer's title as individual landlords had pressured copyholders in England. The scope of Governor Andros' operation made the Dominion of New England a nightmarish exaggeration of the troubles of English husbandmen. That the men behind the designs on the land were placemen and not landlords was of small moment; the avaricious of whatever status would go for land as for the jugular. The Dominion experience perpetuated the anxieties of Old England in Massachusetts. All that was missing to complete the picture Adams had drawn was a descriptive language that evoked feudal images: lordships, vassals, tenantry. And that simply was not there.

No general threat of such large proportions recurred in Massachusetts before the Revolution, but events did not permit New England's privileged yeomanry to sink into complacency. They began the eighteenth century with the vulnerability of their freehold status freshly in mind, and a combination of forces acting at different points conspired to remind farmers of the precariousness of their position. But in none of them were allusions made to lordships or regression to the feudal law even though circumstances seemed to warrant the use of the language of John Adams' *Dissertation.* In a number of towns, most of them in the older portions of the colony, disputes arose over rights to the town's common lands. In the seventeenth century all the town inhabitants had enjoyed grazing privileges on the large undivided town fields. After the Andros trauma, ownership of the fields tended to pass from the town as a body to specific individuals who claimed sole proprietary rights and attempted to exclude other inhabitants. Though usually the proprietors had the law on their side, the force of custom and the need for access to common pasture and woodlots kept the question of access before the town for many decades. Jonathan Edwards thought it one of the achievements of the Awakening in Northampton that the people came "to an agreement and final issue, with respect to their grand controversy relating to their common lands; which has been, above any other particular thing, a source of mutual prejudice, jealousies, and debates, for fifteen or sixteen years past." Similar controversies occurred in Duxbury, Plymouth, Haverhill, Newbury, Salem, Woburn, Billerica, and Falmouth. Although the controversy pitted one large group of townspeople against the other, not the manor lord against the villagers, the question of control of the common fields obviously had its antecedents in England and could have been an occasion for reviewing memories of the older conflicts. But lordships were never mentioned.[51]

Along the periphery of Massachusetts, settlers in new towns fought for title to their lands with landlords holding under grants from New York or New Hampshire who desired to populate their lands with tenants. As with so many colonial boundaries, the lines between Massachusetts and its neighbors, New Hampshire and New York, were not precisely defined. There was no need for exactitude until population growth pressed people toward the dividing lines. By the third decade of the eighteenth century on the New Hampshire boundary and fifteen or twenty years later in the west settlers began to move on to controverted land, and immediately became pawns in the conflict.

After the Treaty of Aix-la-Chapelle in 1748, Massachusetts sold townships in the Berkshires beyond the Connecticut River in territory over which New York exercised a vague claim. The Hudson River manors reached dimly eastward toward the Connecticut. The lords of those manors, and particularly Robert Livingston, felt compelled to treat squatters from Massachusetts as intruders. When they refused to move off the land, houses and crops were burned and the occupants jailed. Massachusetts men in turn formed militia companies and invaded New York to release the prisoners. Tenants of the manor were hauled off to jail in Springfield. From 1752 to 1758 sporadic raids and retaliations required Livingston in New York and the Massachusetts militia leaders on the other side of the line to fortify their houses and arm themselves as if for war.

The conflict gradually cooled after 1757 when the Lords of Trade recommended to the King that the boundary be fixed twenty miles east of the Hudson. The struggle then shifted from Massachusetts claims to claims of the Stockbridge and Wappinger Indians. Settlers holding Indian deeds refused to pay rents to the proprietors of the Philipse Highland Patent, who claimed part of the Indian land. After the usual tugging and hauling, the barn burning and threats of whippings, a group of farmers from eastern Dutchess County marched on New York City to release some of their number imprisoned there. A show of force turned them back and the arrival of British regulars quieted the riots, which had spread as far north as Albany County. William Prendergast and other leaders were captured and Prendergast was sentenced to death. Lord Shelburne, who was none too sympathetic with the magnates' tactics anyway, saw to it, as was customary, that Prendergast was pardoned, and by 1767 the farmers had either migrated or gone back to paying rent.[52]

New York was more violent than New Hampshire, but the issues were similar. At the colony's northern and eastern borders, Massachusetts freeholders owning their land in absolute fee confronted proprietors who offered tenancies in return for rent or quit-rent. The most advanced form of freehold tenure faced a remnant of feudalism. And yet nowhere in the exchange were lordships at issue. Doubtless the settlers preferred freehold tenure. Cadwallader Colden said, with New Yorkers in mind, that "the hopes of having land of their own and becoming independent of landlords is what chiefly induces people into America. . . ." Massachusetts won over some of Livingston's tenants of many years by offering a fee simple title. The aim of the claimants on the Indian deeds was a longer lease and more secure title as well as lower rents. But never was tenancy or the legitimacy of a manor questioned. Prendergast repeatedly said he wished to make up with the landlords. The principle of allodialism was not at stake. By the same token, the town inhabitants did not charge proprietors of common fields with engrossment or enclosure. Whatever may have lain below the surface, the rhetoric Adams used in the *Dissertation on the Canon and Feudal Law* was not part of the farmers' public vocabulary in these disputes.[53]

So long absent from situations where they might be expected to appear, lordships surfaced at last in Massachusetts in connection with quite another land-related problem. In 1722 an anonymous pamphleteer published in Boston *The Original Rights of Mankind Freely to Subdue and Improve the Earth*. The tract described, with some exaggeration, the plight of farmers who were forced to look in outlying towns for farms for their sons only to discover that speculators monopolized the best land. It was a fact that common lands in many towns were gone, and over the generations farms had shrunk until they were too small to divide further. Building on this reality, the author said these husbandmen had the choice of purchasing nearby lands in the hands of monopolizers or going to the frontier "and there be exposed to the Insults of the Indians." To "set up Idol Self" and "Serve their Lusts," the monopolizers had raised the price so high that "all the Personal Estate the Husbandman or Farmers and their Families can raise from their Farms, is not sufficient to purchase Land for their Children to Settle upon." Were ten farmers' sons a year from each town to buy a hundred acres for twenty shillings an acre the interest alone would be six thousand pounds yearly. "If I may not call it Oppression, is it not a very heavy burden laid upon our blooming Youth, who are both the Strength and Glory of the Province?" The author asked for taxes on dormant lands to hurry sales and for free distribution of land as in the seventeenth-century towns. Failing this relief, the prospective purchasers of the monopolizers' lands would become their slaves, as probably the monopolizers had long intended. "Monopolizers of Dormant Lands would be the Lords of this Continent, and necessitate the Farmers, their Families, and Posterity, to give them the benefits of all their Labours, from Generation to Generation. . . ." The steps from purchase at high prices to slavery are not laid out, but presumably rents or interest would eat up the fruits of the farmers' labor and force a forfeiture. At last "the Continent would be the Monopolizers Property, and all Farmers and their Posterity the Monopolizers Slaves for ever. . . ." America would regress to the older order of lordships and perpetual tenancy.[54]

One bibliographer has speculated that the author of the *Original Rights,* who put only the initials I.M. on the title page, was the Reverend Joseph Morgan of Freehold, New Jersey, a pastor in the area where New Englanders and their descendants contended for ownership with the great Jersey proprietors in a close parallel to the struggles with New York and New Hampshire. If the attribution is correct, the pamphlet is evidence that the notion of a decline into tenancies and lordships lurked in the minds of at least some observers of the title disputes and that the engrossment of frontier lands in Massachusetts evoked the same image.[55] The authorship is of little importance, however, for the idea lacked energy in the context of the land controversies. *Original Rights* had no successors. Its companions are not to be found in the literature of settlement, whether associated with boundary disputes or control of new towns. The conception of lordships received its fullest expression in quite another connection entirely—the Massachusetts currency tracts written between 1716 and 1750—where at last we find precedents for Adams' *Dissertation.*

The author of *Original Rights* had lumped together monopolizers of new land and "biting Usurers." [56] So did a sober pamphlet in favor of a land bank published in Boston in 1716 and entitled *Some Considerations Upon the Several Sorts of Banks Propos'd as a Medium of Trade.* Its author foreshadowed *Original Rights* in observing the effects of "those Gentlemen that have Ingrost vast Tracts of Land, without any design ever to settle them," and explained more fully the connection of speculators with "biting Usurers." "Some that are good Farmers, who observing that the Lands are so generally Ingrost, fear they shall not procure sufficient to settle their Children upon, have straitned themselves, and perhaps run in debt to buy Land. . . ." The author did not blame the creditors or charge them with selfish aggrandizement. Men were forced to be usurers "whose Judgment and Conscience is utterly against it." But the results were the same. The usurers were forced "for failure of paying Debt and Interest, to swallow up the Estates of their poor Neighbours." [57]

The connection of debt and the loss of estates was a commonplace assumption of the currency literature by 1720, transcending partisanship. The pro-bank writers said a shortage of currency made farmers vulnerable to usurers; the anti-bank men believed easy loans secured by mortgages put men's estates at the mercy of the bank. An advocate of belt-tightening and an end to the seductions of paper money observed that in Massachusetts,

> People generally desire to be Freehold, they don't chuse to be Tenants, and pay Rent. But if we take up Money whether of the Province or particular Persons, on our Lands; we so far become Tenants to the Lenders, and pay Rent to them.

[113]

And if we can't pay when what's borrowed is regularly call'd for, but a Course of Law recovers Land from us; possibly more Land will be taken, then we should have been willing to have Sold, for half so much more as we have borrowed. Possibly some who have taken up Money on their Lands, by being uncapable of paying will lose them. . . .

In 1734 an anti-bank man summarized the province's banking experience to that date as being of "pernicious consequences, in affording the unthinking part of the People an opportunity of Morgaging their Lands, and thereby rendeing themselves Miserable, or at best Tenants instead of Freeholders. . . ." Farmers in claiming the right to borrow money also laid claim to "a Right to the Alms-House." "These banks tend to the Ruin of the Province." [58]

For some writers the loss of estates was a simple economic process that followed inevitably on debt of any kind. The pro-bank men more commonly saw the schemes of "griping usurers" behind the ruining of farmers. "A few wretched Misers," a particularly virulent pamphleteer wrote, "stand gaping to devour their Indigent but honest Neighbours, and with hearts more unrelenting by far" than Pharoah's "make their Necessitous Circumstances their cursed opportunity to Enrich themselves. . . ." Their procedure was to lend money to the needy farmer and then to monopolize the bills, "so those who have mortgaged their Estates to them may never be able to redeem them, and so of Consequence such Estates must fall into their Hands for what they will be pleased to allow for them. . . ." The aim of the monopolizers was the "engrossing the whole Trade of New-England, and the best part of the Land too." [59]

Because of the anonymity of the authors, the currency tracts cannot be precisely located in the spectrum of political opinion, apart from their position on currency itself. Many were moderate, reasoned, and industriously researched, their language close to the official diction of the exchanges in the Assembly between the governor and the two houses. Others employed a charged, excessive rhetoric, taking titles like *Massachusetts in Agony* or *The Melancholy State of the Province*. The tone alone ties them to radical writings of England's country party. The author of the one entitled *New News from Robinson Cruso's Island* (1720) was at least familiar with Daniel Defoe, a contributor to the literature of England's country party. Underlying the rhetoric was ordinarily a reasoned argument of some sort but the energy was all in the diction not the logic. Why the opposition to bills of credit, *New News* asked: "Is it any wonder, that a few Muck-worms, who have monopoliz'd vast Hoards of Bills should oppose it; seeing they have so fair a prospect (as they think) of raising their Estates, and building up their Names on the Ruins of their Country? Tho' hereby their Memory will be a Stench in the Nostrils of Posterity." " 'Tis a Gangrene in the Soul, that with a poysonous Heat, consumes the Natural Affections, to supply their room with the most virulent Humours. This furious Desire precipitates Men on to Oppression, Violence and Deceit. . . ." [60]

These excessive tracts—two or three in the 1720s, a growing number in the late 1740s and 1750s—went to the extreme in every respect including an elaboration of the effects of unpayable debts on the social order. "What else can we suppose them so furiously driving at," the author of *New News* asked about the anti-bank men, "but to engross all the Estates in the Island; and themselves being Lords, the rest by consequence their Slaves?" A companion piece of the same year, attributed to Dr. Oliver Noyes, a member of the Lower House in the 1720–21 term, ended his argument against an anti-bank pamphlet with a question about the prospects for the province. "And now let any Man judge" whether currency restrictions "be the way to keep the Estates in many Mens Hands . . . or whether it does not rather look like a design to inslave a People and make a few Lords and the rest Beggars." [61]

The bare conceptions of these writers were not outlandish by conventional political standards. The conservative Edward Wigglesworth in 1720 had recognized the same mechanisms at work when people indebted themselves to a public bank.

> We have found by the unhappy Experience of the Publick Bank, that if there be but a Bank to run and borrow at, the Ill Husbandry, Vanity and Folly of the People is such; that in a short time most of the Estates in the Country would become involved; and I think it much more for the Strength, Safety, and Interest of the Country both Civil and Religious, that the Estates should continue as at present in many mens hands, than that a few Gentlemen should be Landlords, and all the rest of the Country become tenants.

It was the extravagance of the radicals which distinguished them, not the simple idea of lordships, their sense of an engulfing and ruinous alteration in the social order and the degradation of farmers from freeholders to tenants and peasants. These authors predicted a new structure: we "shall in a little Time have no middling Sort, we shall have a few and but a very few Lords, and all the rest Beggars." This "arch, Shy Set of Men" who had gnawed at the province for fifty years, *A Word in Season* warned in 1748, "have almost ruin'd the Country by using such Means to beggar the Inhabitants, to aggrandize their own private Fortunes, in order to make the Commonalty Slaves and Vassals, and themselves Lords of Mannors, and sole Possessors of our Lands, Liberties &c." "Vincent Centinel" in 1750 drew up an entire scenario with New England farmers the victims of haughty and imperious party men who spurned all beneath them.

> It is unquenchable Torment, to an ambitious Man, who is pretty Rich, to behold his Neighbour happy, and free in the Enjoyment of a few Acres of Land, with his Cow, his Horse, and his Cart,—He actually wants this very Man on his own Farm, working very hard indeed, for just his daily Bread; except he allows him one single Moment to cast one Glance of his Eye upon this Great Lord of the Mannor; his gilded Equipage, Party-coloured Attendants, and himself besmear'd with Gold—If such Men had their Wills, there should no Common Man own a Canoe, Fishing Boat, Sloop, or the like;

but they should Fish, go a Coasting cross the Seas as their
Servants; nor should any Countryman own one Inch of improved land between Boston and the Blue Hills. . . .

"Vincent Centinel" told his readers that the design to cre-
ate this kind of society had preceded the currency debates.
With their ultimate aim already in mind, the rich faction
discovered that "there was no way better to bring this
Scheme about, than to deceive the People into Debt over
Head and Ears. . . ." By hoarding the money or sending it
away, the creditors made repayment impossible. "We must
sell our Lands to pay them; then go, and Work upon their
Farms, or Starve, or go to Seas as their Slaves, or go to—
Jail—" [62]

The pamphlet debate over the money supply occurred
at a high level and city men largely conducted it. Beyond
the fact that "Vincent Centinel's" *Massachusetts in Agony*
was reprinted once, we cannot know its circulation or how
country towns received it. [63] There is no equivalent of the
replies to the Committee of Correspondence for the currency debate. We do know, however, that the desire for
additional currency was not restricted to Boston and the
port towns. In 1730 the Board of Trade ordered all Massachusetts currency issues withdrawn by 1741 and only min-
imal issues of bills of credit thereafter. The Lower House
of the Assembly fought tooth and nail against Governor
Belcher's attempts to enforce the proclamation. When the
Lower House seemed to temporize slightly in 1739 and
1740, the towns purged the representatives and sent back a
more adamant Assembly. The representatives, in turn, in an
unheard of action, refused to reelect sixteen councillors,
who had been the governor's allies. The country representatives understood precisely the unbearable pressures a
shrinking money supply would place on debtors. As the
day of doom approached, the Lower House approved plans
for a private land bank to serve as a surrogate for public issues by lending notes on mortgages to double the value of
the loan. The response was widespread. The first petition
for a bank listed nearly four hundred subscribers, the sec-

ond over eight hundred from towns scattered over the entire province. Nearly twelve hundred different names can be identified among the various land bank petitions and papers. An observer at the time commented that in addition to the partners "five Parts in six of the Countrymen, who were not interested in it, were Abettors of it. . . ." To squelch the private bank, Parliament extended the Bubble Act of 1720 to Massachusetts and thereby forbade stock companies from issuing bills. John Adams later said that there was more turmoil in the province over this action than over the Stamp Act. Threats of uprisings were reported in the Council from nearly a dozen towns, and only by the slightest majority did the land bank partners agree to comply with the law.[64]

Considering the prevalence of debt, there is every reason to believe that Massachusetts farmers were tuned into the issue. The need for currency and capital created a network of communication and interest that reached into virtually every town, informing, educating, and arousing the inhabitants. How vividly each individual in the network pictured with "Vincent Centinel" the "Great Lord of the Mannor; his gilded Equipage, Party-coloured Attendants, and himself besmear'd with Gold" cannot be known. It seems certain that at the very least everyone understood that failure of repayment led to the sale of land at a loss and the danger of tenantry. The pro-bank Oliver Noyes in 1720 said that "every Body else thinks" along with the conservative Edward Wigglesworth that "to keep the Estates in many Mens hands" is "the Strength, Safety and Interest of the Land." Presumably like Noyes and Wigglesworth, every body also knew that foreclosures on debt permitted some men to become lords. People divided over how to avoid that eventuality, but most believed the dynamics of debt drove society in that direction. The Massachusetts men contesting for land along the New York border warned one another to keep clear of debt to the manor lords. The mob enacted an extra-legal statute that unpaid debts were to be satisfied with personal property—cattle or other movables—not real estate. Prendergast understood that while title claims could be contested, the landlords' victory was certain if land had to be forfeited for debt.[65]

Plain farmers in 1765 may not have remembered the early settlers' flight from lordships, even though that impulse was certainly present in the first generation. Nor was everyone touched directly by each one of the challenges to land titles: Andros' invalidation of town grants, boundary contests with New York or New Hampshire proprietors, disputes with town proprietors over excluding some inhabitants from the commons, or speculators' monopolization of land in unsettled areas. But in combination these controversies were sufficient to keep alive the sense of the vulnerability of landholdings and transmit at least in dilute form the distress of the sixteenth- and seventeenth-century English countryside. The value of the freehold and the necessity of defending land against marauders in various guises could never have subsided entirely.

Unlike all these, the currency problems of 1720–50 touched every town and neighborhood, in some areas nearly every family. Commercial opportunities in an expanding economy and the necessity of obtaining distant farms for one's sons tempted a large proportion of the population to go in debt. In the period 1761–65 the annual number of suits in five rural counties equalled 22 percent of the adult male population, most of them for debt. At the western edge of the state in Berkshire County, the number was 76 percent. For some men "all problems of government revolved about the necessity of saving the land from creditors." Even though the actual number of foreclosures (a difficult figure to recover) may not have been high, debt hung over farmers like a dark cloud ready to envelope them in impoverishment and ruin.[66]

By the time of the Stamp Act, the revolutionary language of haughty landlords and cowering peasants was not entirely alien to Massachusetts farmers. If they had not appropriated it for themselves, many had heard it before, and, most important, they understood precisely the steps which the reduction to lordships followed. It is significant that few references to manor lords appear in the disputes centered on land itself, such as the boundary and town commons controversies. Debt and foreclosure was the route from freehold to slavish tenantry. Finance was the method of betrayal rather than head-on title conflicts.[67] This was the background of the immediate and passionate reaction to the Stamp Act. The transfer of fear from debts to taxes was nearly automatic because taxes were a form of debt, and were ultimately collected in the same way, by forced land sales. All of the same mechanisms operated when a shortage of money made it difficult to pay. A minister with unchecked taxing power had farmers at his mercy as fully as an avaricious creditor. A young country pastor in a 1766 Thanksgiving sermon, rejoicing at the repeal of the Stamp Act, noted that if officials were permitted "to take some of our money unconstitutionally, that is, without consent, are we sure they would not have sent for more, and rise in their demands the next time? And why not for all? And then for our real estates? And why not for our wives and children, to make slaves for ever of them?" It was simple for a population familiar with debt foreclosures to envision the relation of taxes and the loss of estates. Geographically the same areas that subscribed to the land bank of 1740 subsequently joined the "country party" in its opposition to the royal governors and imperial taxation. Anxiety about debt blended with the parallel anxieties about Parliamentary taxation.[68]

Boston's efforts to mobilize opposition were abetted by the confluence of opinion in the colonies as a whole. Resistance to the imperial government elaborated and extended the lines along which information flowed into the towns and loaded those lines with messages from all over. News reached inland centers from Philadelphia, Annapolis, and Charleston because events in those places were now important to Massachusetts yeomen. The fact that the ultimate result of taxation was assumed to be the same everywhere confirmed the warning of Boston radicals. Daniel

Dulany, in his 1765 defense of the colonists' exclusive right to tax themselves, observed that if they were "bound by Laws without Restriction affecting the Property they should earn by the Utmost Hazard and Fatigue, they would lose every other Privilege which they had enjoyed in their native Country, and become meer Tenants at Will, dependent upon the Moderation of their Lords and Masters, without any other security. . . ." Even earlier an essay printed in both Pennsylvania and New York spoke of the "deplorable state of your fellow creatures in other countries" where "there is no such things as freeholders. The countrymen are all slaves to the gentlemen. They belong to the landlord . . . and are bought and sold with the land. . . ." Josiah Quincy in 1773 was privately speculating on who would finally be given the overlordship of the continent: "Were I to hazard an eccentric conjecture, it would be that the Penn, Baltimore or Fairfax families will hereafter contend for the dominion—and one of them perhaps attain the sovereignty—of North America." The Adamses and their circle were not required to elaborate on the horrors of lordships when their countrymen were apprised of the danger from many quarters. The Boston letter to the towns in 1772 could simply remind the farmers that "if the breath of a british house of commons can originate an act for taking away all our money, our lands will go next or be subject to rack rents from haughty and relentless landlords who will ride at ease, while we are trodden in the dirt." [69]

It is not necessary to posit a social crisis to explain the passionate reaction to parliamentary taxation. Distress there was in the Massachusetts countryside in 1770 as there was in 1760 and 1720 and as there was to be again in 1785 and 1820, but the farmers' hostility was not in proportion to their deprivation. They were as a group far better off than their counterparts in England, where three-quarters of the land was owned by landlords, and freehold farmers worked only fifteen to twenty percent. They were still farther in advance of that other dominion, Ireland, where two-thirds of the land was owned by absentee landlords and the Irish peasantry exemplified in actuality all the horrors of slavery envisioned by the American imagination. There did not have to be an intensification of suffering in America or an upsurge in tenantry or foreclosures to explain the farmers' anger. The critical point is that they knew the course events would take once an enemy obtained a purchase on their lands through debt or taxes. The descent into tenantry could be all too precipitous. Within the framework of causation engrained by the colonists' long wrestle with debt, small events assumed large dimensions. The sale of a single farm revealed the mighty forces bearing on them all and foretold the disaster in which any one could be engulfed. Moreover, the American farmers' exceptional privileges in comparison to England or Ireland were unsettling rather than comforting. At the forefront of liberty, the colonial freeholder by the same token was exposed and vulnerable, forever in danger of being reduced to the normal condition of agricultural life in the empire—tenantry and lordships.[70]

In their writings, patriots in Boston and Hubbardston alike dwelt on the colonists' constitutional rights. The assertions, the evidence, the arguments in the replies to the Committee of Correspondence concentrated on strengthening the wall between the colonies and British power. But the Whig writers did not emphasize constitutional privileges out of a peculiarly legalistic frame of mind or a pure commitment to abstract rights. They valued the constitution for the barrier it erected against material threats. Ashby typically wrote Boston on May 13, 1773 that "the people of this Province as also the British Colonies in General have a full Right with the people of Great Britain to Enjoy and dispose of their own property. . . ." Underlying the flat assertion of the rights of property was an intricate complex of anxieties and preconceptions. The alternative to disposing of their own property was for aliens to dispose of it, the remote British parliament in the first instance, and more immediately the officials sent from afar forcibly to collect and freely to allocate the colonists' wealth. The "artfully projected" plan of the ministry, Amherst wrote in 1774, would "open the gates for the Admission of Tyranny and oppression with all their rapacious Followers to Stalk at large, and uncontrouled to ravage our fair and dear bought Possessions—." [71] With rapacity at the gate it was not against impoverishment alone that the right of property protected the colonists, but against a fundamental reordering of the colonial social order on the pattern of a feudal past: first the formation of hierarchical dependencies from the servile underlings who clung slavishly to the men in power, and then the degradation of Massachusetts freeholders to the status of tenants and labourers, vassals to those who monopolized the land. Taxation without representation meant ultimately the creation of a class of masters to dominate the countryside and to wrest from an American tenantry the fruits of their toil. This degradation and exploitation, to the rural imagination of the 1770s, was slavery, the last and only resting place of tyrannical ambition.

John Adams and Daniel Leonard were not far from the mark when they spoke of New England's hereditary aversion to lordships. Adams' summary of the colony's history, however, was lacking in one respect. It underplayed the publicists' tutelage of the populace in the pre-revolutionary years. The countryside seemingly was aware before 1765 that their privileged freehold status could be lost and farmers revert to laborers or tenants. They did not, however, ordinarily use the word "feudal" to describe the law and order that followed on financial ruin through debt or taxes. That word was a contribution of radical Whigs and probably was alien still in country towns until after independence. As it infiltrated the countryside, however, it helped to crystallize the new nation's self-conception. "Feudal" as an analytical term distorted the true condition of England and Europe in the eighteenth century, but such subtleties were unimportant to a nation just creating itself. Feudalism fixed a pole at the opposite end of the earth from America. Europe was the land of great lords and landless peasants; America was a country of freeholding, independent farmers. Americans used the term for the same reason John Adams relished the extravagances of Scottish and German romances which showed "in a clear light the horrors of feudal aristocracy"—to sharpen convictions about themselves.[72]

That self-identification was one of the forces impelling a strain of political economy that ran profusely through the speeches of Thomas Hart Benton, the advocate of cheap western land, and surfaced in a 1779 constitutional proposal in Massachusetts to restrict landholdings lest the owners "denominate their landed estates manners or lordships, as has been practised in other parts of the world." [73] That strain of thought ceaselessly reminded Americans that government policy must protect and foster independent yeoman freeholders, lest its opposite, the feudal manor, fasten itself upon America.

The idea of feudal lords also fed into that most pungent form of political opprobrium in the early republic, labeling an enemy "aristocratic." Enfolding within itself the detested image of lordships along with its other Revolution-inspired meanings, the word "aristocrat" was flourished constantly by American politicians and did its part to chasten, to discredit, and finally to retire from politics the class of men who while tinged but slightly with the qualities of true lordship were destined to go down before the equalizing impulses released in the American Revolution.

The American Revolution as a
Crise de Conscience:
The Case of New York

❖

Michael Kammen

In a Controversy of so long a standing and of such awful
Moment the political Sentiments of all but the most incon-
siderable Characters must be known—And Subscriptions
and Oaths at this late Day will in general be rather Masks
to hide than Tests to discover the real Opinions of such as
are not endued with an undaunted Integrity.

> William Smith, Jr., July 4, 1776

Called on R R L [Robert R. Livingston] and told him of
my Summons Warrant & Resolution. . . . R R L intimated
his Wonder at my Choice. Said Conscience had no Concern
in Forms of Govt. . . . I then refused the Oath as contrary
to my Conscience, my Honor, & my Love to the Country.

> William Smith, Jr., July 4 and 6, 1778

In revolutions, every man had a right to take his part. He
is excusable, if not bound in duty to take that which in his
conscience he approved.

> William Tilghman for a plaintiff in 1805 (the case of
> *McIlvaine* v. *Coxe*)

I. An Historiographical Context

IT would not be profoundly insightful to assert that the American Revolution was a complex event, or that the actual War for Independence—especially in its non-military aspects—has not been easy to comprehend. Nevertheless, that is where one must begin; because the proliferation of new scholarship is so overwhelming that we do not now have a coherent picture of this pivotal event in our national history. Moreover, since much of the new literature is not entirely compatible either with the old or with other pieces of the new, for that matter, we do not even seem to be ready for a fresh synthesis. Problems of contradictory evidence, as well as inconsistent interpretations, remain to be resolved; and there are entire substantive dimensions, unlikely as it may seem, still inadequately perceived and understood. Much of this essay will attempt to define and describe one such dimension.

In order to appreciate that dimension properly, however, we must pause for just a moment in order to take our historiographical bearings, with respect both to the Revolution in general and to revolutionary New York in particular. It was, after all, a very famous monograph about the Revolution in New York which set the terms within which much of our twentieth-century discussion has been fixed. I am referring, of course, to Carl L. Becker's doctoral dissertation, published in 1909, wherein he confidently asserted that from 1765 until 1776 "two questions, about equally prominent, determined party history. . . . The first was the question of home rule; the second was the question, if we may so put it, of who should rule at home." [1]

Although we have come a long way since 1909, we are further now than we were then from achieving a consensus about the nature and dynamics of political society in the Anglo-American world of the 1760s and 1770s. For a decade past we have had one school of thought, whose most prominent spokesman is Bernard Bailyn, which argues that a complex ideology (involving a profound mistrust of

power) *alone* "explains why at a particular time the colonists rebelled, and establishes the point of departure for the
constructive efforts that followed." [2] Others have extended
the application of Bailyn's argument well beyond 1776 as
well as back to the years before 1763. Still others have argued that even the Loyalists shared in the Whig inheritance
of political thought. Their cosmology was fundamentally
the same, and they differed only in their understanding of
what was to be done in the particular circumstances of
1775–76.[3] Although these scholars do not all agree upon every jot and tittle of interpretation, they share a common
cluster of important assumptions, and it seems reasonable
to designate theirs an *ideological* interpretation.[4]

They have been challenged, especially in the past few
years, by a group whose mentor has mainly been Merrill
Jensen and whose counterthrust has centered upon the notion of political economy.[5] They do not dismiss the impact
of ideology; but they do deny its axial importance and insist that sources of income, vocational identity, geographical location, and substantive economic issues did more to
determine social attitudes and political behavior. As Joseph
Ernst has written, "a new generation of historians should
come to recognize that the Revolutionary years were a
time of repeated economic crises. While the precise dimensions and the causes of these crises are open to debate, the affected classes in America ultimately turned to
the political sphere for a solution to their problems. The
outcome was an integration of economic and political concerns firmly rooted in a system of elitist politics that was
essential to the Revolutionary movement." [6] The advocates
of this focus have themselves designated it the approach
through *political economy*.[7]

Sniping—almost a kind of cold war—has been going on
between partisans of the two groups for half a dozen years,
at least, and seems to have intensified with the blossoming
of Bicentennial symposia.[8] The ideologues minimize class
conflict; but the political economists emphasize it. The
ideologues stress the energizing sea change of Western po-

litical thought when brought across the Atlantic, while their opponents utilize modernization theory, adapted from political sociology, as a way of explaining the major shifts in American public life during the second half of the eighteenth century. The advocates of political economy (also called neo-Progressives because of their updated affinity for Becker and Beard) like to quote such remarks by participants as this one: "The ties of blood, religion, or patriotism will not avail against self-interest." [9] By contrast the intellectual historians prefer to cite John Adams's retrospective view that the Revolution took place in the minds and hearts of the people well before 1776.[10] In sum, Bailyn and his disciples are fond of the cerebral Adams, whereas Jensen and his students turn to the likes of Adam Smith, who neatly defined political economy as the business of managing the resources of a people and their government.

Neither side has a fully persuasive case, as yet, because each one tends to look rather selectively at certain sorts of social groups for evidence and alignments. The ideologues are inclined to read pamphlets, sermons, and broadsides, while the neo-Progressives look more to legislative records, financial decisions, and collective career lines.[11] In both cases, however, they tend to watch committed leaders —either the intellectual elite or else prominent political partisans—and therefore neglect the fabled one-third (or was it two-fifths?) which was supposedly apathetic or simply expedient.

John Shy, on the other hand, has made a most persuasive case that a majority of the American population was uncertain, indecisive, and unwilling to commit themselves to one side or the other until the war actually touched their localities, indeed, their very homes.[12] Shy's view adds an aspect of cynicism (regarding motives) and an element of ambiguity (about public willingness to support the war effort). His angle of vision, added to those of the ideologues and the political economists, makes the geometry of revolutionary historiography literally (and perhaps figuratively) three-dimensional.

When we turn to the particular case of New York, we find equally intense disagreements. The issues are not quite a microcosm of those just described, however, because the structure of political society there and New York's place in the imperial system made the circumstances in that important colony somewhat different, in fact, almost peculiar. Our understanding of the Revolution in New York is also odd because for half a century after Becker's famous formulation his view prevailed. In fact, it seems to have almost stifled research and creative writing, for very little of any importance was published about New York until 1960. Then the modern deluge began, much of it explicitly revisionist against Becker.[13]

Was there really a double revolution in New York, both internal and external? Was there really intense class conflict, as Becker had suggested, with a privileged elite attempting to restrain the lesser groups? Milton Klein found (1959) that the middling classes enjoyed more political responsibility than Becker had believed, thereby having less cause for resentment and being less manipulable by their "betters," a conclusion affirmed for the Hudson River Valley by Sung Bok Kim in 1970. Don Gerlach asserted (1964) that the most significant lines of conflict occurred *within* the elite. Roger Champagne, in a series of essays based upon his 1960 doctoral dissertation, reached similar conclusions; and added that the extremist radicals, such as Isaac Sears, Isaac Low, and Alexander McDougall, were hardly a homogeneous group either.[14]

Following these revisionist lines, Bernard Mason agrees that Becker exaggerated the extent of class solidarity. Mason, in fact, finds divisions within every social stratum, rural as well as urban. He argues, indeed, that collaboration across class lines helped ultimately to defeat British imperialism. Alfred F. Young's massive monograph, which has a very different focus and thrust, tends to reinforce many of Mason's conclusions. Young perceives a three-tiered contest: first, colonial Whigs versus the British and their Loyalist sympathizers; second, popular (radical)

Whigs versus conservative Whigs; and finally, tenants versus landlords.[15]

Still others, meanwhile, have resurrected segments of the neo-Progressive emphasis upon class conflict in New York: Staughton Lynd for both Dutchess County and New York City; Jesse Lemisch for the working-class elements as a radical monolith; Bernard Friedman for the coherently middle-class character of revolutionary radicalism; and Gary Nash within the crucible of urban politics.[16] Each of these scholars has a distinctive line of argument, and I do them all an injustice by compressing and so crudely categorizing them. My point is simply to indicate the multiplicity of approaches to revolutionary New York during the past fifteen years. There are still others which I have not even mentioned.

From the standpoint of political economy, it is clear that class, vocation, and other economic considerations did, in fact, play an important part in the politics of revolutionary New York. What about ideology? It is significant, I think, that advocates of an ideological approach tend to cite fewer sources from New York than from New England, Pennsylvania, Virginia, and South Carolina. If the Livingston and DeLancey factions are representative of New York's elite, as most believe they are, then it is noteworthy that expediency mattered more to them than ideology. Maintaining political supremacy was paramount; adherence to abstract principles was secondary.[17] Ideological statements certainly issued from the Sons of Liberty in New York, but even at that level we have come to realize that economic competition (from British soldiers) for employment was a very real stimulus to the constitutional assertions of 1768–70.[18]

What are we to make of all this complexity, of so much apparent disorganization in politics and society? First, that there was internal disagreement within each class and every social group. Second, that alignments and coalitions altered in composition according to the dictates of economic imperatives (for some) and ideological issues (for others). Third, that so long as we continue to debate within the framework of Becker's 1909 dissertation, certain sorts of questions will not even be posed, never mind resolved.

Becker's thesis has been fundamentally demolished by an abundance of evidence to the contrary. The story of the Revolution in New York is clearly far more complicated than his simplistic dualism permits us to contemplate; and I have argued elsewhere that the framework of his dissertation be quietly put to rest.[19] Ironically, a much briefer and less notorious essay, also by Becker, seems to me to present questions which are *still* worthy of our attention, and particularly the fascinating matters of motivation, loyalty, anxiety, and inertia.[20] In a very real sense, I believe, we have been "hung up" on the wrong Becker: the 1909 historian of political parties rather than the 1919 historian of mentalities. Even with the new attention being given to Loyalists, especially in New York, we still have no appreciation of the many persons for whom the Revolution brought an agonizing, sometimes paralyzing, often tragic inability to make a full commitment to *either* side.[21]

I am interested, essentially, in the very considerable number of people, profoundly affected by the War for Independence, who nonetheless were reluctant partisans. For so many of them the American Revolution comprised a *crise de conscience*, which is something rather distinct from either economic self-interest or the internalization of an ideology that was part of what Alfred North Whitehead called "the climate of opinion." Nor does a crisis of conscience involve a mere merging of the two, although elements of both may have been present in the decision-making process of those caught in this dilemma. The people I have in mind came from all stations of society and may well have been among the most interesting of any who lived in the revolutionary generation. They suffered from psychic tensions which can illuminate our understanding of the subtle spectrum of opinion in 1776, of the Anglo-American tradition of conscientious dissent, and of the poignant tragedy which occurs when Society feels compelled to violate the sanctity of even a single Soul.

II. The Conceptual Context

In Carl Becker's charming bagatelle entitled "John Jay and Peter Van Schaack," he remarked that the historian interested in causation "must penetrate to those more subtle and impalpable influences, for the most part unconscious and emotional, which so largely determine motive and conduct." [22] Although that observation was written more than half a century ago, far more work has been done since then on the confiscation of property in revolutionary New York than on violations of conscience there.[23] There may well have been, however, more instances of the latter than of the former. Perhaps the discrepancy simply provides one more indication that property values are held in higher regard than what Nathaniel Hawthorne once described as "the sacredness of a human heart."

Be that as it may, my concern here is with the great number of persons for whom the Revolution provoked a moral crisis of considerable proportions. To some degree this problem touches the lives of Loyalists like Thomas Hutchinson and William Smith, Jr., who have already received extended treatment. To some degree it touches the kinds of persons, such as John Dickinson and Joseph Galloway, who had to contend with the competing pulls of Virtue and Obligation, both of which were powerful pole–stars in the universe of eighteenth-century political thought. But most of all I am interested in the matter of *involuntary allegiance*, especially where it involved compulsory oath-taking, for at that point religion and politics became entangled with the question of conscience. My intention, then, is to focus upon the particular moment when public affairs most poignantly affect an individual's inner life.

The concept of conscience, however elusive it may seem, can be defined both historically as well as contemporaneously. Most simply it is understood to be knowledge within oneself; or, an inmost thought or conviction. More complex is the notion of a moral sense, a consciousness of right and wrong. Here are some alternative variations provided by the Oxford English Dictionary: internal recognition of the moral quality of one's motives and actions; the sense of right and wrong as regards those things for which one is responsible; and, the faculty which pronounces upon the moral quality of one's actions or motives, approving the right and condemning the wrong.

The concept was explicitly embedded, moreover, in the Anglo-American tradition of the seventeenth and eighteenth centuries. For the Puritans, such as William Ames, conscience meant "a man's judgment of himself, according to the judgment of God of him." John Rodgers contended in 1650 that "magistrates' laws bind us by virtue not of them, but of God; we must obey them, and all their good laws bind our consciences; but why, and how? because they be mens laws? No; for no man hath power over the conscience, but by virtue of a commandment of the Lord who hath set them, and given them a power to make laws for His worship, and for civil things agreeable to His law, and bid us obey them." [24] Conscience was thus linked to the cause of civic duty, and implied a profound obligation of personal accountability to God and, as a function of that, to one's fellow man.

The history of conscience (or acts of conscience) in America is a complex and worthy subject which considerably antedates the abolitionists, pacifism at the time of the two world wars, and dissident protest during the years of our Vietnam involvement. On October 12, 1644, when the little community of Wenham, Massachusetts, was organizing its church, the Reverend John Fiske wrote these words in his notebook: "it was agreed by unanimous consent (considering the weight of the work, the paucity of the numbers, and the great temptation that lay upon us) to neglect all ordinary occasions of our own to attend these meetings with all care and diligence and conscience (the Lord only preventing it by some special hand)." [25] When the Massachusetts Bay Colony was threatened, in 1683, with the revocation of its cherished charter, Increase Mather recorded in his autobiography that "the deputies of Boston and several others requested me to be present and to give my thoughts as to the case of conscience before them." [26]

In 1749, at the youthful age of fifteen, George Washington admonished himself to "labor to keep alive in your Breast that little spark of Celestial Fire called Conscience." And finally, coming to the moment in time which most concerns us, we find William Eddis, a young English-born member of the governor's circle in Maryland, putting these words in a letter written from Annapolis on March 13, 1775:

> If I differ in opinion from the multitude, must I therefore be deprived of my character and the confidence of my fellow citizens, when in every station of life I discharge my duty with fidelity and honor? DEATH, the certain tax on all the sons of men, were preferable to so abject a state. No—'twere better to suffer all that "age, ache, penury, imprisonment, can lay on nature," than resign that glorious inheritance of a free subject—the liberty of *thinking, speaking,* and *acting,* agreeable to the dictates of conscience! [27]

Eddis merely echoed his more eminent countrymen at home, who had been contemplating the nature of conscience for much longer than a century. Thomas Hobbes had done so in *Leviathan* (1651), and John Locke's *Essay Concerning Human Understanding* (1690) stated that conscience "is nothing else but our own Opinion or Judgment of the Moral Rectitude or Pravity of our own Actions." Edward Hyde, the Earl of Clarendon, had reflected upon the concept in his influential *History of the Rebellion and Civil Wars in England* (1702); and Bolingbroke's *Dissertation Upon Parties* (1735) insisted that when dissenters engage in politics, "*Conscience* alone determines their Conduct." Most vividly and visibly of all, however, there was Jonathan Swift's sermon "On the Testimony of Conscience," published in 1745 and reprinted many times thereafter.[28] After taking an epigram from Second Corinthians—"For our Rejoicing is this, the Testimony of our Conscience"—Swift begins by asserting that "there is no Word more frequent in the Mouths of Men, than that of Conscience." Observing that its meaning is generally understood, he then adds that it was also a "Word extreamly abused by many People." Therefore he wishes to define it "in the clearest Manner I am able."

> The Word *Conscience* properly signifies that Knowledge which a Man hath within himself of his own Thoughts and Actions; and because, if a Man judgeth fairly of his own Actions, by comparing them with the Law of God, his Mind will either approve or condemn him, according as he hath done Good or Evil; therefore the Knowledge or Conscience may properly be called both an Accuser and a Judge. So that, whenever our Conscience accuseth us, we are certainly guilty; but we are not always innocent, when it doth not accuse us; for very often, through the Hardness of our Hearts, or the Fondness and Favour we bear to ourselves, or through Ignorance, or Neglect, we do not suffer our Conscience to take any Cognizance of several Sins we commit.

There can be no doubt, I believe, that most literate Americans of the revolutionary generation were in some sense aware of this concept of conscience. They may not all have read Dean Swift, but they would have heard the idea expressed at some time in the context of sermons and essays, pamphlets, or public discourse generally.[29] It would often have been linked, moreover, with discussions of the nature of authority and an individual's obligations. In developing the Puritan doctrine of conscience, for example, William Ames had emphasized the sacredness of oaths. "There is a double obligation in every promissory oath," he wrote, "one to God, another to man." [30] The individual who makes a commitment to the State, to Society, or to another individual, binds himself by taking an oath to render God as the guarantor of his integrity—and thereby to suffer the consequences if his integrity should be found wanting in the purview of the supreme Judge.

Despite this common understanding, or perhaps precisely *because* of it, oaths had long been a controversial issue in

English public life. A terrific ruckus arose under James I, for example, over the Oath of 1606. It required the acknowledgement of James as "lawful and rightful King," but also abjuration of the doctrine of the deposing and absolving power along with rejection (by the swearer) that this deposition could be effected by the people. That last, a contradiction of Divine Right, must be condemned under oath as impious, heretical, and therefore damnable. Such a requirement placed English Catholics as well as many Puritans in an impossible position.[31]

After the Glorious Revolution of 1688–89, oaths became a fundamental issue once again. The new monarchs, William and Mary, required an oath of allegiance. Failure to take it by August 1, 1689, brought suspension from any office in the realm, civil or ecclesiastical. Six more months of persistent refusal brought absolute deprivation of office on February 1, 1690. A rich debate kept the printers busy for two more years, and thereby left a heated public legacy for the eighteenth-century mind to contemplate.[32] To the Anglican non-jurors of 1690, High-churchmen who felt themselves morally bound by the oaths they had sworn to James II, there were subsequently added the High Tory nonjurors of 1715, men whose conscience would not permit them to take the oath of allegiance to George I, who had just arrived from Germany to establish the new House of Hanover as Britain's royal bloodline.[33]

Oaths and the need for well-defined allegiance, meanwhile, became problematic in America as well. Almost all of the colonies had assumed the right to naturalize aliens and did so, by and large, on terms much more generous than those required in England. Nevertheless the oath of allegiance which was insisted upon at home carried over into provincial practice. It posed little problem for most trinitarian Protestants; but for Quakers, Roman Catholics, Jews, and others who scrupled at swearing oaths of any sort, the naturalization procedures often threatened a violation of conscience.[34] Similarly the colonial colleges, each of which had some denominational affiliation, often required

their tutors to take an oath or else face immediate dismissal.
At a meeting in 1753, for example, it was determined that
all fellows at Yale College must publicly consent to the
catechism and Westminster Confession of Faith according
to a particular "Formula." What justification was needed?
Very simply that Yale's purpose was to train ministers "according to the Doctrine, Discipline and Mode of Worship"
then practiced in the churches of Connecticut. President
Clap then added the rationale that a similar formula served
the same purpose within the Church of Scotland.[35]

During the troubled prelude to revolution, there were
numerous premonitions of more serious conflicts yet to
come. To begin with, it is clear that even outside of New
England, oaths were still taken very seriously in the rather
more secularized atmosphere of the 1760s and 1770s. Here
is an excerpt from an angry "Notice" served upon Lieutenant Governor Cadwallader Colden of New York on the
evening of November 1, 1765:

> The People of This City and Province of New York, have
> been inform'd that you bound yourself under an Oath to be
> the Chief Murderer of their Rights and Privileges, by acting
> as an Enemy . . . to Liberty and Mankind in the Inforcement
> of the Stamp-Act. . . . We can with certainty assure you of
> your Fate if you do not this Night Solemnly make Oath be-
> fore a Magistrate, and publish to The People, that you never
> will . . . endeavour to introduce or execute the Stamp-Act.
> . . . So help you God.[36]

On Sunday morning, November 3, this anonymous warning, stuffed into an oyster shell, was found at the fort gate
by a sleepy sentry.

> Sir
>   As one who is an enemy to mischief of all kinds, and a
> Well wisher to you and your Family, I give you this Notice
> that Evil is determined against you and your Adherents and
> will in all human Probability take Effect, unless Speedily pre-
> vented by your public Declaration upon Oath, That you will
> never, in any Manner, countenance, or assist, in the Execution
> of the Stamp Act, or anything belonging to it; and also, that

[137]

you will, to the utmost of your Power, endeavour to get it repeal'd in England, and meanwhile prevent its taking Effect here. Your life may depend upon the Notice you take of this Advice.[37]   BENEVOLUS

Later that month a Maryland stamp distributor who had fled to New York with a promise of protection from Colden was "visited" by about a hundred Sons of Liberty. He formally resigned his ignominious office and took an "oath of sincerity" before Justice William Smith, Sr.[38]

By 1767 the imperial crisis had brought oaths to the foreground on both sides of the Atlantic. When Parliament considered an act to suspend New York's Assembly that year, George Grenville offered an amendment. It would have expanded the official oath so that all colonial officers would be obliged to affirm parliamentary supremacy before they could take up their positions.[39]

In 1774–75 the Continental Association, as the movement to protest British policies was known, developed oaths of allegiance by which patriots might be sworn to the cause. In New York at least three different versions of that oath were offered, and local committees tried to canvass the colony house by house in order not to miss a soul. The result, as Bruce Bliven has observed, was that "a good Associator might have refused the third version because he had already taken the first or the second; and some men who had sworn in 1774 had since changed their minds and might be getting credit, in 1775, that they no longer deserved. Moreover, some inimicals had sworn loyalty to the Association falsely, just to get rid of the canvasser." [40]

As the crucible of conflict got hotter during the winter of 1774–75, there were increasing indications of intolerance and therefore of a protracted struggle in which the cause of conscience would be a hapless victim. Individuals from several different colonies suggested, even sought, that the Continental Congress should establish a generalized loyalty oath. An assemblyman from Maryland wondered whether it would not be best "to have one general test for all America?" Massachusetts delegates, in turn, urged "a test by which all persons inimical to the rights and liberties of America shall be distinguished from their friends." The Congress took no action at this time, however.[41]

In New York, meanwhile, at a moment when patriotism was becoming synonymous with non-importation, non-exportation, and non-consumption of British products, nonjuring would be trampled with contempt and considered tantamount to treason. Samuel Seabury, the Loyalist "Westchester Farmer," published in December 1774 this blast at the newly formed committees of inspection:

> Here, gentlemen, is a court established upon the same principles with the *popish inquisition*. No proofs, no evidence are called for. The committee may judge from *appearances* if they please—for when it shall be made appear to a majority of any committee that the Association is violated, they may proceed to punishment, and *appearances*, you know, are easily *made*; nor is the offender's *presence* necessary. He may be condemned unseen, unheard—without even a possibility of making a defense. No jury is to be impannelled. No check is appointed upon this court;—no appeal from its determination.[42]

By the middle of 1776 Seabury's personal situation, as an Anglican minister and a supporter of the Crown, had become impossible. Sitting at White Plains in July, New York's Constitutional Convention passed a resolution to impose upon Loyalists the proper penalty for treason—death. Some fifty armed men were then stationed by the Convention at Westchester, looking Seabury in the eye with the muzzle of a gun. He subsequently explained his dilemma to the secretary of the Society for the Propagation of the Gospel, who was in London:

> If I [publicly] prayed for the King, the least I could expect was to be sent into New England: Probably something worse, as no Clergyman on the Continent was so obnoxious to them. If I went to Church & omitted praying for the King, it would not only be a Breach of my Duty, but in some Degree countenancing their Rebellion, & supporting that Independency which they had declared. As the least culpable Course, I de-

termined not to go to Church, & ordered the Sexton on Sunday Morning to tell any Person who should enquire, That till I could pray for the King, & do my Duty according to the Rubrick & Canons, there would be neither Prayers, nor Sermon. About half a dozen of my Parishioners, & a dozen rebel Soldiers came to the Church: The rest of the People, in a general Way declared, That they would not go to Church till their Minister was at Liberty to pray for the King.[43]

What the Convention had decided at White Plains was important in establishing a fundamental link between aberrations of allegiance and their working definition of treason. Anyone "owing allegiance" to New York "who shall levy war against the said State within the same, or be adherent to the King of *Great Britain* . . . are guilty of treason against the State, and being thereof convicted, shall suffer the pains and penalties of death." [44]

Public opinion, however, went way beyond this sharp division of the political world into saints and sinners. By the later part of 1776 it had palpably begun to categorize neutrality as an unacceptable option. In the minutes of the Committee for Detecting Conspiracies, sitting at Fishkill, New York, on December 21, we find the observation that four prominent individuals of the Albany area "have long maintained an equivocal Neutrality in the present Struggles and are in General supposed unfriendly to the American Cause. . . ." [45]

One of the most interesting and symptomatic characteristics of the language of politics throughout the war was this intimate association of "equivocal" as an inevitable modifier of "neutrality." The patriots very clearly viewed neutrality in a pejorative light, and would respect neither its integrity nor its viability as a legitimate option during the conflict. Here is John Jay interrogating Beverly Robinson, at Fishkill, on February 22, 1777: "Sir, you having observed an Equivocal Neutrality through the Course of your conduct the Committee is at a Loss to know how to Rank you." [46] After Robinson explained that he had confined himself to his estate "in order to keep myself from a necessity

of Expressing my Sentiments," Jay proceeded to make explicit the Committee's reasoning as to why neutrality was an
unacceptable posture: "Sir, we have passed the Rubicon
and it is now necessary [that] every man Take his part, Cast
off all alliegiance to the King of Great Britain and take an
oath of Alliegiance to The States of america or Go over to
the Enemy for we have Declared our Selves Independent." [47]

A visitor to Fishkill who found numerous people imprisoned there because they refused to swear an oath of allegiance to the United States summed up the patriot attitude
as he perceived it in 1778: "The Americans are so oppressive, they will not let any one remain neuter; and they compel every inhabitant, either to take the oath, or quit the
country." [48]

So it was that Hector St. Jean de Crèvecoeur, who lived
in Orange County, across the Hudson from Fishkill, and
who wished to remain a non-combatant, aroused the deep
suspicion of his neighbors because he failed to throw in his
lot with their cause. Only in this context can we fully appreciate the poignancy of his last *Letter from an American
Farmer*, entitled "Distresses of a Frontier Man." He wrote
that he felt torn "between the respect I feel for the ancient
connection, and the fear of innovations, with the consequence of which I am not well acquainted. . . . As to the
argument on which the dispute is founded . . . much has
been said and written on both sides, but who has a judgment
capacious and clear enough to decide? The great moving
principles which actuate both parties are much hid from
vulgar eyes . . . nothing but the plausible and the probable
are offered to our contemplation." [49]

Crèvecoeur must have shared the Tory sympathies of his
wife's family, the DeLanceys, and of some close friends;
but he also felt a strong affection for his adopted land, as
well as revulsion from the suffering caused by war. His
home at Pine Hill was just a few miles distant from a large
camp for prisoners of war. In 1778, after three years of uneasy coexistence with his hostile neighbors, he gained per

mission to go to British-controlled New York City, and from there, hopefully, to France. Reaching the city early in 1779, at last, he discovered that paranoid persecutors were not to be found on the patriot side *alone*. An anonymous informant told the Tory authorities that Crèvecoeur might have made a map of New York harbor, had once persuaded a neighbor to take the oath of allegiance to New York's rebel government, and had corresponded with George Washington. We do not know whether the allegations were entirely true; but they persuaded the British to arrest and imprison Crèvecoeur for three months in a jail reserved for political suspects and prisoners-of-war. Later in 1779, his farm in Orange County in flames, Crèvecoeur left the New World he had loved for three decades. In 1781 he finally reached his native Normandy: impoverished, sick, and sadly disillusioned.[50]

That generation was hardly unique, however, in its mistrust of neutrality. Such apprehension had a long and even elegant history in Western thought. Solon, the Greek tyrant, is supposed to have been responsible for a law which disenfranchised any person "who, in time of faction, takes neither side." According to Aristotle's *Constitution of Athens*, the policy was that "whoever, in a time of political strife, did not take an active part on either side should be deprived of his civic rights and have no share in the state."[51]

By the seventeenth century a profound mistrust still existed, at least in the texture of English thought, of man's capacity to be genuinely neutral. Partisanship seemed inescapable. Here is Shakespeare writing in *Macbeth* (II, iii, 115):

> Who can be wise, amaz'd, temperate, and furious,
> Loyal and neutral, in a moment? No man.

And here is his contemporary, Joseph Hall, the Bishop of Norwich: "Neutrality in things good or evil is both odious and prejudicial; but in matters of an indifferent nature is safe and commendable." Coming down to the moment which concerns us directly, we find Edmund Burke heaping scorn upon the likelihood of anyone achieving neutrality without hypocrisy. "I remember an old scholastic aphorism," he wrote, "which says, 'that the man who lives wholly detached from others must be either an angel or a devil.' When I see in any of these detached gentlemen of our times the angelic purity, power, and beneficence, I shall admit them to be angels." [52]

As the War for Independence opened, then, many participants shared this long-established mistrust of neutrality. Hence the felt need to take a fixed position. The fact that some sincere contemporaries could not, however, is attested by this poem, called "The Pausing American Loyalist," published on January 30, 1776, but most likely copied from a version which had appeared a year before. The dilemma is whether or not to sign the Continental Association.

> To sign, or not to sign!—That is the question:
> Whether 't were better for an honest man
> To sign—and so be safe; or to resolve,
> Betide what will, against 'associations,'
> And, by retreating, shun them. To fly—I reck
> Not where—and, by that flight, t' escape
> Feathers and tar, and thousand other ills
> That Loyalty is heir to: 't is a consummation
> Devoutly to be wished. To fly—to want—
> To want?—perchance to starve! Ay, there's the rub!
> For, in that chance of want, what ills may come
> To patriot rage, when I have left my all,
> Must give me pause! There's the respect
> That makes us trim, and bow to men we hate.
> For, who would bear th' indignities o' th' times,
> Congress decrees, and wild Convention plans,
> The laws controll'd, and inj'ries unredressed,
> The insolence of knaves, and thousand wrongs
> Which patient liege men from vile rebels take,
> When he, sans doubt, might certain safety find,
> Only by flying? Who would bend to fools,
> And truckle thus to mad, mob-chosen upstarts,
> But that the dread of something after flight

(In that blest country, where, yet, no moneyless
Poor wight can live) puzzles the will,
And makes ten thousands rather sign—and eat,
Than fly—to starve on Loyalty!
Thus, dread of want makes cowards of us all;
And, thus, the native hue of Loyalty
Is sicklied o'er with a pale cast of trimming;
And enterprises of great pith and virtue,
But unsupported, turn their streams away,
And never come to action.[53]

The fact that significant numbers of sincere contemporaries could not choose one side or the other is also attested by evidence presented in the sections which follow. That evidence reveals just how agonizing it is to be forced to make a public choice when the polity has disintegrated almost to a state of nature, and when the consequences—for society and for conscience—are so unclear.

III. The Need to Detect Conspiracies

Late in September 1776 the New York State Convention resolved that "a committee be appointed for the express purpose of inquiring into and detecting all conspiracies which may be formed in this state against the Liberties of America." With John Jay in charge, this committee quickly became an energetic body. It deputized secret agents to spy upon suspicious persons in rebel-controlled areas of the state as well as within the new English zone of occupation around New York City. It recruited its own special company (consisting of thirty military men) in order to have an arm of enforcement. And finally, it established subcommittees in the various counties and communities as a means of achieving high visibility and sanctions against disloyalty to the rebel cause.

The commissioners created a loyalty oath as a means of testing people accused of disloyalty, of rehabilitating converts from Toryism, and of assimilating British soldiers who had been captured or wished to defect. Such persons were required to repudiate any allegiance to George III, swear obedience to New York State and the Continental Congress, and promise to expose all "Treasonable Plotts and Conspiracies." Here, for example, is one version of the oath which many would sign in 1778 and 1779.

> I do solemnly swear and declare in the presence of Almighty God that I ought not and do not acknowledge any Allegiance to the King of Great Brittain, his Heirs or Successors or any power or Authority of the Parliament of the said Kingdom of Great Brittain, and that I will bear true faith and Allegiance to the State of New York as a free and Independant State, and that I will in all things to the best of my knowledge and Ability do my Duty as a good Subject of the said State ought to do, So help me God.[54]

By the early part of 1777 these committees were fully functional and extremely active. With the state's provisional government hard pressed to survive—its very legitimacy somewhat tenuous until a constitution was promulgated late in April and Burgoyne's army beaten at Saratoga in October—it often relied upon units of the state militia and of the Continental army to court-martial disloyal citizens, thereby ignoring even the perfunctory procedures that the committees were supposed to follow. Military justice was used to dispose summarily of presumed traitors. The fact that some of them carried certificates showing that they had previously taken Whig loyalty tests mattered very little, if at all. Nor did Article XIII of the state's new constitution, prepared by a convention sitting at Kingston: "That no member of this state shall be disfranchised, or deprived of any rights or privileges secured to the subjects of this state by this Constitution, unless by the law of the land, or the judgment of his peers." [55]

By the middle of 1777 the state offered an "act of grace" to those convicted traitors who would take its oath of allegiance. In 1778 the rebel government created a second (and permanent) Commission for Detecting and Defeating Conspiracies. It enjoyed even broader powers than its predecessor, and was more closely integrated with other units of state administration, especially those concerned with the confiscation of property. These two commissions thus spanned the entire period of the war, 1776–83, and their members comprised many of the most powerful men in New York, including Gouverneur Morris, Jeremiah Van Rensselaer, Philip Livingston, John Beekman, and Leonard Gansevoort, in addition to John Jay. Without acquiring their confidence and passing their loyalty test, one could not vote, hold office, or practice law or any other licensed profession. In sum, one could not enjoy the privileges of residence, citizenship, and property-holding. Make no mistake, moreover, about the commissioners' interpretation of their charge. They equated non-juring with outright disloyalty to New York and the new nation.[56]

Very little has been written about these bizarre circumstances, and what we do have tends to pick up the story, in piecemeal fashion, with the first commission created in September 1776. To do so, however, is to ignore a statewide pattern which had been established in the localities more than fifteen months before. Although many of the worst violations of conscience occurred in 1777 and 1778, the climate of suspicion and the language of loyalty began to emerge at least a year before New York reluctantly ratified the Declaration of Independence. In Tryon County on the northern frontier, for example, we find this oath being sworn on June 17, 1775:

> We the subscribers, Respective Freeholders of the said County, do hereby solemnly declare, and acknowledge the same on our Oaths, when Required that we will support our American Liberties to the utmost of our power in Company and association with our Neighbors and Fellow Freeholders of our said County.

Following the names of several signatories, an ominous and prescient notice was then added.

> The Question was put to all those, who signed at this meeting respectively the [continental] association and the last men-

tioned particular Declaration, Whether they had signed by Motives of Force or Fear, and being assured that they were in no Danger, in case they should refuse . . . They jointly & severally declared, that they acted of their own free Will and Accord.[57]

On August 25, 1775, we find "new Chosen Members" from the Palatine District of the county joining older members in swearing the oath; and the next day we read of men taking the oath in order to testify against partisans of the Crown. One John Vedder "heard the Sheriff often say that the King's people fight for Glory, but the Country doth fight with the halters on their necks." [58]

On November 24, 1775, James Cameron, a recent Scottish immigrant, was examined by the County Committee at the home of Gose Van Alstyne. With Nicholas Herkimer serving as chairman, at least thirty-six members somehow squeezed into this modest home. Only two enrolled members were absent, in fact, and the five sections of the county were carefully denoted by geographical groups: Mohawk, Palatine, Conajohary, Kingsland, and German Flats. The illiterate Cameron had to explain his presence the previous May at the home of Colonel Guy Johnson, as well as his role as an escort on a trip Johnson made to Montreal. Cameron insisted that he had refused invitations to enlist in the King's service, and that he declined to join Colonel John Butler's band of men. He then declared on oath that he would never "take up arms against the Country's Cause, nor do anything consequential in the favor of the Country's Enemies, but rather be always ready to defend the American Liberty with the Friends of our Country." Whereupon the committee released him.[59]

Over in Schenectady on July 14, 1775, Benjamin Hilton was brought before Justice Cornelius Cuyler to give an affidavit. After being duly sworn, Hilton declared that he had

> never entertained or harboured an opinion inimical or unfriendly to the just constitutional rights and liberties of Amer-

ica; that he looks upon the claim which the British Parliament has set up in the present reign by statute, to bind the Colonies in all cases whatever, as unconstitutional and subversive of American liberty; that the measures taken by administration for the enforcement of the several statutes passed against America, in general, and some of the Colonies in particular, in his opinion will justify opposition; that he is a friend to his country and the invaded rights and liberties thereof, (though he believes by many without foundation, taken to be an enemy thereto) and wishes it all the success in this unhappy and unnatural conflict that any real friend to the common cause can.

The Albany County Committee of Safety worried this one around for some while, like a big dog with a small bone. Ultimately it informed the Schenectady committee that Hilton had shown "an unwarrantable exultation in the distress and defeat which he supposed a part of the Continental army had sustained," and decided that his sentiments were "inimical" to the liberties of New York. Even so, it disdained Hilton's "impotent attempts . . . to traduce the proceedings of the northern army," and so dismissed him from further prosecution.[60]

During the late winter and early spring of 1776, the deepening military crisis may have been responsible for a diminution of compassion and scrupulousness. Certainly harshness by patriotic civilians toward suspicious partisans was encouraged by the behavior and attitudes of highly placed military personnel. On March 5, 1776, for example, General Charles Lee wrote from New York City requesting Colonel Isaac Sears to send Tories from Queens County to Connecticut for confinement there in jails. Lee believed that a substantial British army was on its way. Therefore, he wrote,

> I should be responsible to God, my own conscience and to the Continent of America, in suffering, at so dangerous a crisis, a knot of professed foes to liberty and their country, to remain any longer within our own bosom, either to turn openly against us in arms in conjunction with the enemy, or

covertly to furnish them with intelligence and carry on a
correspondence to the ruin of their country. I must desire
that you will offer the enclosed test to the people of whom
I send you a list. Their refusal must be considered an avowal
of their hostile intentions. You are therefore to secure their
persons, and without loss of time to send them up as irre-
claimable enemies to their country, to close custody in Connecticut.[61]

The letters from persons subsequently imprisoned at
Fairfield are among the most revealing documents from this
first phase of the war. Here, to take just one illustration,
are excerpts from a very long letter written by Samuel Gale
to John McKesson of the Provincial Congress on April 12,
1776.

> I have applied to two different attorneys for a *habeas
> corpus,* that the nature of my detention might be inquired
> into. But, to my entire astonishment, they informed me that
> writ never issued in this government, nor was there any law
> of the Colony that could administer any relief.
>
> What then in the name of Heaven is to be done?
>
> I am strangely mistaken if it has not, even heretofore, been
> looked upon as the essential rights of a free people, that every
> individual should enjoy unmolested the liberty of doing and
> saying whatever was not prohibited by some law or rule pre-
> scribed. I also conceive that the greatest severity which rea-
> sonable creatures could with any degree of colour inflict on
> any offender, was the penalties which they had previously
> affixed to his crime. I recollect no rule, nor (though I have
> inquired as well of Mr. Burr who detains me, as of others,)
> can I find any, published by any man or body of men, that I
> have ever broken. Nay, the whole that is, or can be laid to my
> charge, appears by one of the addresses of the Congress in
> 1774, to have been at that time an undoubted right inherent
> in every freeman. And it will doubtless be granted that there
> must be a law, before there can be any transgression. . . .
>
> Let Heaven and earth bear witness, while the generous
> man, and the brave, of what nation or language, rank or con-
> dition, denomination, or party soever, shall lay his hand upon
> his soul and answer—are not these things intolerable? Especially
> let him answer—after finding them to be directly contrary to

all public laws, resolves and orders, both ancient and modern; and still continued, notwithstanding his release, and the illegality of his being taken, has been long since determined on, by a resolve of that body which holds the supreme rule of the Province to which he belongs, and from whence he was forcibly taken.

What in the world can these persecutions mean? or what can they be intended to produce? an alteration of faith? I shall ever hold myself open to conviction, and when I am convinced of any error, I shall frankly acknowledge it. But if this be a specimen of modern freedom, you would doubtless consider me a hypocrite of the first magnitude, should I tell you that I preferred it before the ancient system. Is it meant to secure the safety or exchange of prisoners? Such notions must have been founded in error and mistake, nor could they ever be produced but by a round about application through the channel of the civil officers; for, neither of His Majesty's States, military or maritime, know any thing of my even being in existence; at least, if they do, it is totally without my knowledge or application.

Or is it (as appears to me most likely) that some of my persecutors want to dip their hands in the blood of a martyr? If so—it would in my opinion be far less criminal both in the sight of God and man, for them to let it flow in decent streams, than thus (with dastardly meanness) to drag it from me drop by drop.[62]

How did the hounds of conspiracy and disloyalty get the scent of their quarry? Where most people protested their innocence or neutrality, why were *some* persons suspect? In certain cases because they would not take a pledge to bear arms in defense of the colonies. This happened at Kinderhook in May 1776 to men who had themselves been members of the Kinderhook Committee of Safety.[63] Elsewhere, those who had held appointive offices at the pleasure of the Crown were presumed to be obligated to Great Britain. In June 1776, for example, the Provincial Congress cited fifty-five men from the five lower counties who

by reason of their holding offices from the King of *Great Britain*, from their having neglected or refused to associate with their fellow-citizens for the defence of their common rights, from their having never manifested by their conduct a zeal for and attachment to the *American* cause, or from their having maintained an equivocal neutrality, have been considered by their countrymen in a suspicious light, whereby it hath become necessary, as well for the safety as for the satisfaction of the people, who, in times so dangerous and critical, are naturally led to consider those as their enemies who withhold from them their aid and influence,

and resolved that they be summoned "to show cause, if any they have, why they should be considered as friends to the *American* cause." [64]

Out on Long Island a terrific contest of wills developed over the swearing of oaths, the control of weapons, and the very legitimacy of New York's Provincial Convention. In Brookhaven, at the Manor of Saint Georges and the Patentship of Moriches, a Committee of Observation appeared as early as June 1775. It consisted of sixteen persons who were elected to act for the town "in the prospective deliberations on political matters." The community was bitterly divided over the proper response to British policies, but by September the patriots had gained the upper hand. They resolved at a meeting—apparently still in search of consensus—that "all such persons as had not signed the General Association before the 15th of July have still a right to sign it, and ought to be Received as associates when they Do sign the same." [65]

In April 1776 that Committee of Observation was superseded by a Committee of Safety. On May 13 a rumor was reported that within the district some "private plots" had been hatched and secretly carried into execution "by some unfriendly person dangerous to the Liberty's of America." An inquiry was made, and some of those interviewed were found "unwilling to be sworn or pass an examination." Whereupon the Committee resolved that any persons

refusing to be sworn, or to answer to any questions that shall be asked . . . this Committee will take such effectual measures as they shall think proper, to secure or confine such person, or Persons, until they will comply with whatever resolves relative to proceeding with persons unfriendly to the rights of America are or shall be made for the purpose of obtaining Evidence of such plots & dangerous proceedings.

Some inhabitants of Brookhaven appeared before the committee in order to give testimony against their neighbors, as Daniel Nash did against Andrew Patchin. Thomas Fanning was interrogated about suspicious correspondence with his brother, Edmond, "and other our enemies." Although the committee ordered Thomas to produce the suspected letters, he resolutely refused. He stated, in fact, that he "would not shew them if he had his flesh all pul'd off with hot pinchers." More than that, he even "Deny'd the Authority and Legality of this Committee." Subsequently Fanning indicated that "if he had a hundred Lives, he would Venture Ninety & Nine of them on the side of the King's Forces, rather than one on the part of the Congress." Try as it would, the Committee could not cajole Fanning into *any* demonstration of sympathy or innocence. When the members asked him "for Bonds or other promissory written obligations" to satisfy the community of his good behavior, he refused to "make any verbal concessions except a promise of passive obedience as a Prisoner to obtain a short space upon his Parole of honor." Consequently he was sent before the Provincial Congress, presumably to be chastened.[66]

Ten days later the same sort of war of nerves was waged before the committee by Daniel Davis, Jr., patriotic informer, and Captain Jonathan Baker, who spoke slightingly of the Congress and threatened to raise a company of volunteers even "if they quartered or Cut him in Inch Pieces for so doing." On May 31 the committee arrested Baker and some friends as "Enemies to the American Cause." At his trial in early June, Baker spilled out his contempt for the local committee, and "Dispised their Conduct." They, in turn, voted unanimously to send him and his accomplice, Stephen Fountain, to New Haven for confinement. At a meeting on June 21, 1776, however, one William Longbottom confronted the committee and stated his belief that "all the Combinations & Inlistments were for the purpose of Neutrality & call'd them a Club of Sivility that intended to fight on nither side." Apparently the Brookhaven Whig directorate was vulnerable to criticism from extremist partisans of both persuasions. If so, that may have been a sign that it was doing a reasonably judicious job.[67]

John Jay, who had been so reluctantly drawn to the anti-British side during 1774 and 1775, began to shed his mantle as a moderate during these middle months of 1776. He advocated the arrest of subversive persons, the detention of those who voted against sending delegates to Congress, and the disarming of dissidents. Starting in late September the Committee for Detecting Conspiracies became one of his most absorbing preoccupations. He served for the next four and one-half months with William Duer of Charlotte County, Charles DeWitt of Ulster County, Leonard Gansevoort of Albany, and Zephaniah Platt and Nathaniel Sackett of Dutchess County in zealously gathering intelligence from local agents who informed the committee about Loyalist sympathizers and recruiters for the British army. Jay's board examined witnesses, jailed suspects, issued paroles, and decided upon the deportation of selected prisoners already in custody. By January 1777 seven more members had been added; and on February 11 of that year the committee was replaced by a new commission which fulfilled the same functions.[68]

It is difficult to say just when Jay passed from moderation to militancy. Expediency, dictated most especially by military realities after the British occupation of New York in September 1776, must have made a difference. So, too, did his growing correspondence with other colonial leaders. Early in December, for example, he received from Philadelphia a letter written by Edward Rutledge. "A pure Democracy may possibly do when patriotism is the ruling Passion," wrote Rutledge, "but when a State abounds in Rascals . . . you must suppress a little of that Popular Spirit." A letter from Egbert Benson in March 1777 expressed anxiety that joining the enemy might become or seem to become, an *"honorable"* pursuit.[69] By that time, however, Jay himself had declared neutrality unacceptable. He said so to Beverly Robinson on February 22, 1777, as we have seen; and on March 21 Jay explained his position to Mrs. Susanna Robinson in greater detail.

> Mr. Robinson has put his own and the Happiness of his Family and Posterity at Hazard, and for what? For the Sake of a fanciful Regard to an Ideal Obligation to a Prince, who on his Part disdains to be fettered by any obligations, a Prince who with his Parliament, arrogating the Attributes of Omnipotence, claim a Right to bind you and your Children in all Cases whatsover. Persuaded that all former Oaths of Allegiance were dissolved by his usurpations, does he not daily attempt to bind the Inhabitants of this Country by new ones? If he deemed the former Oaths valid, why this Exaction of new Obligations of Allegiance? [70]

Jay was referring to efforts by the British army of occupation to have the Americans under their jurisdiction reaffirm oaths of allegiance taken to George III. I shall discuss such attempts in a separate section below. What should be noted here, however, is the fact that March 1777 was a month of intensification in terms of the Revolution as a *crise de conscience*. On March 7 the New York Provincial Convention resolved that those among the neutrals or Loyalists who had "been sent into some or one of the neighboring States, or confined within this State by parol or otherwise," would be asked once again to take an oath of allegiance to the state. Failing to do so they would "receive a pass and be directed to repair, with their families, apparel and household furniture, to the city of New-York, or some other place in the possession of the enemy." [71] In essence, the Loyalists and neutrals would be banished from their homes.

There were many among the Whigs, moreover, who protested that the Convention had been too generous. Egbert Benson, Melancton Smith, and Jacobus Swartwout, who had been named to the Commission for Detecting Conspiracies on February 11, 1777, wrote a letter of protest to the Convention on March 19. The recent resolution, they pointed out, actually permitted non-jurors to take their clothing and furniture with them.

> We could wish they were restricted to such only as is necessary, and leave us to determine that from the particular circumstances of each person. . . . The obstinate and inveterate spirit indicated by such a conduct, we conceive has precluded these people from all indulgence, and numbers of them have clothing and bedding more than is requisite for their immediate use, and much wanted in the present exigencies of the country.[72]

Upon receiving this appeal the Convention reconsidered, and on March 21 instructed the commissioners "to use a discretionary power in granting the indulgences," and that those who chose to pass behind British lines "be not suffered to carry with them more apparel and household furniture than are necessary for their comfortable accommodation." [73]

Because oaths had become, by March 1777, such a cynosure of integrity, we must pause to examine the nature of the oath itself, its manner of administration, and, most important of all, contemporary understanding of the meaning and reliability of oaths.

IV. The Meaning and Consequences of an Oath

During the Salem witchcraft trials in 1692, the only way to be acquitted or released had been to confess guilt. A person of inner conviction who insisted upon his or her innocence was most likely to be hanged. The same obtained in the context of New York's infamous slave "conspiracy" crisis of 1741. Expedient slaves "confessed," while naïve ones made the fatal mistake of insisting upon their innocence. In revolutionary New York, those who swore the requisite oath of allegiance were blithely "discharged" from arrest or confinement; but those who pleaded their conscience, for whatever reason, were almost always "remanded." What presumptions underpinned such paradoxical behavior? [74]

There are grave problems involved in trying to determine the sincerity of the oath-takers—problems every bit as beguiling, say, as the Puritans' efforts in Massachusetts Bay to make the visible church correspond with the body of invisible saints. Who could know for sure whether the conversion experiences being described were authentic or merely formulaic? Who could say whether hypocrites were slipping into the congregation, only to pollute by their presence the purity of communion (and other sacraments as well) for those true members of God's Elect Nation? The same sort of intense social drama described for Massachusetts Bay by Perry Miller, Edmund S. Morgan, and Robert G. Pope was very much present, but in a more secular setting, during the War for Independence in New York.[75] Many participants remarked upon the difficulty of knowing who had sworn the oath with conviction, and who was simply being pragmatic in order to save his property or his skin.

To begin, the oaths often had strong religious overtones, and pious people therefore took them very seriously. One oath opened, for example, "I do swear upon the holy Evangelists of Almighty God that I will be true to the State of New York," and concluded, of course, "So help me God." [76] On certain occasions the administering committees showed some consideration for the capacity or sincerity of persons under scrutiny. It was deemed inappropriate, for example, to administer an oath to someone under the age of sixteen, for such youths were not yet mature enough to know their own minds.[77] There were also occasions when men asked for additional time in order to weigh the decision to take the oath. Depending upon the mood of the particular committee, it might be granted. On May 24, 1777, for example, Joseph Mabbit appeared before Melancton Smith and Peter Cantine, Jr., and "desired Ten Days time to consider of Taking the Oath of Allegiance to this State."

They permitted him to "return home on his parol, to appear before this Board again within that Time from This Date." [78]

Often, of course, the oath was administered under coercive conditions: either military coercion, or threat of economic confiscation, or else enormous social pressure to conform. Nevertheless, or perhaps *on account of*, such intimidation, most oaths concluded with a declaration that they were voluntarily sworn without any mental reservation. In many cases such forced hypocrisy only compounded the violation of conscience. Sometimes the victim was candid with his committee. On March 21, 1777, for instance, Michael Ryer, who had improperly purchased two horses and passed through patriot lines, explained his anxiety. He had fully intended to apply to General Alexander McDougall for a pass, he said, and added

> That he has always, from the beginning of the present Troubles been warmly attached to the American Cause, & was he not restrained by Oath of Allegiance which he lately took to the King of Great Britain he would do all in his power to promote & advance it—that he took the Oath of Allegiance [to George III] only as a means to preserve his life, as he would upon refusal have been thrown into Gaol and probably have perished there.[79]

The view seems to have been widely held, however, that one oath, no matter how solemnly sworn, could be renounced in favor of another—even a contradictory oath. The Committee to Detect Conspiracies was always pleased when individuals "on Oath renounc'd all allegiance to the King of Great Britain" and pledged instead "to support the measures of the Congress." [80] Cases of perjury clearly abounded—there would be numerous accusations of perjury among the Loyalists at war's end—and yet intriguing gestures of good faith were made on the basis of oaths which in retrospect seem to have been suspect. One Isaac Vail appeared before the board on February 27, 1777, and informed them that he had heretofore taken the Oath of Allegiance to this State before the Committee and confin'd by their Order, and now pray'd that he might be permitted to go at large and he having made a candid & open confession of his having deserted the Guards on his way to Exeter, and of his having since been in the City of New York & on Long Island, and declaring that he had changed his Sentiments, and this Board having confidence in him that he will agreeable to his profession conduct himself as a True Friend to the American cause.[81]

The committee decided to release Vail "from his present confinement on his Farm," and permitted him "to go at Large." Cases such as this one, where the suspect seems so obviously unreliable, suggest that some board members, at least, may have regarded the oath as formulaic, perfunctory, or both. In either case, they most certainly used it as a means of intimidation, but with mixed success.

Therefore we must ask next: what sorts of responses did the oath of allegiance elicit? What was achieved by those persons who took it? What was risked by those who rejected it? And, most interesting, what *reasons* were given by those who refused it? The responses were diverse and complex, but of compelling importance for a full understanding of the revolutionary experience.

To begin, the oath provided a straightforward route to rehabilitation for most neutrals or Loyalists who had undergone a change of heart—or at least claimed that they had. There are innumerable references to such persons as Eli Crosby who had been "sent away as a disaffected person to Exeter [New Hampshire], having return'd, and giving this Committee reason to suppose that he has chang'd his Sentiments, and Voluntarily taking the oath of Allegiance, was discharg'd." [82] Then there were those whose public behavior had been deviant, often anti-authoritarian, like Thomas Bemus, who had been committed for "damning the Congress." Brought before the board after two months in detention, he offered to take the oath, was allowed to do so, and was discharged.[83] Prisoners were also released upon swearing allegiance to the state. Many of them had been held aboard the "fleet prison," a colloquialism for the horrible floating jails.[84]

In the Albany area such prisoners had commonly been arrested by local "rangers." After a period of unpleasant confinement, the "Tory Prisoners" often "prayed that they might be restored to favour & Voluntarily Swore allegiance to the free and Independant States of America in return for the protection of their Laws." In some instances, also, a fee had to be paid for the privilege of subscribing to the oath and being released.[85] On December 5, 1777, twenty-four members of the Albany committee resolved that it should be considered a crime to recruit or persuade people for service to the enemy, "or of having taken the benefit of the late Act of Grace," or to swear allegiance to the "late" British government. One month after that, however, the same board modified its position considerably. The language used to describe the new conditions is very revealing.

> Many Persons went over to the Enemy and took an Active part in their favour, some thro' Fear, some thro' the persuasions of artful and designing Persons, others thro' the Allurements of Gain and the prospect of seeing their oppressed Country in the Hands of its base Invaders. However infamous the Conduct of those Persons have been, be their Motives what they may . . . we would remind our Countrymen, that the God of Justice has declared Victory in our favour, & put many of our Enemies in our power. . . . Let us also now Exercise Mercy (one of the attributes of Heaven) as far as is Consistant with the Good or Safety of our Country and by Acts of Clemency forgive our Offending Brethren provided they shew Signs of Contrition for their past Offences and promise of Amendment in future; those who have taken the Oath of Allegiance and perjured themselves, or such as have seduced others from their Allegiance to the State we are of Opinion ought not to interfere in our Elections.[86]

Once that wondrous victory at Saratoga the preceding October had been fully savored, its implications absorbed, and the area made more secure, a certain swagger and close-fisted magnanimity began to be apparent. When some of General Burgoyne's British soldiers sought to remain in Albany, hoping to pursue their peacetime vocations, the committee required them to swear allegiance to New York and then permitted them to stay.[87]

Beginning in the spring of 1778, one senses a pattern of perhaps some gradual relaxation of tension. Individuals who had been confined or suspected of disloyalty were liberated, commonly "on entering into Recognizance for future good Behaviour & Monthly Appearance," and always provided that they took the oath.[88] In some cases the individuals seem to have been nervous about retribution or retroactive injustice, and so expressed their willingness to swear allegiance in exchange for a promise of amnesty. The board appears to have been unsure about its power to award "Indulgence," however, and "resolved to take the Opinion of the Judges of the Supream Court thereon." [89]

The war's impact upon family relations also emerges with some clarity from these Albany area cases. On August 24, 1778, for example, Joseph and Benjamin Greenman came before the commissioners, "and upon examination it appeared that they had been with the Enemy at Rhode Island and had been seduced thereto by their Father, that they upon the first oppertunity offering made their escape from the Enemy and prayed that they might be admitted as Subjects of the State." [90] The board administered the oath of allegiance to them. Early in November of that year we find the case of Duncan McDugall, who had been restricted to his brother's farm in Tryon County. Because the commissioners had "heard no Complaints alledged" against McDugall since his original release from restriction to the "farm arrest," his full freedom was restored.[91]

By the spring of 1779 the state was making special provision for persons who had previously refused to take the oath but now were willing to do so.[92] On July 19, 1779, the board heard the case of one Jacob Haines, who had been jailed for provisioning unpatriotic "robbers." The members ordered his release upon interesting terms: an oath

> that he will not Aid Comfort or assist any Person or Persons whom he knows or Suspects to be Robbers or who are disaffected to the American Cause or who in Order to screen themselves from doing Milatary Duty keep & skulk in the Woods or who have deserted from the Continental Service & that he will upon Discovery of any of those Persons immediately give notice thereof to the Commissioners of Conspiracies or some other Authority in this State & on his entering into a Recognizance for the next two Years to keep the Peace.

And the sum of £200, as well, for his bail.[93]

Similarly, William Halenbeeck was discharged on August 5, 1779, after taking an oath that he would not thereafter harbor "Tories or Robbers," and that he would notify the "Board of all such Persons of that Denomination as may come to his House." There were subsequent instances in 1780 and 1781 of persons being freed (after taking the oath) on amounts of bail ranging from £100 to £500.[94]

All of these varied cases, ranging from early in 1777 until the end of 1781, concern people who originally had pro-British sympathies, or wished to remain neutral, or had been unable to support the rebel cause from the outset—but eventually, for one reason or another, "saw the light" and took the oath. What happened to those who finally *refused*, however, or refused with finality? In a word: punishment. In several: ostracism, imprisonment, expropriation of property, and eventually, exile.

Meeting on December 21, 1776, the First Commission for Detecting and Defeating Conspiracies, chaired by John Jay, resolved that persons who still considered themselves subjects of Great Britain or refused the oath should be removed, "under the Care of some discreet Officer to the Town of Boston at their own Expence and there to remain on their Parole of Honour," to await future action by the committee or the state convention; and that a copy of their parole be sent to the selectmen of Boston.[95] On March 19,

1777, when Matthias Cook refused a second request to swear the oath, he was given ten days to get "his Family, Apparel & Household furniture to the City of New York or some other place in the possession of the Enemy." Similar action was taken ten days later in the case of the Reverend James Sayre of Fredericksburgh Precinct, with members of the local committee there prepared, at Sayre's departure, to "take Charge of the residue of his Estate." The same thing happened two days later to the Reverend Epenetus Townsend, an Anglican missionary living and working at Cortlandt Manor.[96]

The comparable case of the Reverend John Beardsley is interesting, but frightening and tragic, too. On June 7, 1777, he appeared before the board and refused to take the oath. Ten days later, with only two members present, the board ordered Beardsley to be confined to his farm. The next day, with Egbert Benson joining Melancton Smith and Peter Cantine, the commissioners decided that they were obliged to have Beardsley as well as "all those of the People called Quakers, who have lately been to Long Island and are returned, to be apprehended and sent under guard to the fleet prison at Esopus Creek." Beardsley must have somehow slipped away to New York City; but on September 5 we learn that he had returned. Egbert Benson, sitting alone and constituting the board, issued a summons for Beardsley's prompt appearance. He was released on parole, and seems to have been on good behavior for the next ninety days. Nevertheless, some assistant commissioners reported on December 4 that "the spirits of the people are up so that I fear they may injure him in his person." The two deputies pleaded from Poughkeepsie that "it is not in our power to ease the minds of a set of men who are exceeding troublesome in this place, and therefore think it advisable to send him to New-York." [97]

Finally, on December 11, the disposition of this case reached the State Council of Safety (meeting at Hurley), which instructed the assistant commissioners summarily. Beardsley should not be allowed to sell his property in or-

der to pay debts to local inhabitants. All property left behind by departing Loyalists "must be subject to disposition
by the authority of the State." What about the possessions
of Beardsley's children? The council decided "that they
can not be considered as exempted from seizure, because
the father, who is an enemy to the State, can not be the
proper guardian of their effects, especially as he is no longer
a subject of this State, and is on the point of being sent out
of it." The council then summarized its directive: banish
the family, and "permit them only to take off their wearing
apparel and necessary bedding and provisions for their passage, and no other goods or effects whatsoever." [98]

It is not entirely clear why some people who refused to
take the oath were exiled, like Beardsley, while many others
were simply stuck in local jails, or in the "Guard house," or
placed under house arrest.[99] In certain instances a first refusal required the latter, a second meant imprisonment, and
a third brought banishment. But it would be misleading to
imply any clear-cut pattern. Local practice varied, for one
thing, especially in response to the military exigencies of
the moment. Moreover, persons of higher social status and
those of British birth, such as Anglican clergymen, were
more likely to be expelled. It was not uncommon, besides,
for propertied people to find that "the Time fixed for their
Departure is so short as to put it out of their Power to settle their necessary Affairs." [100]

Still other "disaffected persons" and neutrals were held
by the commissioners, under the direction of state authorities, to be used in exchange for patriot prisoners of war.
On December 7, 1778, for instance, we discover that John
Cumming, who had refused to take the oath

> as prescribed to be taken by Persons of Neutral and equivo-
> cal Characters & was in Consequence thereof to be removed
> within the Enemies Lines but was detained by his Excellency
> the Governor for Exchange made Application to the Board
> to be permitted to go and reside at Kats Kill with his Family
> and their being no Prospect of an Exchange taking Place
> as yet for the said John Cumming therefore ordered that the

said John Cumming enter into a Parole to remain within the Limits and Bounds of the District of Grote Imboght and abide by such Restrictions as are in the said Parole specified.[101]

The variations upon all of these actions were virtually infinite. On March 17, 1777, six men were detained by the Committee at Claverack "for Contumaciously refusing to give Evidence respecting a Supposed conspiracy," and were sent before Egbert Benson, sitting as a one-man board.[102] Then, too, there were apparent backsliders. On June 25, 1777, an affidavit was obtained that Abraham Van Aelen, who had previously taken the New York oath, "has declared himself a Subject of the King of Great Britain." A resolution for his immediate arrest passed promptly. On July 4 of that same year, the Albany committee read a letter stating that Coenradt Ten Eyck, "after taking the Oath of Allegiance has drank damnation to the Congress." The culprit appeared, confessed, was briefly jailed and then "Liberated upon his entring into Bond for his future good behaviour." [103]

There are even cases which indicate that swearing the oath provided no absolute assurance against harassment or restriction of freedom. In October 1777, at Rhinebeck Precinct, a number of men who voluntarily took the oath of allegiance were released, but to the confinement and personal supervision of an acceptable relative or householder.[104] A few months earlier one Dennis Kennedy wrote to the Council of Safety complaining of mistreatment by the Commissioners of Sequestration. The particulars of his case are less interesting than his appeal.

> Now gentlemen, being conscious within myself of having asserted nothing but the truth, it seems reasonable to me, to conclude that the commissioners refrained writing merely because they had nothing to say against me, except their private opinions, as above mentioned, which I did not pretend to dispute, relying upon the determination of this Honourable Board, who I trust will consider me, a true and well affected subject of this State; suffering under many difficulties which

you alone can redress. . . . It has been insinuated by some
people who know nothing of the matter, that I was compelled to take the oath of allegiance; but some of the members
of this council, who were present at the time, will remember
it was not so. I was no prisoner nor under difficulties, but
from convictions that it was my duty; I did it freely and
voluntarily, and have never yet repented, and was it to do
over again, I would take it as readily as before; will therefore
request the favour of a certificate, that there was no compulsion, &c.[105]

Kennedy's case brings us, finally, to the very core of our
inquiry: the expressions of integrity professed by so many
of these participants. Kennedy claims to have taken the oath
quite willingly. There were others, however, who could not
do so under any circumstance, and who stated categori-
cally, with Cadwallader Colden, Jr.: "I Did not in my Conscience think that I was absolved from my former oaths of
Allegiance." [106] The son of a prominent provincial politician,
Colden lived on the family farm near Newburgh. By April
of 1775 he saw that his views conflicted with those of his
neighbors, who happened to include George Clinton. When
Colden attempted to withdraw to a neutral position, he
found himself arrested, a circumstance that continued, almost without a break, from June 1776 until September
1778.[107]

While confined at Kingston, Colden became familiar
with the case of two fellow prisoners, Jacobus Rose and
Jacob Midagh. Accused of acting for the British to recruit
soldiers in Ulster County, they were tried by court-martial
at Fort Montgomery on April 30, 1777, and condemned to
death by New York's Provincial Convention. While await-
ing execution, Rose spilled out his thoughts to Colden, who
recorded them in his journal:

He told me that it was true he hardly thought they would be
so Mad as to put him to Death, yet, should that be the Case,
he should Die with an Easy Conscience with Respect to what
he was to Suffer for, for that he had not taken the Part he
did from any Lucrative Motive, or the Sake of gaining any

[165]

Preferement, but that he thought his Country would never be happy again till Reduced to a Proper Obedience to its former State of Government, and that the sooner this be brought about the better.[108]

Ten days later Colden wrote to John Jay in an effort to explain that hanging Rose and Midagh "will not make one Man change his Sentements in Your favour, But the very Reverse." As for himself, Colden reiterated his "determined Resolution to keep a Clear Conscience by Takeing no active Part on Either Side of the Controversy. . . ." [109]

Soon thereafter Colden was paroled from the fleet prison to his farm, and on September 22, 1777, he wrote to Governor Clinton, imploring him "to grant me what Larger Limitts or indulgence you think Proper." Just as he had insisted to Jay in May, nothing had changed.

> You may be inform'd if you Please to take the Trouble of Enquireing, that Notwithstanding my Long Confinem't there has not been any Charge much Less Prooff appeared against me of my haveing accted in opposition to (what is Call'd) the American Cause, Since the Declaration of Independency, Nevertheless I Cannot Devest myself of my Private Opinion, and it is hard to wrack a man's Conscience.[110]

A month later, hauled before the Council of Safety, sitting at Marbletown, he was offered the chance to repudiate his allegiance to George III. Colden's written response, prepared after an opportunity for reflection, provides an ambiguous yet categorical statement of divided loyalties: to both his remote sovereign as well as the realities of his native land.

> I shall ever look upon myself to be a faithful and true subject to that state from which I receive protection; and though I am bound by my oath to be a subject of the king of Great Britain, yet as that part of the province of New York in which I reside is now under an independent government entitled the state of New York, I do hereby promise to be a true and faithful subject to the said state so long as it shall remain an independent state and I reside therein.[111]

This waffling dualism was exemplified in the contradictory behavior of his sons. One, his namesake, fought on the patriot side; the other, Thomas, joined the Tories. In September 1778 the commission exiled Colden. He returned to Coldenham in 1784, however, and lived out his remaining years there until 1797.[112]

The cases of Henry and Peter Van Schaack may very well be the best documented of all those persons whose conscience would not permit them to swear allegiance to the new state of New York. In 1774 Peter had opposed the punitive policies of Lord North's administration. He even helped write a binding loyalty oath to the patriot cause in 1775. Quite soon, however, he came to believe that he could not himself take such an oath; and later, on May 29, 1776, he refused to sign the Continental Association. Required to travel to Albany in order to be examined, his non-juring stance before the board brought him banishment to Boston and detention there. Eventually he was recalled for a hearing in Kingston before the Provincial Convention, which paroled him to his home in Kinderhook. He remained there under considerable harassment until the summer of 1778, when the Banishing Act passed in June forced him to abandon his residence in patriot-controlled New York.[113]

As he reluctantly departed for England, however, he continued an interesting and revealing exchange of views with John Jay which had been going back and forth for some months. In April of 1778, for example, Jay had explained that Governor Clinton's sense of "duty" militated against either freedom of movement or neutrality. When, in August, Clinton permitted exile abroad for Van Schaack (so that he could have an eye operation for removal of a cataract), the neutralist explained his beliefs to Jay in explicit detail. The statement is so succinct, lucid, and important that it is worth excerpting at some length.

Dear Sir:
    I owe it to the friendship which formerly subsisted between us, to explain myself on a very serious subject, before I quit this country, perhaps forever. The charitable construction

which every man would wish to be put upon his own conduct, will, I hope, induce you to do justice to *my* principles;
principles not formed without consideration; not dependent
on undecisive events, and not to be deserted at the approach
of danger.

I suffer, sir, as you must see, for a difference of opinion
merely, on a question wherein I am not only justifiable, but
under the most sacred obligation to exercise my own private
judgment. In a case like this, involving considerations of moral
duty, there can be no *choice*, and he who disobeys the dictates of his own mind, stands convicted. Punishment by the
civil power for a difference of opinion in the abstract, will be
reprobated by every liberal man; but, in the present case, its
justice is derived from the dangerous tendency of those
opinions, in that they uphold a supremacy *foreign* to the
government of the state. They are *but opinions*, nevertheless;
and that their evil tendency cannot be restrained, or prevented, without so harsh a measure as the present, I believe
will not, when considered without passion, be believed: and
if it *can*, the government (which, too, is not exempt from
obligation,) is bound to adopt more lenient methods. . . .

Whatever may be urged in favor of the act, I must think
that I suffer, even in the sense of my prosecutors, for an
involuntary error of the mind, or, at most, for the omission
of a *moral* duty—neither of which are cognizable by the civil
authority. In the thirty-eighth article of your Constitution,
the rights of conscience are separated by a clear boundary,
from matters of civil cognizance.[114] All religious professions
are placed on the same foot, without discrimination. . . .

With the loyalist, however, the case is different; for *he*,
consistent with his principles, may be laid under obligations
affording ample security to the public; which, according to a
well-informed conscience, are binding; and I must think that
he, no more than other men, is to be farther punished than
necessity (which alone can justify *any* punishment) requires.

I readily waive any arguments drawn from the *belief* the
oath requires, of the independency of this State both of *right*
and in *fact;* the latter, in one sense at least, dismembered as
the State is, is not true; the former is yet *sub judice*, and
undecided. I am willing to consider it, for my own part, as
a simple oath of allegiance; and in that view, I think it is

manifestly improper to tender it to persons of opposite principles, because it is a temptation to perjury, in attacking
human weakness in its most vulnerable parts; because, if taken,
it adds no obligation in point of morality upon the man it is
tendered to, since a man by his voluntary act cannot discharge
himself from a prior duty, and because, therefore, it gives no
security to the public; and I think this measure most cruel,
because it is carried on at a time when no *state necessity*
(which, though sometimes a reality is oftener a phantom, to
which numbers of virtuous men have been made victims,) can
be pretended to justify it. It is cruel, because it operates
against men in that situation, whereto they are reduced, not
by choice, but by a different way of thinking, on a subject
they had a right to judge and determine upon. . . .

I have not *affected* but *maintained*, as far as I could, a
neutrality. I was your prisoner, and under parole to do so;
and surely it argued no poverty of spirit, or undue attachment
to property; nor was it "unmanly or ignominious," to adhere
to the faith I had given you, nor did I want to "shelter myself
under your government;" and if it was known that I had en-
deavored to "undermine or subvert it," (and without being
known it ought not surely to have been asserted,) I was ame-
nable to your courts.

I say, I have, as far as I *could*, maintained a neutrality; for
this has not been left at my option. Notwithstanding my local
restrictions, notwithstanding my being disarmed, I have been
compelled to pay sums of money, and have been tried by a
court martial for not marching in arms, and doing the duties
of a soldier. Does not this remind one of the bed of Pro-
crustes? and surely a very small share of gratitude would
suffice for *such* protection. Permit me to observe, by the by,
that many instances of the breach of faith you have met with,
I fancy have arisen from like treatment; added to this consideration, that persons of opposite sentiments have never
known the extent of their punishment, nor were placed in any
situation where they could have that reasonable assurance of
their safety, which is necessary to enjoy peace of mind in
society.

Whatever the policy may be of banishing me from my
native country, I dare confidently say that my political principles are not incompatible, either with the just rights of

government, or the liberties of a free people. I may have erred in the application of them in a contested point, but as they have been formed with all the consideration I was master of, I hope I may say that I am *innocent* in this respect; at least, I think that in a question depending on *opinion* only, and wherein every man has a *right* and is *bound* to determine according to *his own* opinion, he is accountable only for the fair and impartial exercise of his judgment; and as no human tribunal can examine this, so they ought not to punish him for the result. Motives of *self-preservation* alone can justify a State in banishing a man who is chargeable, not with transgression of law, but with a mere difference of opinion; every severity besides, as an act of vindictive justice, is unpardonable.[115]

His brother Henry, meanwhile, had his own problems. In May 1777 he failed to appear before the Commission for Detecting Conspiracies. The commission's adjutant promptly apprehended and imprisoned him, though it kindly permitted a parole period of sixteen days so that Henry could attend to his land sales as well as two thousand bushels of wheat which he had contracted for sale to the commissary general. In June the board dismissed him on parole once again, this time with a maximum of twenty days to depart for New England, "and in the mean time, that he be permitted to go at large for the purpose of settling his affairs." [116] He removed to Massachusetts in the hope that his neutral conduct "will one day be considered in a favorable light." His difficulty inhered in the oaths he had taken before the Revolution as a public official. Not only had he taken them, but he had been accustomed to administering them to others, as well. Starting in 1770 he had been commissioned (along with Sir William Johnson) by Lieutenant Governor Colden to give the oaths of allegiance and supremacy to all officials in Albany County. He believed that these oaths had a solemn character; copies of several of them were found among his papers after his death in 1823. Van Schaack had himself sworn, after all, and had sworn many others to "defend to the utmost of his power against all traitrous conspiracies and attempts what-soever," which might be made against the King.[117]

When he refused to take the oath prescribed on June 30, 1778, by the Banishing Act—"An Act more effectively to prevent the mischiefs arising from the Influence and Example of Persons of equivocal and suspected Characters in this State"—he was sent to enemy lines. In September he wrote to Theodore Sedgwick, a friend who lived in the Berkshires, and commented with rueful irony upon his last appearance before the commissioners. They admitted publicly that he "was charged with no crime; but they were obliged to consider me as coming within the description of the Act as a neutral; and, as they were conscience bound, they were obliged to banish me." [118]

As the war was nearing its close, in April 1783, Henry sent Sedgwick yet another letter. Van Schaack did not wish to join the British army in evacuating New York City for England, and stated that the "hour of peace" at last made possible his acceptance of the now legitimate regime. "The old government being annihilated," he explained, "those who are not yet members of the new establishment and wish to remain here, have now no ties of honor or scruples of conscience to withhold the most unequivocal allegiance to the American empire." [119] In November he moved to Great Barrington, Massachusetts, underwent an examination before two justices, took an oath of fidelity, and became a citizen of the Commonwealth. There he found tranquility, happiness, and—better than both, apparently—splendid conditions for commerce. "We have no house-breaking, robberies, cursing, swearing, tavern-haunting, or scarce a scene of immorality," he wrote. "Besides, my affairs stand much better than I feared they would when I left New York." Van Schaack proclaimed his particular admiration because Massachusetts had not, during the war, "executed a single man for his political principles. When this fact is handed down to posterity, by the faithful pages of history, ages hence will rank the Massachusetts among the first people of the world. This is a theme I could be copious on, but business forbids it." [120]

In addition to Cadwallader Colden II and Henry and Peter Van Schaack, there is also the case of Sir John Johnson (the son of Sir William), who proclaimed on October 27, 1775, that "before he would sign any association, or would lift up his hand against his King, he would rather suffer, that his head shall be cut off." [121] I do not wish to imply, however, that these crises of conscience occurred only, or even primarily, to persons of high status who owed their eminence and perquisites to the Crown. What is most striking are the numerous instances of protest from very ordinary people, such as John McCord. Sent before the Committee for Detecting Conspiracies, meeting at Connors Tavern in Fishkill on January 2, 1777, he insisted that he was "a Friend to his Country but neither Whig or Tory and that his Conscience wont let him fight on either Side." The board consigned him into custody once again.[122]

Albany County provides endless examples of ordinary citizens who felt passionately about their bonds of obligation:

> Peter Miller declared on May 23, 1776, "that he had taken an oath which would oblige him to join the Kings Troops when called upon by any of his Officers, and to kill his best Friends if they were in opposition to him."
>
> Jonathan Owens (of Claverack) confessed on January 22, 1777, "that he had taken an Oath of Allegiance to the Crown of Great Britain and Consequently could not take an Oath of Allegiance to this State, and that in Point of Conscience he cannot take up arms against the Forces of the King."
>
> Benjamin Baker refused to take the oath on July 23, 1778, because "if he did he would perjure himself." The commissioners deemed his declaration "a high Contempt and Insult upon the Authority of this State," and had him jailed.
>
> John Drummond was "adjudged a person of a Suspicious Character and dangerous to the safety of the

State." Appearing before the board on October 8, 1780, he denied that he posed any danger to New York but professed "his principles in Favour of the Crown of Great Britain" and declared "his intention of not taking up Arms in Defence of the American Cause." He, too, was imprisoned.[123]

In a very real sense, those who denied the privileges of neutrality placed the concept of duty—and collective security—above the sanctity of conscience. John Jay put it this way to Peter Van Schaack in 1782:

> my Heart has . . . been on more than one occasion, afflicted by the Execution of what I thought, and still think was my Duty. I felt very sensibly for you and for others; but as society can regard only the political Propriety of Men's Conduct, and not the moral Propriety of their motives to it, I could only lament your unavoidably becoming classed with many, whose morality was convenience, and whose Politicks changed with the aspect of public affairs.[124]

V. Turnabout Is Foul Play

It would be a grievous mistake, however, to conclude that the civil government of New York had a monopoly —or an exclusive fixation—upon constraint of conscience. The British could be equally callous. Therefore we must devote at least one section of this essay to a comparison of the two military forces in requiring oaths of allegiance. We must recognize, for example, that all the British proposals for compromise and settlement that emerged between 1775 and 1781 required the rebels to seek the King's pardon and swear an oath of allegiance.

In the autumn of 1776, soon after the British conquest and occupation of New York City, a report received in London contained this ominous announcement: "There is a broad R put upon every door in *New-York* that is disaffected to Government, and examples will be made of its inhabitants; on the other hand, every person that is well affected to Government, finds protection." [125] Also in October, one thousand Loyalists petitioned General Howe for the restoration of civil government; but their request was merely pigeonholed and ignored. By what right did Howe assert his authority? He found legal justification in Parliament's Prohibitory Act of January 1776, which, the military commanders contended, not only curtailed colonial trade but deprived them of all civil and political rights as well. In the language of the day, they were considered to be beyond the "King's peace." [126]

The British army made a house-to-house canvass in the area now under control. One Whig who escaped to Philadelphia reported on October 23 that General Howe "makes every one of the inhabitants swear to submit and be obedient to the laws of the *British* Parliament, in all cases whatsoever." In a proclamation dated November 30, 1776, the brothers Howe prescribed an oath of allegiance to be taken within sixty days by anyone seeking pardon from the Crown. In December Governor Tryon administered his own "oath of allegiance and fidelity" to militiamen in Suffolk County, Long Island; and in January 1777 Tryon began trying to administer the same oath to *all* residents of British-occupied New York. By February 11, 1777, no less than 5,600 persons had taken this oath in Manhattan, Staten Island, Long Island, and Westchester County.[127]

Early in February there were even outraged complaints in Albany that copies of Howe's oath had somehow been printed and "industriously propogated thro' this City & perhaps of this County & other Counties by some evil minded Persons." [128] These pre-printed documents had blanks for the insertion of names and dates. Here, for example, is the form used by David Mathews, the Loyalist mayor of New York City.

> I DO hereby Certify, That *David Brinkerhoff* has, in my presence voluntarily taken an OATH, to bear Faith and true Allegiance to HIS MAJESTY KING George the Third,—and to defend to the utmost of his Power, His sacred Person, Crown and Government, against all Persons whatsoever.

Given under my Hand at New-York, this 15 Day of *May* in the Seventeenth Year of HIS MAJESTY'S reign, Anno. Dom. 1777. *D. Mathews* Mayor of the City of New-York.[129]

Needless to say, the patriot side did not look with favor upon anyone known to have administered the Tory oath of allegiance, regardless of the reason. On March 11, 1777, for instance, Nathaniel Underhill, who had been arrested by the patriots in Westchester County, was hauled before the Committee for Detecting Conspiracies. His neighbors were brought to testify about him. A Dr. Daniel White related that

the said Underhill was reputed unfriendly to the American Cause, previous to the Enemys coming into West Chester— That after they had taken possession of that place, This Deponant understood that the said Underhill assisted as a Magistrate in administering the Oath of Allegiance to the King of Great Britain, to divers Inhabitants of the Borough of West Chester,—That notwithstanding this, he had heard the said Underhill in a Conversation had with him, a few days after his assisting as above and while the British Army was in possession of the Borough of West Chester, find great fault with Governor Tryon for requiring the Inhabitants to swear Allegiance, and further the said Underhill had informed this Deponant, that he had been desired to furnish a List of the persons who had taken the Oath, which he refused, and declared that no Man should know from him who had taken the Oath, as the exposing of them, might subject the Inhabitants to Inconvenience & Injury. This Depon[t] further saith, that he has frequently heard the said Underhill declare, that he did not consider himself as a Magistrate, nor would he act in that Office while the present Troubles lasted—That he farther informed this Deponant that on a certain Time he had been sent for to go to Kingsbridge to administer the Oath to some people who had gone down out of the Country, which he utterly refused—and farther this Deponant saith, that he has reason to believe, that the said Underhill did many kind & benevolent Offices to the Inhabitants who were reputed friendly to the American Cause, while the British Troops were Quartered among them and in their Neighbourhood.

Joshua Pine then corroborated this testimony; and ten days later Underhill explained to the committee, on his own behalf,

> that notwithstanding he was present and attended to the administring the Oath of Allegiance to the Crown of Great Britain to sundry Inhabitants of the Borough of West Chester when lately in the possession of the Enemy, his intentions were not to promote or advance the cause & Interest of our Enemies, but that he was solely influenced by motives to assist the Inhabitants & prevent their being plundered. That he never return'd the Roll of the persons who took the Oath, but destroyed it in order that Governor Tryon might not know who the persons were, and does insist that notwithstanding many parts of his conduct may appear unfriendly & inimical, that he is still a true & hearty friend to our Cause, & wishes prosperity to the Measures pursuing by the United States for the preservation of their Liberties.

The board decided to parole Underhill to his home, stating that he should be considered a prisoner there and prepared to surrender whenever called for by the committee or any authorized body.[130]

Massive confusion, not to mention moral and legal complexity, occurred wherever the British had occupied an area temporarily and then departed, leaving the rebels in control. Some people who had sworn neutrality so that their homes would not be burned by General Howe subsequently re-swore the rebel oath.[131] What happened when multiple oaths conflicted? Did double swearing tax tender consciences? Did one loyalty oath take precedence over another? Opinions varied, few dared to speak with assurance, and it is very difficult to untangle their attitudes in retrospect.

Still another complicated and related problem, of a jurisdictional nature, arose in 1776 and 1777: was the administration of loyalty tests most properly the responsibility of civil or military officials? Both did so, of course; but at a time when the very nature and locus of sovereignty was so uncertain, men of contradictory opinions became very agitated about the matter. John Jay and Alexander Hamilton felt strongly that the whole loyalty program ought to remain under civilian control. "To impose a test is a sovereign act of legislation," Jay explained to General McDougall, "and when the army become our legislators, the people that moment become slaves." [132]

The issue had become so nasty because in February and March 1776, under the aggressive supervision of General Charles Lee, loyalty oaths had been administered in the New York City area and on Long Island. The Provincial Congress protested vigorously, denounced any arrests made without its consent, and elicited from Lee an interesting justification for some of his precipitous actions.

> the Congress will not suppose that I am aiming at an authority superior to theirs. . . . I respect them as the true representatives of the people . . . but, sir, the information I have received from Cambridge, and the orders I have received from the Continental Congress, will justify me in most humbly entreating the Congress not to enjoin me to assent (so much against my conscience,) to any intercourse of any kind with Mr. Tryon.[133]

Echoing the language of his letter to Isaac Sears, written a day earlier (see pp. 148–49, above), Lee petulantly insisted upon his determination to "put this city and its environs in a state of defence," and decreed imprisonment for all of the Long Island Loyalists.

> When the enemy is at our door, forms must be dispensed with; my duty to you, to the Continental Congress, and to my own conscience, have dictated the necessity of the measure. If I have done wrong, and I confess the irregularity, I must submit myself to the shame of being reputed foolish, rash, and precipitate. I must undergo the censure of the public, but I shall have the consciousness in my own breast that the most pure motives of serving the public cause, uncontaminated by pique or resentment to individuals, have urged me to the step.[134]

What Lee really seemed to be saying was that he willingly would violate the conscience of many other people in order to pacify his own and dutifully fulfill his orders. Although he acknowledged that a disaffected person or proto-Loyalist might swear falsely, Lee did not doubt his own ability to separate the "desperate fanatics" (who refused to take the oath) from the "reclaimable" citizens (who consented to take it).[135] The military mind may not be unique in claiming omniscience; but in the name of national security it does tend to take liberties with civilian sensibilities.

New York instructed its delegates to the Continental Congress to protest in Philadelphia against Lee's behavior. Whereupon the Congress did, in fact, pass a resolution to the effect that no military officer under its control should force test oaths upon civilians.[136] General Israel Putnam, however, wrote from his headquarters at Peekskill, on June 21, 1777, to the president of New York's Provincial Convention. "There is an order of the Convention," he explained, "that no person in the military line shall administer the oath of allegiance to this State except an officer of militia." Such civil-military figures were not always available, he pointed out, "and we are frequently put to much difficulty on this account." He earnestly hoped that the inconvenience would be removed. A committee of the Convention responded amicably that "any officer of this State, civil or military may administer the oath, consequently a proper person may at any time be found at Peekskill, where there are the officers of two regiments of this State." The committee did express concern, however, about the danger of forged certificates "if too many persons are permitted to administer the oath, since in such case it would be impossible to detect those forgeries, especially if the names of officers living in States very remote should be put to them." [137]

One gets the feeling that the real issue was not so much civilian versus military mastery over loyalty, but control over New Yorkers *by* New Yorkers rather than by officers of the Continental line who were outsiders. In any case, oaths continued to be a troublesome issue within the military sector. In 1778, for example, twenty-six officers in one Continental brigade refused to take the standard oath of abjuration, allegiance, and office. They gave four reasons to their superiors.

1. "The tenor of the oath they in some measure consider an indignity . . . as it presupposes that some of them have acted contrary to their sentiments; it may be unnecessary, for those officers, who ventured their lives and fortunes in support of American Independence, could have no other reason but the apparent one."

2. "As many officers at present are injured in their rank, and cannot possibly continue in the army exactly in their present situation, they apprehend it would be an impropriety in them to swear to continue in their present posts, as the rank of the juror is to be taken when the oath is administered."

3. "Would not the oath debar an officer from the privilege of resigning when circumstances might render it indispensably necessary that he should quit the army?"

4. "The taking of the oath, while the present establishment continues, most of the subscribers are of opinion, would lay them under a pointed restraint in endeavoring to procure a change, which the whole army have long, not only most ardently wished for, but conceived absolutely necessary for its preservation; a change, that would put them on an honorable and advantageous footing."

George Washington's communication to Lafayette on this sensitive and threatening matter, dated May 17, 1778, is both judicious and intensely interesting.

As every Oath should be a free act of the Mind, founded on the conviction of the party, of its propriety, I would not wish, in any instance, that there should be the least degree of compulsion exercised; or to interpose my opinion in order to induce any to make it, of whom it is required. The Gentlemen therefore, who signed the paper, will use their own discretion in the matter, and swear or not swear, as their conscience and feelings dictate.

At the same time, I cannot but consider it, as a circumstance of some singularity, that the scruples against the Oath should be peculiar to the Officers of one Brigade, and so very extensive.

The Oath in itself is not New. It is substantially the same with that required in all Governments, and, therefore, does not imply any indignity; And it is perfectly consistent with the professions, Actions, and implied engagements of every Officer.

The objection, founded on the supposed unsettled Rank of the Officers, is of no validity (rank being only mentioned as a further designation of the party swearing); Nor can it be seriously thought, that the Oath is either intended, or can prevent their being promoted, or their resignations.

The fourth objection stated by the Gentlemen, serves as a Key to their scruples, and I would willingly persuade myself, that their own reflexions will point out to them the impropriety of the whole proceeding, and not suffer them to be betrayed in future into a similar conduct. I regard them all, and cannot but regret that they were ever engaged in the measure. I am certain they will regret it themselves.[138]

Once again George Washington seems to justify his reputation as a very unflappable, non-vindictive, leader of men.

The pattern persisted throughout the war, at least in New York, that persons joining the military would be required to take an oath of allegiance. Moreover, deserters from Burgoyne's army were absorbed into the state's population—"they have Permission to go at large"—upon accepting the oath. Even Hessian mercenaries who had fought with Burgoyne were "tendered an Oath of Neutrality" in 1778, and thereafter were considered as non-threatening persons.[139] The only respectable way to achieve neutral status in revolutionary New York, apparently, was to have been an enemy of non-British nationality. Then one could swear neutrality and look good. In an atmosphere of anxiety and suspicion, paranoia and persecution, personal reputations as well as rumors of good or bad behavior counted for much. Common lore came to mean more than the common law.

VI. Pangs of Conscience

For many who would not swear an oath of allegiance contrary to their true beliefs, and for others who could not take an oath contradictory to one given previously, the act of swearing was considered both solemn and sacred. To some of these the oath still carried its explicitly religious connotations, especially from the controversies of Reformation Europe. To others the oath had become secularized and carried more a burden of responsibility between man and society than an obligation made by man in the sight of God. It is often difficult to distinguish between the two; yet we must not lose sight of the fact that for certain denominations the Revolution threatened violations of conscience for fundamentally religious reasons.

There are occasional episodes of some interest which arise among the Anglicans, Dutch Reformed, and Presbyterians of New York.[140] The groups that were troubled *as sects*, however, were the Quakers, Moravians, and Shakers. Since their role in the Revolution has already been told—to some degree, at least—its significance for our context can be interpolated briefly.

For conscientious Quakers in New York, the Revolution brought serious problems. They could not pay taxes in the knowledge that their money would be used for military purposes. In 1777 the pacifist Quakers of New York City refused to supply funds which would be used to purchase stockings for the British army, and subsequently they would not accept rent which the British authorities repeatedly thrust upon them for their use of Friends' meetinghouses in an area requisitioned for army purposes. In 1782 Quakers were unwilling to take their turn in the city's security watch. And in rural New York during the final phases of the war, when most overt fighting had ceased, some Quakers began to take part in town meetings, believing that participation no longer conflicted with their witness to peace. The Society's leadership strongly disapproved, however, contending that "in the present commotions of public affairs, Friends being in any ways active in government is inconsistent with our principles." [141]

In certain important respects, nevertheless, the Quakers in New York did receive consideration as a group specially circumstanced. The New England, Philadelphia, and Baltimore area meetings, for example, required their local, subordinate meetings to disown members who willingly paid war taxes. The New York yearly meeting, however, while recommending non-compliance, did not call for disownment. British military authorities would not, for the most part, impose conscription upon Friends; and the Provincial Convention eventually agreed to allow twelve non-Quakers to swear as proxy for each Friend who could not take an oath.[142]

When Quakers were called before the patriotic Committee for Detecting Conspiracies, their inability to swear an oath was commonly respected and affirmations accepted instead.[143] For the most scrupulous Friends, however, even making an affirmation was extremely difficult. During the summer of 1777 the commissioners directed that Quakers be released "on their taking an affirmation of allegiance to the State, and paying costs, which they inform'd the [Provincial] Council they could not comply with, as they believed the taking an Affirmation to either party while contending for the Authority by the Sword, would be inconsistent with the peaceable principles they professed." [144]

There is also evidence that Quakers were physically abused for refusing to comply with military requisitions made by the patriot command:

> such as supplying with Horses for the use of the Armies, or going themselves or Sending a person to drive their Teams when taken from them for that purpose, and for refusing other demands, which they apprehended they could not comply with, without letting Fall the Testimony we have to bear against the nature and Spirit of War; for such refusal, tho done in great Meekness some suffered imprisonment, some were Cruelly beatten, and others were exposed to great dangers from Officers and Soldiers, who could not brook to have their Commands not obeyed, altho ever so unreasonable, therefore to effect a complyance, very Harsh Means have been used, Pistols and drawn Swords have been held up in view to some, with severe threats unless they complyed.[145]

Finally, we know that New York's Friends suffered special difficulties in travel and communication. They commonly had to cross the area between the two contending armies in order to attend their monthly, quarterly, or yearly meetings. There they were preyed upon by the "Cowboys" and "Skinners," ruthless brigands who exploited helpless persons passing through the "no man's land." [146]

For the Moravians, war meant that the sanctity of their places of worship would be desecrated, as in November 1776, when the British quartered soldiers in the Moravian meetinghouse at New York City. The pastor applied to Governor Tryon for relief, but without receiving any satisfaction.[147] For the Shakers, sharp conflict emerged in 1780 —six years after the arrival at New York City of Mother Ann Lee and eight companions. They had settled at Watervliet (near Albany), gained a following, and began their missionary work, which included opposition to war. In July 1780 the Commissioners for Detecting and Defeating Conspiracies intervened when an angry mob seized a Shaker convert as he was driving a herd of sheep from New Lebanon to Niskayuna, New York. Three Shakers who were called before the Albany County board explained that fighting violated their religious convictions. "It was their determined resolution," they insisted, "never to take up arms and to dissuade others from doing the same." Later that month six more Shakers, including Mother Ann Lee, were arrested for preaching pacifism. They, too, gladly pleaded guilty. Most were soon released, but Ann Lee was detained until year's end.[148]

There is, of course, one final paradox: New York's attitude and policy toward the Iroquois amidst all this. A very few Indians, raised as Christians, took the state's oath of allegiance. The vast majority, however, insisted upon the integrity of their own sovereignty, and leaned increasingly toward pro-British partisanship and participation. Therefore the Provincial Convention and subsequent policymakers after 1777, while being so contemptuous of "an equivocal neutrality" in white Americans, tried desperately to secure Iroquois neutrality during the war. Failure to achieve that goal made the Revolution in upstate New York an especially bloody affair.[149]

VII. Conclusions and Legacies

It ought to be obvious by now that the problem of allegiance—voluntary and involuntary—played a very significant role in revolutionary New York. Loyalty oaths fostered patriotism in some people and alienated others. They helped to polarize Americans, made neutrality an untenable position, and exacerbated a tendency to perceive the conflict in terms of Devils and Angels.

We must not be naïve, of course, and assume that every person who administered or refused to take an oath was doing so exclusively to satisfy the sanctions of conscience. Hypocrisy and expediency were present, to be sure, perhaps in abundance. In the course of my research I have been struck by the appearance of persons, at least in New York, who fought on *both* sides during the course of the war. I have also been impressed by the numerous persons who casually swore several contradictory oaths over a period of time and who did not hesitate to perjure themselves. We know that military hangmen executed British "traitors" even when they carried certificates attesting that they had previously taken Whig loyalty tests. One might infer that the patriot side did not always take seriously its own oath, or respect the sincerity of those who had subscribed to it.

The reality was more complex, however, than such critical comments would allow. For the partisans on both sides were not innocents, and their leaders least of all. They knew that people changed their hues as the winds of warfare shifted. They often referred to someone, or to a category of duplicitous people, as the Vicar of Bray, referring to the sixteenth-century English clergyman who was twice a Protestant and twice a papist in successive reigns. There

was, for example, a wonderful parody written late in the
Revolution which ends with these six lines:

> So Congress till death my King shall be,
> Unless the times do alter.
>> For this is law I will maintain
>> Until my dying day, Sir;
>> Let whatsoever King will reign,
>> I'll be a Vicar of Bray, Sir.[150]

There is also evidence that a certain disillusionment
about oaths had taken hold by the 1780s. A Frenchman had
written these cynical remarks to Benjamin Franklin in
June, 1776, about a courier with a diplomatic dispatch who
had given Barbeu Dubourg

> his word of honour that at least it shall not fall into the en-
> emy's hands. . . . He would have given me his oath for it,
> if I laid stress upon oaths; but I have never regarded them
> otherwise than as the last resource of liars. Was it not for
> that, I would swear, in this within your hands, a full homage
> and an inviolable fidelity to the august Congress of the most
> respectable Republick which ever existed.[151]

In 1785 Franklin echoed these remarks in a letter to Francis
Maseres. Maseres had written that Americans seemed
vengeful toward the Tories and should have "restored their
estates upon their taking the oaths of allegiance to the new
governments." Franklin replied that it was scarcely surprising that resentment still existed, and suggested that "the
opposition given by many to their re-establishing among
us is owing to a firm persuasion, that there could be no re-
liance on their oaths." [152]

Others among Franklin's contemporaries, however,
looked back upon the great divisive issues with realism
and renewed friendship. In the autumn of 1782 John Jay
and Peter Van Schaack resumed their correspondence. "As
society can regard only the political propriety of men's
conduct," Jay explained, "and not the moral propriety of
their motives to it, I could only lament your unavoidably

becoming classed with many whose morality was convenience, and whose politics changed with the aspect of public affairs." [153] Van Schaack replied a month later from London with a long letter that has the ring of authenticity.

> I would rather be the patient sufferer, than run the risk of being the active aggressor; and as I should rather be even a figure for the hand of scorn to point its slow and moving finger at than to destroy the peace of my own mind, I concluded, rather than to support a cause I could not approve, to bear every distress that might result from the part I took; and if America is happier for the revolution, I declare solemnly that I shall rejoice that the side I was on was the unsuccessful one.[154]

Van Schaack's willingness to become "a figure for the hand of scorn" deserves our notice because those neutrals who chose to return after the peace settlement did indeed bear a strong mark of stigma, of what Erving Goffman has called "spoiled identity." [155] Those whose professions of loyalty or neutrality had been genuine and consistent looked back with pride, little regret, and a clear conscience. Near the end of Henry Van Schaack's life, in 1823, he received a beautiful letter from Hendrick Frey, a Tryon County man who had been faithful to the Crown during the war. Nearly blind at the age of ninety, Van Schaack's eyes must have watered at the sentiments that his old friend shared.

> It is unnecessary to touch upon Revolution impositions which we have under gone, that such have been many is obvious, that we Did not do as many have done who held Civil Commissions under George the third is in my opinion in our favor, that cost us Sums of money and time, when we were still in Active life. But it has Left us a comfortable Substitute that is a Clear Conscience.[156]

Perceiving the American Revolution as a crisis of conscience may help to open a series of windows upon that complex phenomenon, and thereby admit both fresh air and new light. Customarily we have asked, what was different about the Loyalists and their situation: greater wealth? higher social status? positions of power held at royal pleasure? If the historian seeks only differences, he is likely to find and stress only differences. His conclusions will be predetermined. In the approach pursued in this essay, partisans on each side, and neutrals too, are assessed by the same standard. I have found intolerant Torquemadas in both camps, persons constrained by conscience in both, and expedient hypocrites in both, to boot.

Another window opened by this approach illuminates the lives of *ordinary* folk affected by war. They are not quite the "inarticulate" that we have lately been urged to rediscover, because their voices are not entirely mute. They include, however, obscure farmers and workingmen, not just the affluent, articulate, and prestigious. Many of them were totally illiterate and could only scratch their "mark" upon the transcript of their oral testimony. Many were rude and isolated country people in whom we discover strong feelings about the issues of the day. In April 1777, for instance, one James Campbell joined the company of a group of militiamen carousing at a home. A number of them, he later related,

> Drank success to King George, & Confusion to the American Arms, that they said the American Money was good for Shin paper. That this Deponant upon hearing their Conversation, Express'd his Sentiments very freely in favour of the American Cause, upon which, one Isaac Wood came up to him & Calld him a Damn'd Rascal for opposing so good a King, & with his sword (sheathed) struck him a Blow on the side of his head, which knock'd him down on A Bed. That before this Deponant could recover from that Blow, said Wood, struck him with his fist in the face, which brot him to the floor, & beat & Bruised him while he was down.[157]

And a few weeks later, to the north at Kingston, a petition emerged from the jail, sent by one Samuel Townsend to the Provincial Convention. He tried to explain the circumstances of his arrest:

That ye petitioner some few days ago went from home upon some business and happened to get a little intoxicated in liquor, and upon his return home inadvertantly fell in company upon the road with a person unknown to yr petitioner and discoursing and joking about the Tories passing through there and escaping, this person says to yr petitioner that if he had been with the Wigs, [they] should not have escaped so. . . . To which your petitioner, being merry in liquor, wantonly and in a bantering manner told him that in the lane through which they were then riding five and twenty Whigs would not beat five and twenty Tories and, joking together, they parted, and yr petitioner thought no more of it. Since, he has been taken up and confined and he supposes on the above joke.

Being conscious to himself of his not committing any crime or of being unfriendly to the American cause worthy of punishment. . . . That yr petitioner is extremely sorry for what he may have said and hopes his intoxication and looseness of tongue will be forgiven by this honorable convention as it would not have been expressed by him in his sober hours.[158]

Yet another window opened by this approach may very well encourage a more systematically comparative examination of the social and cultural history of revolutionary America. We have materials similar to those I have used for Connecticut, New Jersey, Pennsylvania, and the Carolinas, to cite just several examples. Close examination of those sources, and careful comparisons with New York, should help us to separate what was generally pervasive from what was peculiarly regional (or local) about the wartime experience.[159]

Looking to the broader course of American history, it is noteworthy that current interest in what Richard Hofstadter called the "paranoid style in American politics" has largely overlooked the issues examined in this essay.[160] Until quite recently, with the partial exception of Civil War historiography, the literature of American history has not been notable for a sense of the tragic. Much more attention has been devoted to progress and success in our national past. Alongside our newly heightened understanding of the suffering involved in chattel slavery, and of the tragedy of American foreign policy (including Indian policy at home), we may come to view the American Revolution as a crisis of conscience. In addition to the displacement of persons, the separation of families, and the arbitrary confiscation of property, there is a history of inner turmoil which is suffused with tragic power because it is so very personal and deeply felt. Ultimately, it can be appreciated only case by case, family by family, and community by community. It is an intimate part of the painful birth of our nationality—a story not without voices of anguish.

Notes

Introduction

1. See, for example, Ted Robert Gurr, *Why Men Rebel* (Princeton, 1970).

2. David Ramsay, *The History of the American Revolution* (Philadelphia, 1789).

3. Charles Francis Adams, ed., *The Works of John Adams* (Boston, 1850–56), X, 171, 181–82, 282–83.

4. The McClellan Lecture series was created in 1968 by a gift of $25,000 to Miami University from Ruby Geunther Stratton of Stillwater, Oklahoma. Mrs. Stratton (Miami '19) wished to establish a memorial to her first husband, Edward Earl McClellan, a longtime teacher of history in Preble County, Ohio. Mr. McClellan attended Miami University and received baccalaureate degrees in 1920 and 1921. Devoted to selected topics in American history, the annual memorial lectures were begun in 1971. In addition to the three scholars whose essays appear in this volume, other McClellan lecturers include Professors Paul Gaston, University of Virginia (1971), and Robin Winks, Yale (1972).

5. Greene's lectures at Miami University were given April 3–5, 1973.

6. Bushman delivered his lectures April 8–9, 1974.

7. Kammen was the McClellan lecturer April 23–24, 1975.

Notes (pages 14–17)

Society, Ideology, and Politics

* This essay is a revised and somewhat extended version of "The Rules of the Game," Chapter One of a projected but uncompleted book on "Virginia Politics in the Era of the American Revolution, 1760–1790," to be written in collaboration with Dr. Keith B. Berwick. The chapter was initially written in 1964 and owes much in its conception to discussions with Dr. Berwick as well as the many other scholars who were then working in colonial Virginia history, including especially Professors Thad W. Tate, Emory G. Evans, and Robert Polk Thomson, and Drs. Edward M. Riley, and Jane Carson. The research was supported by grants-in-aid from Colonial Williamsburg, Inc., in 1959, 1960, and 1961, as well as from the Social Science Research Council in 1960–61 and the Henry E. Huntington Library in 1962. Professors John Hemphill, Rhys Isaac, and Marvin Whiting have contributed in important ways over the past decade to enlarge the author's understanding of some of the social determinants of colonial Virginia's political culture.

1. Bernard Bailyn, "Politics and Social Structure in Virginia," in *Seventeenth-Century America: Essays in Colonial History*, ed. James M. Smith (Chapel Hill, 1959), pp. 90–115; Jack P. Greene, *The Quest for Power: The Lower Houses of Assembly in The Southern Royal Colonies, 1689–1776* (Chapel Hill, 1963), pp. 22–24, and "Foundations of Political Power in the Virginia House of Burgesses, 1720–1776," *William and Mary Quarterly*, 3rd ser., XVI (1959), 485–506; Robert E. and B. Katherine Brown, *Virginia 1705–1786: Aristocracy or Democracy?* (East Lansing, 1964), pp. 7–31; Hugh Jones, *The Present State of Virginia*, ed. Richard L. Morton (Chapel Hill, 1956), p. 81; James Reid, "The Religion of the Bible and Religion of K[ing] W[illiam] County Compared," [1769], in *The Colonial Virginia Satirist: Mid-Eighteenth-Century Commentaries on Politics, Religion, and Society*, ed. Richard Beale Davis (Philadelphia, 1967), p. 48.

2. *Journal and Letters of Philip Vickers Fithian, 1773–1774: A Plantation Tutor of the Old Dominion*, ed. by Hunter D. Farish (Williamsburg, 1943), p. 35; Carl Bridenbaugh, *Myths and Realities: Societies of the Colonial South* (Baton Rouge, 1952), pp. 1–53, and *Seat of Empire: The Political Role of Eighteenth-Century Williamsburg* (Williamsburg, 1950); Louis B. Wright, *The First Gentlemen of Virginia* (San Marino, 1940); Charles S. Sydnor, *Gentlemen Freeholders: Political Practices in Washington's Virginia* (Chapel Hill, 1952); Daniel J. Boorstin, *The Americans: The Colonial Experience* (New York, 1958), pp. 99–143; and Greene, "Foundations of Political Power," pp. 485–506.

3. See especially John Ferdinand D. Smyth, *A Tour in the United States of America*, 2 vols. (London, 1784), pp. 65–69; Thomas Anburey, *Travels through the Interior Parts of America*, 2 vols. (Boston and New York, 1923), pp. 215–17; Marquis de Chastellux, *Travels in North America in the Years 1780, 1781 and 1782*, ed. Howard C. Rice, Jr., 2 vols. (Chapel Hill, 1963), p. 437; and Brown and Brown, *Virginia 1705–1786*, pp. 32–59.

4. Smyth, *Tour*, pp. 65–69; Fithian, *Journal and Letters*, pp. 211–12. On poverty in Virginia, see Chastellux, *Travels*, p. 437.

5. "Journal of Josiah Quincy," ed. Mark A. DeWolfe Howe, Massachusetts Historical Society, *Proceedings*, XLIX (1916), 467; Chastellux, *Travels*, pp. 435–36.

6. See St. George Tucker to William Wirt, Sept. 25, 1815, *William and Mary Quarterly*, 1st ser., XXII (1914), 252–53; "Observations in Several Voyages and Travels in America," July 1746, *ibid.*, XVI (1907), 158–59. A superb exploratory discussion of the "social style" of the gentry is in Rhys Isaac, "Evangelical Revolt: The Nature of the Baptists' Challenge to the Traditional Order in Virginia, 1765–1775," *Wm. and Mary Qtly*, 3rd ser., XXXI (1974), 348–53. See also "My Country's Worth," [1752], in *The Poems of Charles Hansford*, ed. James A. Servies and Carl R. Dolmetsch (Chapel Hill, 1961), p. 57.

7. See, for instance, James Maury to John Camm, Dec. 12, 1763, in *Journals of the House of Burgesses of Virginia*, ed. Henry R. McIlwaine and John P. Kennedy, 13 vols. (Richmond, 1906–15), *1761–65*, pp. li–liii; James Wood to George Washington, July 7, 1758, in *Letters to Washington and Accompanying Papers*, ed. Stanislas M. Hamilton (Boston and New York, 1898–1902), III, 149; *The Diary of Colonel Landon Carter of Sabine Hall*, ed. Jack P. Greene, 2 vols. (Charlottesville, 1965), Feb. 12, 1774, II, 795; and [John Randolph], *Considerations on the Present State of Virginia* ([Williamsburg], 1774), p. 3.

8. Landon Carter's Reply to Election Poem, Nov. 1, 1768, Sabine Hall Collection, Alderman Library, University of Virginia (Charlottesville); *The Life of Reverend Devereaux Jarratt* (Baltimore, 1806), p. 16; Reid, "Religion of the Bible," p. 57.

9. Hansford, "My Country's Worth," pp. 56–57.

10. Brown and Brown, *Virginia 1705–1786*, pp. 136–50.

11. Bland to Theodorick Bland, Sr., Feb. 20, 1745, in *The Bland Papers*, ed. Charles Campbell, 2 vols. (Petersburg, 1840–43), I, 4.

12. Edmund Randolph, *History of Virginia*, ed. Arthur H. Shaffer (Charlottesville, 1970), pp. 178–83; and, esp., William Wirt, *Sketches*

of the *Life and Character of Patrick Henry* (Philadelphia, 1818), esp. pp. 32–67.

13. Tucker to Wirt, Sept. 25, 1815, pp. 252–53.

14. Chastellux, *Travels*, p. 397, See also Johann David Schoepf, *Travels in the Confederation* [1783–84], trans. and ed. Alfred J. Morrison, 2 vols. (Philadelphia, 1911), I, 63–65, for similar observations.

15. See, for instance, Hugh Jones, *Present State of Virginia*, p. 84; Andrew Burnaby, *Burnaby's Travels Through North America*, ed. Rufus Rockwell Wilson (New York, 1904), pp. 53–55; Thomas Jefferson, *Notes on the State of Virginia*, ed. William Peden (Chapel Hill, 1955), p. 164; Chastellux, *Travels*, pp. 435–36; and Reid, "Religion of the Bible," pp. 45–68.

16. David Griffith, *Passive Obedience Considered* (Williamsburg, [1776]), pp. 6, 12; William Stith, *The Sinfulness and Pernicious Nature of Gaming* (Williamsburg, 1752), pp. 14–15; [John Randolph], *Considerations*, pp. 22–23; Jonathan Boucher, *A Letter from a Virginian* ([New York], 1774), pp. 7–8.

17. Sir William Gooch, *A Dialogue Between Thomas Sweet-Scented, William Orinico, Planters, . . . and Justice Love-Country* (Williamsburg, 1732), p. 17; James Horrocks, *Upon the Peace* (Williamsburg, 1763), p. 8; Griffith, *Passive Obedience*, p. 13. For instances of questioning the political abilities and wisdom of the middle and lower sorts see James Wood to George Washington, July 7, 1758; [Randolph], *Considerations*, pp. 22–23; Chastellux, *Travels*, pp. 435–36; and [Boucher], *Letter from a Virginian*, pp. 7–8.

18. Greene, *Quest for Power* and "Foundations of Political Power"; Sydnor, *Gentleman Freeholders*; Tucker to Wirt, Sept. 25, 1815, p. 253; George Webb, *The Office and Authority of a Justice of the Peace* (Williamsburg, 1736), pp. 200–202.

19. John Camm, *A Review of the Rector Detected* (Williamsburg, 1764), p. 7; Reid, "Religion of the Bible," pp. 56–57; Fithian, *Journal and Letters*, p. 35; [Randolph], *Considerations*, pp. 22–27; [Gooch], *Dialogue*, p. 14; Landon Carter's essay on refusal of Councilors to join the Association, [1775?], Sabine Hill Collection; Landon Carter to George Washington, Feb. 12, 1756, in Hamilton, *Letters to Washington*, I, 195; Robert Carter Diary, July 5, 1723, Vol. 12, Virginia Historical Society (Richmond); *Virginia Gazette* (Williamsburg), Sept. 29, 1752. For an insight into the influence of the leading men in a county on the nomination of burgesses see Theodorick Bland, Jr., to John Randolph, Jr., Sept. 20, 1771, Bryan Family Papers, Alderman Library.

20. Sydnor, *Gentleman Freeholders*, pp. 39–59; Reid, "Religion of the Bible," pp. 50–51, 54; Robert Munford, *The Candidates*, ed. Jay B. Hubbell and Douglass Adair (Williamsburg, 1948), pp. 17, 20, 24, 40; Webb, *Office and Authority*, pp. 17–18; *The Acts of Assembly* (Williamsburg, 1752), p. 51.

21. Munford, *Candidates*, pp. 20–21, 32; Hansford, "My Country's Worth," pp. 60–61; David Hume, *Essays*, I, 487, as quoted in Douglass Adair, " 'That Politics May Be Reduced to a Science': David Hume, James Madison, and the Tenth *Federalist*," *Huntington Library Quarterly*, XX (1956–57), 352. For three divergent views on the nature of Virginia elections see Sydnor, *Gentlemen Freeholders*, pp. 11–59; Brown and Brown, *Virginia, 1705–1786*, pp. 145–242; and Lucille Blanche Griffith, *Virginia House of Burgesses, 1750–1774* (Northport, Ala., 1963), 53–79.

22. Shoepf, *Travels*, pp. 56–57; Greene, "Foundations of Political Power," pp. 485–506. On the importance of oratory, see Randolph, *History of Virginia*, p. 192, and *Diary of Landon Carter*, May 14, 1755, I, 120. For an extended analysis of the ingredients of political leadership in colonial and revolutionary Virginia, see Jack P. Greene, "Character, Persona, and Authority: A Study of Alternative Styles of Political Leadership in Revolutionary Virginia," in *The South During the American Revolution: Essays in Honor of John R. Alden*, ed. W. Robert Higgins (Durham, 1976).

23. Munford, *Candidates*, pp. 24, 43; *The Defence of Injur'd Merit Unmasked* (1771), p. 9.

24. George Washington to James Wood, [July 1758], in *The Writings of George Washington*, ed. John C. Fitzpatrick, 39 vols. (Washington, 1931–44), II, 251; Munford, *Candidates*, p. 38: [Mercer] "Dinwiddianae," [1754–57], in Davis, *Colonial Virginia Satirist*, p. 23.

25. Samuel Davies, *The Curse of Cowardice* (Woodbridge, N.J., 1759), p. 21; [Gooch], *Dialogue*, pp. 14–15; Stith, *Sinfulness of Gaming*, pp. 14–15, 24; Landon Carter to Purdie and Dixon, Fall 1769, Carter Family Papers, College of William and Mary Library (Williamsburg); *Diary of Landon Carter*, Nov. 6, 1771, Oct. 6, 1774, Mar. 15, 1776, Feb. 15, 23, 1777, II, 638, 866–67, 1001–1002, 1084; Hansford, "My Country's Worth," pp. 63–64.

26. "Common Sense" to the printer, *Virginia Gazette*, Oct. 3, 1745; Reid, "Religion of the Bible," pp. 51–52; Dedication of Landon Carter to Robert Wormeley Carter, 1753, in *A Collection of all the Acts of Assembly, Now in Force, in the Colony of Virginia* (Williamsburg, 1733), Library of Sabine Hall (Warsaw, Va.); William Leigh, *An Oration in Commemoration of the Founders of William and Mary*

College (Williamsburg, 1771), p. 8; Charles S. Sydnor, *Political Leadership in Eighteenth-Century Virginia* (Oxford, England, 1951), p. 3.

27. *Diary of Landon Carter,* Nov. 23, 1762, I, 242.

28. Pendleton to Citizens of Caroline County, Nov. 1798, in *The Letters and Papers of Edmund Pendleton, 1734–1803,* ed. David J. Mays (Charlottesville, 1967), II, 650; Chastellux, *Travels,* p. 428; [Boucher], *Letter from a Virginian,* p. 7. Other examples of similar feelings toward the gentry may be found in Hansford, "My Country's Worth," pp. 50–59; and Roger Atkinson to Samuel Pleasants, Oct. 1, 1774, in "Letters of Roger Atkinson, 1769–1776," ed. A. J. Morrison, *Virginia Magazine of History and Biography,* XV (1908), 354–57.

29. For a more extended discussion of this point see Greene, *Quest for Power,* pp. 22–31; Bridenbaugh, *Myths and Realities,* pp. 1–53; and Robert Detweiler, "Politics, Factionalism and the Geographic Distribution of Standing Committee Assignments in Virginia House of Burgesses, 1730–1776," *Virginia Magazine of History and Biography,* LXXX (1972), 267–85.

30. See esp. Schoepf, *Travels,* pp. 62–63; *Diary of Landon Carter,* March 10, 1752, I, 81; Randolph, *History of Virginia,* p. 158; Dawson to Virginia Clergy, Jan. 15, 1746, *Virginia Gazette,* Jan 9, 1746; Reid, "Religion of the Bible," p. 54. The standard account of Virginia religious development is George Maclaren Brydon, *Virginia's Mother Church,* 2 vols. (Richmond, 1947–52). For the development of religious "discord" in Virginia, see Brown and Brown, *Virginia, 1705–1786,* pp. 243–70; and, esp., Rhy Isaac, "Religion and Authority: Problems of the Anglican Establishment in Virginia in the Era of the Great Awakening and the Parsons' Cause, *William and Mary Quarterly,* 3rd ser., XXX (1973), 3–36, and "Evangelical Revolt," *ibid.,* XXXI (1974), 345–68.

31. Tucker to Wirt, Sept. 25, 1815, p. 253.

32. Jack P. Greene, "The Opposition to Lieutenant Governor Alexander Spotswood, 1718," *Virginia Magazine of History and Biography,* LXX (1962), 35–42.

33. Paul Lucas, "A Note on the Comparative Study of the Structure of Politics in Mid-Eighteenth-Century Britain and Its American Colonies," *William and Mary Quarterly,* 3rd ser., XXVIII (1971), 305.

34. Randolph's speeches, Aug. 24, 1734, Aug. 6, 1736, in *Burgesses Journals, 1727–40,* pp. 175–76, 241–42; David Mossum, Jr., "Ode," *Virginia Gazette,* Nov. 26, 1736.

35. John Markland, *Typographia: An Ode on Printing* (Williamsburg, 1730), pp. iii, 9–10; and Randolph's speech, Aug. 6, 1736, *Burgesses Journals, 1727–40*, pp. 241–42.

36. Randolph's speech, Aug. 6, 1736, *Burgesses Journals, 1727–40*, pp. 241–42. For the normal pattern of executive-legislative relations in the colonies, see Jack P. Greene, "Political Mimesis: A Consideration of the Historical and Cultural Roots of Legislative Behavior in the British Colonies in the Eighteenth Century," *American Historical Review*, LXXV (1969), 337–60. For Gooch's ideas on the proper stance of governors toward local establishments, see his remarks on Sir William Keith, "A Short Discourse on the Present State of the Colonies in America," [ca. 1730], in *Great Britain and the American Colonies, 1606–1763*, ed. Jack P. Greene (New York, 1970), 196–214.

37. Markland, *Typographia*, p. 7.

38. *Ibid.*, p. 8; Randolph, *History of Virginia*, pp. 116, 176; Jones, *Present State of Virginia*, pp. 82–83; Philo Patria [Richard Bland] to George Washington, 1756, in *Letters to Washington*, I, 394.

39. Horrocks, *Upon the Peace*, pp. iii–iv; [Landon Carter], *A Letter to the Right Reverend Father in God, the Lord B - - - - p of L - - - - n* (Williamsburg, 1760), p. 35. A conventional assessment of executive power in Virginia during the late 1750s may be found in Memorial of James Abercromby, read by Board of Trade, Nov. 21, 1759, Colonial Office Papers 5/1329, ff. 343–49, Public Record Office (London).

40. Jones, *Present State of Virginia*, pp. 80–82; Fithian, *Journal and Letters*, p. 211; Landon Carter, *The Rector Detected* (Williamsburg, 1764), p. 24; Schoepf, *Travels*, pp. 61–62, 91–95; [Boucher], *Letter from a Virginian*, pp. 9–10; Horrocks, *Upon the Peace*, p. 12; "Observations in Several Voyages and Travels in America," [1746], *William and Mary Quarterly*, 1st ser., XVI (1907), 158.

41. See esp. Wright, *First Gentlemen of Virginia;* Robert Manson Myers, "The Old Dominion Looks to London: A Study of English Literary Influences upon the *Virginia Gazette* (1736–1766)," *Virginia Magazine of History and Biography*, LIV (1946), 195–217; and Elizabeth Christine Cook, *Literary Influences in Colonial Newspapers, 1704–1750* (New York, 1912), pp. 179–229.

42. Examples of this conception of human nature and the function of government are [Carter], *Letter to B - - - - p of L - - - - n*, pp. 6, 17, 43; *A Letter from a Gentleman in Virginia, to the Merchants in Great Britain, Trading to that Colony* (London, 1754), pp. 5, 16; *Maryland Gazette* (Annapolis), Oct. 28, 1754; and *Letter to a Gentleman in*

London from Virginia (London, 1759), pp. 15, 20–21; *Diary of Landon Carter*, Sept. 28, 1770, Sept. 11, 1775, I, 505, II, 940–42; Common Sense [Richard Bland], *The Colonel Dismounted or the Rector Vindicated* (Williamsburg, 1764), p. 13: [Gooch], *Dialogue*, p. 13; *Defence of Injur'd Merit*, p. 9; [Nicholas], *Considerations on the Present State of Virginia Examined*, pp. 24–25; Griffith, *Passive Obedience*, pp. 6–14, 18–19, 23; speech of Sir John Randolph, Aug. 6, 1736, *Burgesses Journals, 1727–40*, pp. 241–42.

43. [Carter], *Letter to a Gentleman in London*, pp. 20–21, *Letter to B - - - - p of L - - - - n*, pp. 6, 46, 55, and *Rector Detected*, pp. 16, 22; Camm, *Review of "Rector Detected,"* p. 16; [Bland], *Colonel Dismounted*, p. 14; Introduction by Richard Henry Lee to John Dickinson and Arthur Lee, *The Farmer's, and Monitor's Letters to the Inhabitants of the British Colonies* (Williamsburg, 1769), p. i; [Nicholas], *Considerations*, p. 28–29; [Boucher], *Letter from A Virginian*, pp. 9–10; Griffith, *Passive Obedience*, p. 12; and George Mason to George Washington, Sept. 15, 1756, in Kate Mason Rowland, *The Life of George Mason*, 2 vols. (New York, 1892), I, 66.

44. [Carter], *Letter from a Gentleman in Virginia*, pp. 29, 35, and *Letter to B - - - - p of L - - - - n*, pp. 29, 35; Bland, *Colonel Dismounted*, pp. 21–23, and *A Fragment on the Pistole Fee, Claimed by the Governor of Virginia, 1753*, ed. by Worthington C. Ford (Brooklyn, 1891), pp. 36–37.

45. Bland, *Fragment on Pistole Fee*, pp. 37–38; [Gooch], *Dialogue*, p. 13; and [Carter], *Letter from a Gentleman in Virginia*, 12, 19, 22–23, *Letter to B - - - - p of L - - - - n*, p. 44, and *Letter to a Gentleman in London*, pp. 14, 19–20.

46. See Conway to Mr. Parks, *Virginia Gazette*, June 24, 1737; Alexander Spotswood to Sir John Randolph, *ibid.*, Dec. 10, 1736; speech of Sir John Randolph, Aug. 6, 1736, *Burgesses Journals, 1727–40*, pp. 241–42; [Nicholas], *Considerations*, pp. 24–25; Randolph, *Considerations*, pp. 5–8; [Boucher], *Letter from a Virginian*, pp. 7–10; *Virginia Gazette* (Purdie), June 27, 1766; [Bland], *Colonel Dismounted*, p. 14.

47. Richard Bland, *A Letter to the Clergy of Virginia* (Williamsburg, 1760), pp. 15–16, 18; Bland to John Camm, Oct. 25, 1763, in [Bland], *Colonel Dismounted*, p. ii; and [Carter], *Letter to a Gentleman in London*, pp. 20–21, *Letter to B - - - - p of L - - - - n*, pp. 6–7, 19, 46, 50–51, and *Rector Detected*, p. 30. For a report of a similar argument by Patrick Henry see James Maury to John Camm, Dec. 12, 1763, *Burgesses Journals, 1761–65*, p. liii.

48. [Boucher], *Letter from a Virginian*, pp. 9–10, 15; *Diary of Landon Carter*, May 9, 1774, II, 808; and [Carter], *Letter to a Gentleman in London*, pp. 10, 19, *Letter to B - - - - p of L - - - - n*, p. 29, and *Rector Detected*, p. 22.

49. James Madison, *An Oration in Commemoration of the Founders of William and Mary College* (Williamsburg, 1772), p. 6; [Boucher], *Letter from a Virginian*, pp. 9–10; [Randolph], *Considerations*, pp. 3–5, 22–23; Conway to Parks, *Virginia Gazette*, Nov. 17, 1738; *Diary of Landon Carter*, Oct. 17, 1754, I, 116–17.

50. *Defence of Injur'd Merit*, p. 7; *Diary of Landon Carter*, March 21, 1752, Jan. 31, 1776, Aug. 8, 1777, I, 89, II, 970, 1121–22; [Carter], *Letter from a Gentleman in Virginia*, pp. 3–5, 21–22, 27, 35, *Maryland Gazette*, Oct. 28, 1754, *Letter to a Gentleman in London*, pp. 6–7, 9, 14, 27, *Letter to B - - - - p of L - - - - n*, pp. 5, 10, 53, *Rector Detected*, 24; and Landon Carter to Councilors, [1774–75], Sabine Hall Collection; Richard Bland's Poem to Landon Carter, June 20, 1758, in Moncure D. Conway, *Barons of the Potomack and Rappahannock* (New York, 1892), pp. 138–41; [Randolph], *Considerations*, pp. 7–8; George Washington to Mrs. Mary Washington, Aug. 14, 1755, to Speaker John Robinson, Dec. 1756, and to Governor Robert Dinwiddie, Sept. 15, 1757, in *Writings of Washington*, I, 159, 532–33, II, 133; Robert Carter Nicholas to Washington, Aug. 18, 1756, Philo Patria [Richard Bland] to Washington, 1756, and John Robinson to Washington, Nov. 15, 1756, in *Letters to Washington*, I, 338, 391, 394–95, II, 1–2; epitaph of William Byrd, n.d., in *The Writing of "Colonel William Byrd of Westover in Virginia Esqr."*, ed. John Spencer Bassett (New York, 1901), p. xli; Randolph, *History of Virginia*, p. 273; Burgesses' Oath, *Virginia Gazette*, Nov. 24, 1738; Sir John Randolph to Alexander Spotswood, *ibid.*, Oct. 29, Dec. 17, 1736; essay on "an honest Man," *ibid.*, Sept. 29, 1752.

51. *Diary of Landon Carter*, March 6, 9, 13, 1752, Feb. 15, 1770, June 6, 1773, May 10, 1774, I, 75–78, 84–85, 357–58, II, 755–56, 808–9; [Carter], *Letter to a Gentleman in London*, pp. 12, 27–28, *Letter to B - - - - p of L - - - - n*, pp. 1, 8, 40; Landon Carter to "My Friend," n.d., and to Councilors, [1774–75], Sabine Hall Col., and to Purdie and Dixon, Fall 1769, Carter Family Papers, Folder 3; Stith, *Sinfulness of Gaming*, pp. 11–12, 25; [Randolph], *Considerations*, p. 3; [Nicholas], *Considerations*, pp. 37–38; Bland, *Letter to Clergy*, p. 9; Burnaby, *Travels*, p. 20; Schoepf, *Travels*, p. 55; William Nelson to Washington, Feb. 22, 1753, and Landon Carter to Washington, Oct. 7, 1755, in *Letters to Washington*, I, 1, 108; Randolph, *History of Virginia*, pp. 178, 193, 197; The Monitor, "On Good Nature," *Virginia Gazette*, Jan. 28, 1737; essay on "an honest Man," *ibid.*, Sept. 29, 1752; Reid, "Religion of the Bible," pp. 55, 60–61.

52. See Munford, *Candidates,* pp. 38, 40, 43; [Nicholas], *Considerations,* pp. 37–38; [Randolph], *Considerations,* pp. 3, 5–8; *Diary of Landon Carter,* March 14, 1770, I, 368; Anbury, *Travels,* pp. 200–201; *Defence of Injur'd Merit,* p. 8; Bland's Poem to Carter, June 20, 1758, in Conway, *Barons of Potomack and Rappahannock,* pp. 138–41; Washington to Speaker John Robinson, Dec. 1756, in *Writings of Washington,* I, 532–33; Edmund Randolph, *An Oration in Commemoration of the Founders of William and Mary College* (Williamsburg, 1771), p. 6; Landon Carter to Dixon and Hunter, [May 1776], Sabine Hall Collection.

53. Munford, *Candidates,* pp. 24–25, 36–38, 41, 43; Randolph, *History of Virginia,* p. 173; *Diary of Landon Carter,* April 1, 6, 14–15, 17, 1752, Aug. 22, 1754, May 14, 1755, I, 91, 93, 100–105, 107–14.

54. *Diary of Landon Carter,* Oct. 17, 1754, I, 116–17.

55. Landon Carter to Washington, [April 1756], George William Fairfax to Washington, May 9, 13, 1756, Philo Patria [Richard Bland] to Washington, 1756, and Bland to Washington, [June 1757], in *Letters to Washington,* I, 236, 251, 256–57, 391, 394–95, III, 87–89; *Diary of Landon Carter,* Aug. 22, 1754, I, 107–14.

56. Camm, *Review of "Rector Detected,"* p. 25; Sydnor, *Gentlemen Freeholders,* pp. 39–59.

57. Bland, *Fragment on Pistole Fee,* p. 25, *Letter to Clergy,* pp. 3, 5, and *Colonel Dismounted,* p. 13; Carter, *Letter from a Gentleman in Virginia,* pp. 3–5, *Maryland Gazette,* Oct. 28, 1754, *Letter to a Gentleman in London,* 6–7, 9, 11, 14, 22, 25, 27, *Letter to B - - - - p of L - - - - n,* pp. 5, 53, and *Rector Detected,* pp. 5, 25 27–28, 33; and Bland's poem to Carter, June 20, 1758, in Conway, *Barons of Potomack and Rappahannock,* 138–41.

58. See Greene, *Quest for Power,* pp. 159–65, and "The Case of the Pistole Fee," *Virginia Magazine of History and Biography,* LXVI (1958), 406–22. Stith's toast and comments are in his letter to Bishop of London, April 21, 1753, Fulham Palace Mss., Virginia (Second Box), 13 Lambeth Palace (London).

59. See Thad W. Tate, "The Coming of the Revolution in Virginia: Britain's Challenge to Virginia's Ruling Class, 1763–1776," *William and Mary Quarterly,* 3rd series, XIX (1962), 324–35; *Burgesses Journals, 1752–58,* Nov. 21–28, Dec. 4, 1753, 129, 132, 136, 141; Greene, "Case of the Pistole Fee," *Virginia Magazine of History and Biography,* LXVI (1958), 406–22; Representation of Virginia Burgesses to Francis Fauquier, May 1763, Shelburne Papers, XLIX, 455–66, William L. Clements Library (Ann Arbor, Mich.).

60. Dinwiddie to Board of Trade, Dec. 29, 1753, CO 5/1328, ff. 77–78, 81–82; *Diary of Landon Carter*, April 8, 1752, I, 95. On the agency question see Greene, *Quest for Power*, pp. 280–84.

61. Tate, "Coming of the Revolution in Virginia," pp. 326–32; Bland, *Letter to Clergy*, pp. 15–18; [Carter], *Letter to B - - - - p of L - - - - n*, pp. 6, 19–20, 29, 43–47, 50–51, 59, and *Rector Detected*, pp. 23, 30; Charles Carter to Peter Wyche, [ca. 1760], Guard Book, VI, no. 48, Royal Society of Arts (London), as cited in Gwenda Morgan, "Anglo-Virginia Relations 1748–1764" (M.A. thesis, University of Southampton, 1969), pp. 75–76.

62. [Carter], *Letter to B - - - - p of L - - - - n*, pp. 44–47; [Bland], *Colonel Dismounted*, pp. 21–23, 26. For Patrick Henry's more extreme use of the same argument see Maury to Camm, Dec. 12, 1763.

63. See Horrocks, *Upon the Peace*, p. 6; [Carter], *Letter to a Gentleman in London*, p. 25, and *Letter to B - - - - p of L - - - - n*, pp. 38, 54; Representation of Virginia Burgesses to Fauquier, May 1763, Shelburne Papers, XLIX, p. 455; Robert Carter Nicholas to Washington, Jan. 23, 1756, in *Letters to Washington*, I, 178–79; Bland, *Fragment on Pistole Fee*, p. 35; Randolph, *History of Virginia*, pp. 160–61, 163; [Mercer], "Dinwiddianae," pp. 21, 27.

64. *Virginia Gazette*, May 30, 1751; Arthur Lee to Philip Ludwell Lee, Nov. 5, 1763, in Arthur Lee Papers, I, 2 (Ms. Am 811F), Houghton Library, Harvard University; Randolph, *History of Virginia*, pp. 71, 202. The best treatment of economic conditions in Virginia at the close of the Seven Years' War is Joseph Albert Ernst, "Genesis of the Currency Act of 1764: Virginia Paper Money and the Partition of British Investments," *William and Mary Quarterly*, 3rd ser, XXII (1965), esp. pp. 34–59.

65. See *Virginia Gazette*, April 21, 1738; March 5, 20, April 3, 1752, April 10, 1754; Randolph, *History of Virginia*, pp. 96, 216; Hansford, "My Country's Worth," pp. 65–67; [Mercer], "Dinwiddianae," pp. 30, 32; Reid, "Religion of the Bible," p. 49; "Observations on Several Voyages . . . ," [1746], *William and Mary Quarterly*, 1st ser., XVI (1907), 6–9; Mason, "Scheme for Replevying Goods . . . , Dec. 23, 1765, in *The Papers of George Mason*, ed. Robert A. Rutland, 3 vols. (Chapel Hill, 1970), I, 61–62.

66. Burnaby, *Travels*, p. 55, Fauquier to Board of Trade, Nov. 3, 1762, CO 5/1330, ff. 339–40; [Carter], *Letter from a Gentleman in Virginia*, pp. 28–29; Randolph, *History of Virginia*, pp. 279–80; *Virginia Gazette*, Dec. 29, 1752; Horrocks, *Upon the Peace*, pp. 9–10, 14. See also the extended essay on the same theme, "The Virginia Centenal, No. X" in *Virginia Gazette*, Sept. 3, 1756.

67. Randolph, *History of Virginia*, p. 61; *Virginia Gazette*, Feb. 28, March 28, Sept. 5, 1751; Hansford, "My Country's Worth," pp. 62–64; James Mercer to Daniel Parke Curtis, May 31, 1754, Curtis Papers, Folder 1754–55, Virginia Historical Society (Richmond); Horrocks, *Upon the Peace*, pp. 9–10, 14.

68. *Virginia Gazette*, July 11, 1751; "Observations on Several Voyages . . . ," pp. 15–16; Reid, "Religion of the Bible," pp. 48, 52, 53–57.

69. Samuel Davies, *Virginia's Danger and Remedy* (Williamsburg, 1756), pp. 12, 16, 20–21, 23, 25, 28, 48, *Curse of Cowardice*, pp. 8, 14–15, 33–34, *Religion and Patriotism* (Philadelphia, 1755), pp. 10–12, 27–35, and *The Crisis: or, the Uncertain Doom of Kingdoms at Particular Times, Considered* (London, 1756), pp. 28–35; Stith, *Sinfulness of Gaming*, pp. 11–12, and *The Nature and Extent of Christ's Redemption* (Williamsburg, 1753), p. 31; Horrocks, *Upon the Peace*, pp. 9–10, 14; Camm, *Review of "Rector Detected,"* p. 20. See also "Robert Dinwiddie's Proclamation for a Fast," Aug. 28, 1775, *Virginia Gazette*, Sept. 12, 1755.

Massachusetts Farmers and the Revolution

1. J. M. Stowe, *History of the Town of Hubbardston . . .* (Hubbardston, 1881), pp. 41, 42.

2. *Ibid.*, p. 41.

3. Richard D. Brown, *Revolutionary Politics in Massachusetts: The Boston Committee of Correspondence and the Towns, 1772–1774* (Cambridge, Mass., 1970), pp. 57, 67, 145, 122. Brown has mapped the replying towns, but Hubbardston was not on his list presumably because the copy sent to Boston was lost.

4. Land ownership can be tabulated from the 1771 tax valuation list for Concord in Massachusetts Archives, Vol. 132, State House, Boston.

5. Brown, *Revolutionary Politics*, pp. 29, 51, 144, 97; Robert J. Taylor, *Western Massachusetts in the Revolution* (Providence, 1954), p. 62.

6. Stowe, *History of Hubbardston*, pp. 41, 209, 211–13; Brown, *Revolutionary Politics*, pp. 132, 135, 134.

7. Boston Committee of Correspondence to New Salem, April 6, 1773, Letters and Proceedings received, photo 570; Boston Committee

of Correspondence to Westborough, Jan. 19, 1773, Minute Book, V, 361. Photostats at the Massachusetts Historical Society.

8. Abington, Jan. 11, 1773, photos 1, 2, Letters and Proceedings received, Boston Committee of Correspondence; "By Direction of the Committee of Correspondence for the Town of Boston," Broadside, March 30, 1773, quoted in Brown, *Revolutionary Politics*, p. 140; cf. pp. 99, 106, 113, 121.

9. Stowe, *History of Hubbardston*, p. 27.

10. *The Literary Diary of Ezra Stiles*, ed. Franklin Bowditch Dexter (New York, 1901), I, 480.

11. Thomas Gage to Lord Dartmouth, Boston, Sept. 2, 1774, *The Correspondence of General Thomas Gage with the Secretaries of States* (New Haven, 1931), I, 371.

12. Chatham, Dec. 29, 1772, photo 164, and Andover, June 1, 1773, photo 24, Letters and Proceedings received, Boston Committee of Correspondence; David Foster Estes, *The History of Holden, Massachusetts, 1684–1894* (Worcester, 1894), p. 26; Ashby, May 13, 1773, photo 30, Letters and Proceedings received, Boston Committee of Correspondence.

13. Acton, Jan. 18, 1773, photo 17, Letters and Proceedings received, Boston Committee of Correspondence; Stowe, *History of Hubbardston*, p. 41.

14. Sheffield, Jan. 12, 1773, photo 744, Letters and Proceedings received, Boston Committee of Correspondence.

15. John Wise, *The Churches Quarrel Espoused . . .* , 2nd ed. (Boston, 1715), p. 32; Milton M. Klein, ed., *The Independent Reflector, or Weekly Essays on Sundry Important Subjects . . .* (Cambridge, Mass., 1963), p. 289.

16. Joseph Emerson, *A Thanksgiving-Sermon Preach'd at Pepperell, July 24, 1766 . . .* (Boston, 1766), pp. 23, 26.

17. J. P. Kenyon, *The Stuart Constitution, 1603–1688* (Cambridge, England, 1966), pp. 21–22; Athol, July 20, 1774, photo 34, and Amherst, Jan. 26, 1774, photo 24, Letters and Proceedings received, Boston Committee of Correspondence.

18. Oliver Noble, *Some Strictures upon the . . . Book of Esther . . .* (Newburyport, 1775), p. 17–18.

19. Henry Ashurst to Gurdon Saltonstall, June 27, 1709, *Collections of the Massachusetts Historical Society*, 6th ser., V (Boston, 1892), 195; Wise, *Churches Quarrel*, pp. 65, 8.

20. Jonathan Mayhew, *Observations on the Charter and Conduct of the Society* . . . (Boston, 1763), pp. 155–56.

21. *A Ministerial Catechise, Suitable to Be Learned by All Modern Provincial Governors, Pensioners, Placemen, etc.* . . . (Boston, 1771), p. 5; *Writings of Samuel Adams*, ed. Harry A. Cushing (New York, 1906), IV, 247.

22. *Works of John Adams*, ed. Charles Francis Adams (Boston, 1856), IV, 320, 43; "A Petition of John Ashley," April 12, 1776, in *Massachusetts, Colony to Commonwealth: Documents on the Formation of Its Constitution, 1775–1780*, ed. Robert J. Taylor (New York, 1961), p. 23; "Petition of Pittsfield," Dec. 26, 1775, *ibid.*, p. 18.

23. Noble, *Some Strictures*, p. 8; "An Act for Abolishing the Kingly Office, 17 March 1649," in Kenyon, *Stuart Constitution*, p. 340; Petersham quotation in Lee N. Newcomer, *The Embattled Farmers: A Massachusetts Countryside in the American Revolution* (New York, 1953), p. 33; William Gordon, *A Discourse Preached December 15, 1774* . . . , 2nd ed. (Boston, 1775), reprinted in John Wingate Thornton, *The Pulpit of the American Revolution* . . . , 2nd ed. (Boston, 1876), p. 203.

24. [Daniel Leonard], *Massachusettensis, Letter to the Inhabitants of the Province of the Massachusetts-Bay* (Boston, 1775), p. 15.

25. Adams, *Works*, IV, 54.

26. Brown, *Revolutionary Politics*, p. 62; "A State of the Rights" is most conveniently found in *Tracts of the American Revolution, 1763–1776*, ed. Merrill Jensen (Indianapolis, 1967), p. 241.

27. Leonard, *Massachusettensis*, p. 15; Adams, *Works*, IV, 54.

28. Page Smith, *John Adams* (Garden City, 1962), I, 77.

29. John Adams, *A Dissertation on the Canon and Feudal Law*, in *Works*, III, 450.

30. *Ibid.*, p. 450.

31. *Ibid.*, pp. 450–51.

32. *Ibid.*, pp. 451–53.

33. *Ibid.*, pp. 454–55.

34. *Ibid.*, p. 464.

35. J. G. A. Pocock, *The Ancient Constitution and the Feudal Law: English Historical Thought in the Seventh Century* (Cambridge,

England, 1957), ch. 6 and *passim;* H. Trevour Colbourn, *The Lamp of Experience: Whig History and the Intellectual Origins of the American Revolution* (Chapel Hill, 1965), ch. 1, 2, 4, 5; Smith, *John Adams,* I, 80.

36. Andrew P. Appleby, "Agrarian Capitalism or Seigneurial Reaction? The Northwest of England, 1500–1700," *American Historical Review,* LXXX (June 1975), 592; quotations on wardships from Christopher Hill, *The Century of Revolution, 1603–1714* (Edinburgh, 1961), p. 49; Mildred Campbell, *The English Yeoman under Elizabeth and the Stuarts* (New Haven, 1942), summarizes the feudal incidents to various tenures, pp. 110 ff; for Winthrop in the Court of Wards, see Edmund S. Morgan, *The Puritan Dilemma: The Story of John Winthrop* (Boston, 1958), pp. 22–26.

37. Quoted in Hill, *Century of Revolution,* p. 149.

38. Justice was often on the side of the landlord—his costs rose with prices while rents stood still, and there were usually legal grounds for his claims. The courts were as likely to rule against him as his tenants in title cases because juries were made up of yeomen. If he won, he usually had good cause. Sir Edward Coke said that copyholders' titles were more secure in Elizabethan and Stuart times than ever before. Moreover, agriculture was practiced more efficiently as the myriads of small holders were squeezed out and large-scale capitalist farming took over. Nonetheless, the victims of enclosing, engrossment, or rack-renting suffered at the landlords' hands. At the very least, enclosures, for example, even when compensated, increased the dependence of labourers on their landlords. (Appleby, "Agrarian Capitalism," pp. 549, 591; Eric Kerridge, *Agrarian Problems in the Sixteenth Century and After* [London, 1969], pp. 65–93, 132.) The position of farmers is summarized in Campbell, *English Yeoman,* and Alan Everitt, "Farm Labourers," in *Agrarian History of England and Wales,* ed. Joan Thirsk (Cambridge, England, 1967), Vol. 4, *1500–1640,* pp. 396–465. Jerome Blum makes the point that in the fifteenth and sixteenth centuries, rising prices motivated seigneurs all over Europe to intervene in village life to gain control over land ("The Internal Structure and Polity of the European Village Community from the Fifteenth to the Nineteenth Century," *Journal of Modern History,* XLII [Dec. 1971], 541–76).

39. G. R. Elton, *England under the Tudors, 1485–1603* (London, 1955), pp. 206–7; Everitt, "Farm Labourers," pp. 406–8; Campbell, *English Yeoman,* p. 152.

40. Charles M. Andrews, *The Colonial Period of American History: The Settlements* (New Haven, 1934), I, 405, 417, 57 n.

41. Andrews, *Colonial Period*, I, 57 n.; Irving Mark, *Agrarian Conflicts in Colonial New York, 1711–1775* (New York, 1940), p. 14.

42. Andrews, *Colonial Period*, I, 87; Viola F. Barnes, *The Dominion of New England: A Study in British Colonial Policy* (New York, 1923), pp. 182, 205–8; Marshall D. Harris, *Origins of the Land Tenure System in the United States* (Ames, Iowa, 1953), pp. 116, 3.

43. *Puritan Political Ideas, 1558–1794*, ed. Edmund S. Morgan (Indianapolis, 1965), pp. 164–65. For an explication of the subtleties of hierarchy in colonial Puritanism, see Stephen Foster, *Their Solitary Way: The Puritan Social Ethic in the First Century of Settlement in New England* (New Haven, 1971), ch. 1.

44. *Andros Tracts: Being a Collection of Pamphlets and Official Papers . . . of the Andros Government and the Establishment of the Second Charter of Massachusetts*, ed. W. H. Whitmore (New York, 1868–74), II, 233, 234.

45. Barnes, *Dominion*, ch. 8. Randolph in a characteristic exaggeration said not ten landholders in Massachusetts had good title (*ibid.*, p. 203). In 1685 the General Court tried to remedy the flaws in title by declaring all grants to towns or individuals "were and are intended . . . to be an estate in fee simple, and are hereby confirmed to the said persons and townships . . . forever," and authorizing the affixing of the seal (*Records of the Governor and Company of the Massachusetts Bay in New England . . .*, ed. Nathaniel B. Shurtleff [Boston, 1854], V, 470–71). The court's action came too late, however, as the charter had been previously vacated and the authority to pass laws lost.

46. Barnes, *Dominion*, pp. 188, 176–77, 199; *The Diary of Samuel Sewall, Collections of the Massachusetts Historical Society*, 5th ser., V (Boston, 1878), 231 n.

47. Barnes, *Dominion*, pp. 197–98, 195. Cambridge was appealing its case to the King when Andros was deposed.

48. David S. Lovejoy, *The Glorious Revolution in America* (New York, 1972), pp. 241, 243; Whitmore, *Andros Tracts*, I, 18.

49. J. G. A. Pocock, *The Ancient Constitution and the Feudal Law;* Whitmore, *Andros Tracts*, I, 187; II, 257, 260.

50. Whitmore, *Andros Tracts*, I, 19, 12–16.

51. Roy H. Akagi, *The Town Proprietors of the New England Colonies: A Study of Their Development, Organization, Activities and Controversies, 1620–1770* (Philadelphia, 1924), pp. 142 n., 141–47, 125–38; Jonathan Edwards to Thomas Price, Northampton, Dec. 12,

1743, in *The Great Awakening,* ed. C. C. Goen (New Haven, 1972), Vol. IV, *The Works of Jonathan Edwards,* 557. For the equivalent controversies in Connecticut, see Richard L. Bushman, *From Puritan to Yankee: Character and the Social Order in Connecticut, 1690–1765* (Cambridge, Mass., 1967), pp. 41–53.

52. Accounts of the New York land disputes are Oscar Handlin, "The Eastern Frontier of New York," *New York History,* XVIII (Jan. 1937), 50–75; Mark, *Agrarian Conflicts;* and Patricia U. Bonomi, *A Factious People: Politics and Society in Colonial New York* (New York, 1971), ch. 6.

53. Handlin, "Eastern Frontier," p. 60; Bonomi, *Factious People,* pp. 195, 214–16; "Land Cases in Colonial New York, 1765–1767, The King v. William Prendergast," ed. Irving Mark and Oscar Handlin, *New York University Law Quarterly Review,* IX (Jan. 1942), 175, 177. R. H. Akagi saw opposition to feudalism behind the proprietary disputes: "The whole principle underlying the controversies was, indeed, a defiance against the vestige, so to speak, of feudalism in America" (*Town Proprietors,* p. 299).

54. I. M., *The Original Rights of Mankind Freely to Subdue and Improve the Earth* (Boston, 1722), pp. 14, 12, 18. For the actuality of crowding, see Kenneth Lockridge, "Land, Population and the Evolution of New England Society, 1630–1790; and an Afterthought," in *Colonial America: Essays in Politics and Social Development,* ed. Stanley N. Katz (Boston, 1971), pp. 466–91; Philip J. Greven, Jr., *Four Generations: Population, Land, and Family in Colonial Andover, Massachusetts* (Cambridge, 1970).

55. Charles Evans, *American Bibliography* . . . , reprint ed. (New York, 1941), I, 310; *Catalogue of the American Library of the Late George Brinley* . . . (Hartford, 1878–97), I, 138. Joseph Morgan, though a New Jersey minister, was identified with New England. He published seven works other than *Original Rights* at New England presses, sent his son to Yale, and occasionally preached in New England pulpits (Evans, *American Bibliography,* I, II).

56. P. 18.

57. Andrew McFarland Davis, *Colonial Currency Reprints, 1682–1751* (Boston, 1910–11), I, 344, 345, 347.

58. *Ibid.,* I, 361–62; II, 55; IV, 57; cf. III, 76, 169; IV, 204–5.

59. *Ibid.,* II, 60–61, 325–26; III, 446, 276; II, 128; III, 138; II, 46; cf. II, 41, 67, 385; III, 139–40, 276.

60. *Ibid.,* II, 132, 130–131.

61. *Ibid.,* II, 132, 17.

62. *Ibid.,* I, 439–41; III, 143; IV, 362, 439; cf. IV, 33, 77–78, 369, 443.

63. For reprint information, see *ibid.,* IV, 459.

64. *Ibid.,* IV, 44, 283; "Calendar of Papers and Records Relating to the Land Bank of 1740," *Publications of the Colonial Society of Massachusetts,* IV (1910), 19–21. For the full story of the crisis, see Robert Zemsky, *Merchants, Farmers, and River Gods: An Essay on Eighteenth Century American Politics* (Boston, 1971), ch. 3; and George A. Billias, *The Massachusetts Land Bankers of 1740* (Orono, Maine, 1959).

65. Davis, *Colonial Currency Reprints,* II, 17; I, 439–40; Mark and Handlin, "Land Cases," pp. 171, 174, 189.

66. John M. Murrin, "Review Essay," *History and Theory,* XI (1972), 250–51; Oscar and Mary Handlin, *Commonwealth: A Study of the Role of Government in the American Economy: Massachusetts, 1774–1861,* rev. ed. (Cambridge, 1969), p. 19. For the growth of debt in Connecticut, see Bushman, *From Puritan to Yankee,* p. 297. Charles S. Grant, *Democracy in the Connecticut Frontier Town of Kent* (New York, 1961) reports very few foreclosures in this one town in northwestern Connecticut.

67. The tax drain on yeomen and the lesser gentry was also the cause of concentration of land in England in the eighteenth century (H. J. Habbakuk, "English Land-Ownership, 1680–1740," *English Historical Review,* X [1940], 2–17; Isaac Kramnick, *Bolingbroke and His Circle: The Politics of Nostalgia in the Age of Walpole* [Cambridge, Mass., 1968], pp. 56–63). The rhetoric spilled over into other areas late in the revolutionary era. In 1774 Roger Sherman, protagonist of Connecticut's claims to Susquehannah lands in Pennsylvania, complained of the lack of support from Connecticut's leaders. Why the reticence? "Gentlemen, who love to monopolize wealth and power, think it best for lands to be in a few hands and that the common people should be their tenants" (quoted in Lawrence Henry Gipson, *Jared Ingersoll: A Study of American Loyalism* [New Haven, 1920], p. 325).

68. J. Emerson, *Thanksgiving Sermon,* p. 13; Patterson, *Political Parties,* p. 47.

69. Daniel Dulany, *Considerations on the Propriety of Imposing Taxes in the British Colonies . . . ,* 2nd ed. (Annapolis, 1765), p. 29. The essay from Pennsylvania and New York is quoted in Bernard Bailyn, *The Origins of American Politics* (New York, 1968), pp. 150–

51 n. The author ended on a positive note: "But how different is the case amongst us! We enjoy an unprecarious property, and every man may freely taste the fruits of his own labors under his vine and under his fig tree, none making him afraid. . . ." Josiah Quincy quoted in John M. Murrin, "Anglicization and Identity: The Colonial Experience, the Revolution, and the Dilemma of American Nationalism," paper delivered before the Organization of American Historians, April 1974, p. 30.

70. The most complete statement of farmer distress in the decade prior to the Revolution is Kenneth Lockridge, "Social Changes and the Meaning of the American Revolution," *Journal of Social History*, VI (1972), 403–37. For England, see G. E. Mingay, *English Landed Society in the Eighteenth Century* (London, 1963), pp. 19, 24, 43, 45; cf. Rowland Berthoff and John M. Murrin, "Feudalism, Communalism, and the Yeoman Freeholder: The American Revolution Considered as a Social Accident," in *Essays on the American Revolution*, ed. Stephen G. Kurtz and James H. Hutson (Chapel Hill, 1973), pp. 256–88. The return to the Boston committee from Colrain, a town where Scotch-Irish had settled, spoke of the Tea Act as part of an English plan to enslave the colonies as Britain had already subjected Ireland: "It plainly appears to us that it is the design of this present administration to serve us as they have our brethren in Ireland first to raise a revenue from us sufficient to support a standing army, as well as place men and pentioners, and then laugh at our calamities and glut themselves on our spoile (many of us in this town being eye witnesses of those crewell and remorsless enemies)" (Colrain, January 31, 1774, photo 179, Letters and Proceedings received, Boston Committee of Correspondence).

71. Ashby, May 13, 1773, photo 30, and Amherst, January 26, 1774, photo 24, Letters and Proceedings received, Boston Committee of Correspondence.

72. John Adams to Benjamin Rush, Dec. 27, 1810, *Old Family Letters*, ed. Worthington C. Ford (Philadelphia, 1898), I, 269. The contrast proved useful for a surprisingly long time after the Revolution. Thus an 1821 address to agriculturalists in Erie and Niagara counties, New York, spoke of American "citizens clothed in allodial sovereignty, 'reaping where they have sown, and gathering where they have reapt;' not like the feudal vassals of Prussia and Russia, the serfs of Tuscany, the peasants of Flanders, the boors of Germany, or the tenants of England, compelled to support by their sweat and labor the profligate prodigality of kings, princes, nobles, sinecurists, spies and informants" (Joseph Moulton, *An Address Delivered . . . on the Anniversary Celebration of the Niagra and Erie Society for Promoting Agriculture and Domestic Manufactures* [Buffalo, 1821], p. 25).

73. Quoted in Handlin, *Commonwealth*, p. 87.

The American Revolution as a *Crise de Conscience*

* I would like to thank Kathleen J. Bragdon, my research assistant in 1974–75, for her indispensable help; also Professors Edward Countryman, Douglas S. Greenberg, Clive A. Holmes, Milton M. Klein, and Mary Beth Norton for their critical reading of the essay; and Connie Ingraham for her meticulous preparation of the typescript.

1. Carl L. Becker, *The History of Political Parties in the Province of New York, 1760–1776* (Madison, 1909), p. 22.

2. Bernard Bailyn, "The Central Themes of the American Revolution. An Interpretation," in *Essays on the American Revolution*, ed. Stephen G. Kurtz and James H. Hutson (Chapel Hill, 1973), pp. 15, 27. Bailyn reaffirms his position in *The Ordeal of Thomas Hutchinson* (Cambridge, Mass., 1974), p. x: "recent historical writings have allowed us to see with some clarity the pattern of fears, beliefs, attitudes, and perceptions that became the ideology of the Revolution— which alone, in my judgment, explains why certain actions of the British government touched off a transforming revolution in America. . . ."

3. "The 'American Tory,' " writes Mary Beth Norton, "was in fact a Whig par excellence: he was a vehement supporter of the settlement resulting from the Glorious Revolution and a fervent admirer of the British Constitution. . . . In sum, instead of characterizing the American Revolution as a struggle between Whigs and Tories, I would argue that in ideological terms it should be seen as a contest between different varieties of Whigs, Whigs whose respective world views brought some of them to become revolutionaries and others to become loyalists . . . ("The Loyalist Critique of the Revolution," in *The Development of a Revolutionary Mentality* [Washington, D.C., 1972], p. 130). See also Max Savelle, "Nationalism and Other Loyalties in the American Revolution," *American Historical Review*, LXVII (July 1962), esp. 904–9, 912.

4. Among the principal books in this group are Gordon S. Wood, *The Creation of the American Republic, 1776–1787* (Chapel Hill, 1969); Pauline Maier, *From Resistance to Revolution: Colonial Radicals and the Development of American Opposition to Britain, 1765–1776* (New York, 1972); Richard V. W. Buel, *Securing the Revolution. Ideology in American Politics, 1789–1815* (Ithaca, 1972); Edwin G. Burrows and Michael Wallace, "The American Revolution: The Ideology and Psychology of National Liberation," *Perspectives in*

American History, VI (1972), 167–306; and Alan Rogers, *Empire and Liberty: American Resistance to British Authority, 1755–1763* (Berkeley and Los Angeles, 1974).

5. The stress which Jensen and his students place upon material factors owes as much to the Turner tradition at Wisconsin as Bailyn's emphasis upon the determinative role of ideas derives from a milieu Perry Miller helped to create at Harvard during the 1940s and 1950s.

6. Joseph Ernst, *Money and Politics in America, 1755–1775: A Study in the Currency Act of 1764 and The Political Economy of Revolution* (Chapel Hill, 1973), 360–61. See also Ernst and Marc Egnal, "An Economic Interpretation of the American Revolution," *William and Mary Quarterly*, XXIX (Jan. 1972), 3–32.

7. Among the principal books in this group, in addition to Ernst's, see E. James Ferguson, *The Power of the Purse: A History of American Public Finance, 1776–1790* (Chapel Hill, 1961); Jackson Turner Main, *The Sovereign States, 1775–1783* (New York, 1973), esp. ch. 7; Ronald Hoffman, *A Spirit of Dissension: Economics, Politics, and The Revolution in Maryland* (Baltimore, 1973); Stephen E. Patterson, *Political Parties in Revolutionary Massachusetts* (Madison, 1973); and James K. Martin, *Men in Rebellion: Higher Governmental Leaders and the Coming of the American Revolution* (New Brunswick, 1973).

8. See, for example, Main's review of Wood, *William and Mary Quarterly*, XXVI (Oct. 1969), 604–7; Buel's review of Main, *Political Science Quarterly*, LXXXIX (June 1974), 438–39; Wood's review of Main, *Canadian Historical Review*, LV (June 1974), 222–23; and Gary Nash's review of the Kurtz and Hutson *Essays* (see note 2, above) in *William and Mary Quarterly*, XXXI (April 1974), 311-14.

9. William Graves to Charles Carroll of Annapolis, Jan. 14, 1770, quoted in Hoffman, *Spirit of Dissension*, p. 91.

10. See Edmund S. Morgan, "The Puritan Ethic and the American Revolution," *William and Mary Quartely*, XXIV (Jan. 1967), 3–43.

11. A patch of common ground may be found in J. G. A. Pocock, *The Machiavellian Moment: Florentine Political Thought and the Atlantic Republican Tradition* (Princeton, 1975), ch. 13, "Neo-Machiavellian Political Economy," and ch. 14, "The Eighteenth-Century Debate" (pp. 423–505).

12. John Shy, "The American Revolution: The Military Conflict Considered as a Revolutionary War," in Kurtz and Hutson, *Essays on the American Revolution*, pp. 121–56; Shy, "The Loyalist Problem in

the Lower Hudson Valley: The British Perspective," in *The Loyalist Americans: A Focus on Greater New York*, ed. Robert A. East and Jacob Judd (Tarrytown, 1975), pp. 3–13.

13. See Bernard Mason, "The Heritage of Carl Becker: The Historiography of the Revolution in New York," *New-York Historical Society Quarterly*, LIII (April 1969), 127–47; Robert E. Brown, *Carl Becker on History and the American Revolution* (East Lansing, 1970); and my essay review of Brown's book in *History and Theory*, XI (1972), 359–68.

14. Milton Klein, "Democracy and Politics in Colonial New York," *New York History*, XL (July 1959), 221–46; Sung Bok Kim, "A New Look at the Great Landlords of Eighteenth-Century New York," *William and Mary Quartely*, XXVII (Oct. 1970), 581–614; Don Gerlach, *Philip Schuyler and the American Revolution in New York, 1733–1777* (Lincoln, 1964); Roger Champagne, "Family Politics versus Constitutional Principles: The New York Assembly Elections of 1768 and 1769," *William and Mary Quarterly*, XX (Jan. 1963), 57–79; Champagne, "Liberty Boys and Mechanics of New York City, 1764–1774," *Labor History*, VIIII (Spring 1967), 115–135.

15. Bernard Mason, *The Road to Independence: The Revolutionary Movement in New York, 1773–1777* (Lexington, 1966); Alfred F. Young, *The Democratic Republicans of New York: The Origins, 1763–1797* (Chapel Hill, 1967).

16. Staughton Lynd, "Who Should Rule at Home? Dutchess County, New York, in the American Revolution," *William and Mary Quarterly*, XVIII (July 1961), 330–59; Lynd, "The Mechanics in New York Politics, 1774–1788," *Labor History*, V (Fall 1964), 225–46; Jesse Lemisch, "New York's Petitions and Resolves of December 1765: Liberals vs. Radicals," *New-York Historical Society Quarterly*, XLIX (Oct. 1965), 313–26; Bernard Friedman, "The Shaping of the Radical Consciousness in Provincial New York," *Journal of American History*, LVI (March 1970), 781–801; Gary Nash, "The Transformation of Urban Politics 1700–1765," *ibid.*, LX (Dec. 1973), 605–32.

17. For the most explicit emphases upon the role and coherence of ideology in New York, see *The Independent Reflector . . . by William Livingston and Others*, ed. Milton M. Klein (Cambridge, Mass., 1963), esp. pp. 20–28, 32–48; Friedman, "Radical Consciousness," pp. 781–801; and Maier, *From Resistance to Revolution, passim*. Whereas Becker gave responsibility to the elite for some ideological impetus, Champagne attributes credit to the middle-class Sons of Liberty and Lemisch finds initiative among the lower-class radicals.

18. See Lee R. Boyer, "Lobster Backs, Liberty Boys, and Laborers in the Streets: New York's Golden Hill and Nassau Street Riots," *New-York Historical Society Quarterly*, LVII (Oct. 1973), 280–308.

19. *History and Theory*, XI (1972), 363–64. See also the essay by Milton M. Klein, "Detachment and the Writing of American History: The Dilemma of Carl Becker," in *Perspectives on Early American History: Essays in Honor of Richard B. Morris*, ed. Alden T. Vaughan and George A. Billias (New York, 1973), pp. 142 ff; and Klein, *The Politics of Diversity. Essays in the History of Colonial New York* (Port Washington, 1974), esp. pp. 4–5.

20. Carl L. Becker, "John Jay and Peter Van Schaack," *New York History*, I (Oct. 1919), 1–12, reprinted in Becker, *Everyman His Own Historian. Essays on History and Politics* (New York, 1935), pp. 284–98.

21. See, for example, *Conscience in America: A Documentary History of Conscientious Objection in America, 1757–1967*, ed. Lillian Schlissel (New York, 1968), which includes only two documents from the War for Independence (pp. 39–44), both of them from Pennsylvania.

22. Becker, *Everyman His Own Historian*, p. 287.

23. See, e.g., Harry B. Yoshpe, "The DeLancey Estate: Did the Revolution Democratize Landholding in New York?" *New York History*, XVII (April 1936), 167–79; Yoshpe, *The Disposition of Loyalist Estates in Southern New York* (New York, 1939); Catherine S. Crary, "Forfeited Loyalist Lands in the Western District of New York—Albany and Tryon Counties," *New York History*, XXXV (July 1954), 239–58; Beatrice G. Reubens, "Pre-Emptive Rights in the Disposition of a Confiscated Estate: Philipsburgh Manor, New York," *William and Mary Quarterly*, XXII (July 1965), 435–56; A. Day Bradley, "New York Friends and the Confiscated Loyalist Estates," *Quaker History*, LXI (Spring 1972), 36–39.

24. Both quoted in Larzer Ziff, *Puritanism in America: New Culture in a New World* (New York, 1973), pp. 14, 21.

25. "The Notebook of the Reverend John Fiske, 1644–1675," ed. Robert G. Pope, *Publications of the Colonial Society of Massachusetts*, XLVII (Boston, 1974), p. 3.

26. "The Autobiography of Increase Mather," ed. Michael G. Hall, *Proceedings of the American Antiquarian Society*, LXXI, pt. 2 (Worcester, Mass., 1962), 308.

27. Washington is quoted in Arthur M. Schlesinger, *Learning How to Behave* (New York, 1946), p. 5; William Eddis, *Letters from America*, ed. Aubrey C. Land (Cambridge, Mass., 1969), p. 103.

28. I have used the early edition of his collected *Works*, VIII (1752), 289–302. The quotation which follows is from 289–90.

29. See Philip Furneaux, *The Palladium of Conscience* (Philadelphia, 1773), a British tract which was reprinted twice in the colonies during the years before the Revolution.

30. William Ames, *Conscience with the Power and Cases Thereof* (London, 1639), Book IV, p. 54.

31. See *The Political Works of James I*, ed. Charles Howard McIlwain (Cambridge, Mass., 1918), pp. lii, lv, lxxix; Christopher Hill, *Society and Puritanism in Pre-Revolutionary England* (London, 1964), pp. 382–419.

32. See Charles F. Mullett, "Religion, Politics, and Oaths in the Glorious Revolution," *Review of Politics*, X (Oct. 1948), 462–74; Gerald M. Straka, *Anglican Reaction to the Revolution of 1688* (Madison, 1962), ch. 4, "The Oath of Allegiance and the Origins of Government"; J. W. C. Wand, *The High Church Schism: Four Lectures on the Nonjurors* (London, 1951), pp. 8–19; and L. M. Hawkins, *Allegiance in Church and State: The Problem of the Non-Jurors in the English Revolution* (London, 1928).

33. See *The English Catholic Nonjurors of 1715*, ed. Edgar E. Estcourt (1885; reprinted at Westmead, Hants., 1969). After 1702, when a new oath was imposed upon the English clergy requiring them to abjure all allegiance to "the pretended Prince of Wales," the vulnerability of many churchmen to non-juring doctrine was visibly heightened. See Geoffrey Holmes, *The Trial of Doctor Sacheverell* (London, 1973), pp. 22, 23.

34. Edward A. Hoyt, "Naturalization under the American Colonies: Signs of a New Community," *Political Science Quarterly*, LXVII (June 1952), 255.

35. Thomas Clap, *The Annals, or History of Yale College* (New Haven, 1766; Evans #10262), pp. 61–66.

36. *Collections of The New-York Historical Society for the Year 1923* (New York, 1923), pp. 84–85. On October 31, 1765, Colden had, in fact, appeared before the council and taken the following oath: "You Swear that you shall do your utmost that all and every the Clauses contained in an Act of the Parliament of Great Britain, passed

in the fifth Year of the Reign of our Sovereign Lord King George the Third, . . . be punctually and bona fide observed according to the true intent and meaning thereof, so far as appertains unto you. So help you God" (*ibid.*, p. 64).

37. *Ibid.*, p. 88.

38. Herbert M. Morais, "The Sons of Liberty in New York," in *The Era of The American Revolution: Studies Inscribed to Evarts Boutell Greene*, ed. Richard B. Morris (New York, 1939), p. 275.

39. See Nicholas Varga, "The New York Restraining Act: Its Passage and Some Effects, 1766–1768," *New York History*, XXXVII (July 1956), 247.

40. Bruce Bliven, Jr., *Under the Guns: New York, 1775–1776* (New York, 1972), p. 50.

41. Harold M. Hyman, *To Try Men's Souls: Loyalty Tests in American History* (Berkeley and Los Angeles, 1959), p. 70; Arthur M. Schlesinger, *The Colonial Merchants and the American Revolution, 1763–1776* (New York, 1917), pp. 552–59.

42. Samuel Seabury, *The Congress Canvassed: or, an Examination Into the Conduct of the Delegates, at their Grand Convention* . . . (New York, 1774), pp. 14–16.

43. Quoted in Bruce E. Steiner, *Samuel Seabury, 1729–1796: A Study in the High Church Tradition* (Oberlin, 1971), p. 165.

44. A resolution extracted from the minutes, July 16, 1776, *American Archives: Containing a Documentary History of the United States of America, from* . . . *1776 to* . . . *1783*, compiled by Peter Force (Washington, D.C., 1837–53), 5th ser., I, 447. For the interrogation of Whitehead Hicks and Samuel Martin in June 1776 see *ibid.*, 4th ser., VI, 1159–60.

45. *John Jay, the Making of a Revolutionary: Unpublished Papers, 1745–1780*, ed. Richard B. Morris (New York, 1975), pp. 332–33.

46. *Ibid.*, pp. 347–48.

47. *Ibid.* For other examples of the prejudice against "Persons of neutral and equivocal Characters" see *Minutes of the Commissioners for Detecting and Defeating Conspiracies in the State of New York: Albany County Sessions, 1778–1781*, ed. Victor H. Paltsits (Albany, 1909), I, 180, 186, 268, 286, 295, 310, 311.

48. Thomas Anburey, *Travels through the Interior Parts of America* (Boston, 1923), II, 153–54.

49. Hector St. Jean de Crèvecoeur, *Letters from an American Farmer and Sketches of Eighteenth-Century America* (New York, 1963), pp. 197–204.

50. See Julia Post Mitchell, *St. Jean De Crèvecoeur* (New York, 1916), pp. 45–46; Claude-Anne Lopez, *Mon Cher Papa: Franklin and the Ladies of Paris* (New Haven, 1966), pp. 158–162.

51. Plutarch, "Solon," in *The Lives of the Noble Grecians and Romans*, trans. John Dryden (New York [Modern Library]), n.d., 108–9; Aristotle, *Constitution of Athens*, VIII, 5, trans. Kurt von Fritz and Ernst Kapp (New York, 1950), 76. Solon's law "against neutrality" would be quoted by John Jay during the war and cited in turn by Peter Van Schaack in a letter to Jay, Aug. 14, 1778. See Henry C. Van Schaack, *The Life of Peter Van Schaack . . .* (New York, 1842), p. 122.

52. Edmund Burke, *Thoughts on the Cause of the Present Discontents* (London, 1770), p. 115.

53. Quoted in Moses Coit Tyler, *The Literary History of the American Revolution, 1763–1783* (1897; reprinted New York, 1957, 1970), II, 54–55.

54. This and other oaths are printed in *Minutes of the Commissioners, Albany Sessions*, II, 831–33.

55. *The Constitutional History of New York . . .* , compiled by Charles Z. Lincoln (Rochester, 1906), I, 173.

56. See Hyman, *To Try Men's Souls*, pp. 88–90. Hyman's fourth chapter is much the best previous work in this subject, and I am indebted to his thoughtful, pioneering book. He is not always precise about dates, however, or entirely clear about the phasing of change between 1775 and 1781. One of the ways in which my expanded treatment differs from his is in giving greater attention to matters of chronology and context. Some pertinent material may also be found in two older monographs: Alexander C. Flick, *Loyalism in New York During the American Revolution* (New York, 1901), pp. 130–31, 168–69, 184–85; and Claude H. Van Tyne, *The Loyalists in the American Revolution* (New York, 1902), p. 271.

57. *The Minute Book of the Committee of Safety of Tryon County . . .* , ed. J. Howard Hanson and Samuel Ludlow Frey (New York, 1905), pp. 31–32.

58. *Ibid.*, pp. 49, 56–57, 61.

59. *Ibid.*, pp. 99–100.

60. *Journals of the Provincial Congress, Provincial Convention, Committee of Safety, and Council of Safety of the State of New York, 1775–1777* (Albany, 1842), II, 190–91.

61. *Ibid.*, II, 148.

62. *Ibid.*, II, 183–84. On Dec. 31, 1776, Gale was finally permitted to take the oath of allegiance and was discharged. For an earlier appeal from Fairfield jail, by Angus McDonald, see *ibid.*, II, 76.

63. See Alice P. Kenney, "The Albany Dutch: Loyalists and Patriots," *New York History*, XLII (Oct. 1961), 337, 343.

64. Force, *American Archives*, 4th ser., VI, 1368–69.

65. Minutes of the Committee of Safety, Brookhaven, New York; Manuscript Room, New York Public Library, case 12.

66. *Ibid.*

67. *Ibid.*

68. Morris, *John Jay: Unpublished Papers, 1745–1780*, pp. 13–14, 287–88, 331.

69. *Ibid.*, pp. 322, 350–51.

70. *Ibid.*, pp. 352–53. For Jay's interrogation of Robinson on February 22, see *The Price of Loyalty: Tory Writings from the Revolutionary Era*, ed. Catherine S. Crary (New York, 1973), pp. 148–49.

71. *Journals of the Provincial Congress*, I, 827, 835, 839, 906, 924, 937, 940, 945, 948, 954, 959, 960, 963, 965, 969, 976, 978, 996, 1051, 1071, 1074. See also Morris, *John Jay: Unpublished Papers, 1745–1780*, pp. 349–51. This resolution offering a second chance, as it were, did not extend to those who were "charged with taking up arms against the United States, with enlisting men for the service of the enemy, accepting a warrant or a commission for that purpose, supplying them with provisions, or conveying intelligence to them."

72. *Journals of the Provincial Congress*, I, 844.

73. *Ibid.*, II, 398.

74. See, for example, the fascinating case of David Mathews, mayor of New York, who was accused in the summer of 1776 of conspiring to murder George Washington and betray the city to the British. Mathews would not accept the legitimacy of the patriot court in which he was being tried. "You must therefore use your pleasure," he argued, "for I cannot in my conscience admit of any authority in this body, to try and confine, or punish any subject of England." To

which the court responded: "We are convinced of your guilt, and recommend you to make a confession and repent of your crimes. Your confession may entitle you not only to mercy, but if we discover sincerity in your reformation, a person of your station and influence, may expect every favour from your country." Mathews would accept no favor under dishonorable circumstances, however: "I avow my principles, and shall never swerve from them." *See Minutes of the Trial and Examination of Certain Persons, in the Province of New York, Charged with Being Engaged in a Conspiracy Against the Authority of the Congress* (London, 1786), pp. 41–42, 44.

75. See, for example, Walter Butler's letter to Horatio Gates, October 1, 1777, asking to be released from jail: "The multiplying of words or making declarations which I do not mean my Conscience and Honor forbids . . ." (quoted in Howard Swiggett, *War Out of Niagara. Walter Butler and the Tory Rangers* [New York, 1933], p. 101).

76. Paltsits, *Minutes of the Commissioners, Albany Sessions*, II, 747.

77. *Minutes of the Committee and of the First Commission for Detecting and Defeating Conspiracies in the State of New York, December 11, 1776–September 23, 1778* (New York, 1924), in *Collections of the New York Historical Society for the Year 1924*, LVII, 169 (hereafter referred to as *Minutes of the First Commission for Detecting Conspiracies, 1776–1778*). See also *Minutes of the Albany Committee of Correspondence, 1775–1778*, ed. James Sullivan (Albany, 1923), I, 803.

78. *Minutes of the First Commission for Detecting Conspiracies, 1776–1778*, pp. 107, 304.

79. *Ibid.*, pp. 211–12.

80. January 21, 1777. *Ibid.*, pp. 115–16.

81. *Ibid.*, p. 159. See also, in the same volume, pp. 21, 25, 27, 38, 48, 49, 56, 59, 69.

82. *Ibid.*, p. 86. See also pp. 90, 93, 133, 141, 196, 324, 345, 359.

83. *Ibid.*, p. 152.

84. *Ibid.*, pp. 262, 275, 322, 326, 327, 336, 338.

85. Sullivan, *Minutes of the Albany Committee, 1775–1778*, pp. 599, 751, 760, 762, 765, 766, 768, 769, 775, 790, 792, 796, 921, 1136–37.

86. *Ibid.*, pp. 876, 902.

87. *Ibid.*, p. 905; Paltsits, *Minutes of the Commissioners, Albany Sessions,* pp. 98, 213.

88. *Ibid.*, pp. 91, 102, 104, 171, 185, 186, 188, 195, 197, 228, 310–11, 367, 630–31.

89. *Ibid.*, pp. 189, 194.

90. *Ibid.*, p. 216.

91. *Ibid.*, pp. 275–76.

92. *Ibid.*, pp. 344, 346, 359.

93. *Ibid.*, pp. 388–89.

94. *Ibid.*, pp. 399, 504–5, 712.

95. *Minutes of the First Commission for Detecting Conspiracies, 1776–1778,* p. 39.

96. *Ibid.*, 207, 223, 225.

97. *Ibid.*, pp. 315, 320, 321–22, 373–74, 441, 445–46.

98. *Ibid.*, pp. 447–48. See also William S. Livingston, "Emigration as a Theoretical Doctrine During the American Revolution," *Journal of Politics,* XIX (Nov. 1957), 607.

99. E.g., *Minutes of the First Commission for Detecting Conspiracies, 1776–1778,* pp. 218, 219, 227–28, 231, 232, 234, 235; *Minutes of the Commissioners, Albany Sessions,* pp. 542, 712–13.

100. See Paltsits, *Minutes of the Commissioners, Albany Sessions,* pp. 172, 175, 176, 183, 193–94, 200, 209.

101. See *ibid.*, pp. 281, 286–87, 295, 834–35.

102. *Minutes of the First Commission for Detecting Conspiracies, 1776–1778,* p. 203. On December 16, 1776, the committee for Claverack District had established a general oath of allegiance (*ibid.*, p. 26).

103. Sullivan, *Minutes of the Albany Committee, 1775–1778,* I, 800, 808.

104. *Minutes of the First Commission for Detecting Conspiracies, 1776–1778,* p. 398.

105. Dated June 6, 1777, printed in *Journals of the Provincial Congress,* II, 443.

106. Colden's 196-page letterbook and journal, covering the years 1776–79, is in the Huntington Library, San Marino, California (HM

607). It has no pagination; but see especially (on the microfilm), frames 2, 17–18, 20, 29–30, 40, 101–2.

107. See *Minutes of the First Commission for Detecting Conspiracies, 1776–1778*, pp. 14, 205–6 (proceedings for November 25, 1776, and March 19, 1777).

108. Crary, *The Price of Loyalty*, p. 227. The petition of Rose and Midagh (to the Convention) for a stay of execution, dated May 13, 1777, opens with these words: "altho their conscience doth not in the least accuse them of being Guilty of any sin against God or their Country . . . yet your Petitioners are heartily sorry for having incurr'd the Displeasure of your House in so sensible a manner" (*ibid.,* p. 299).

109. *Ibid.,* p. 228.

110. *Public Papers of George Clinton* (New York, 1900), II, 340.

111. Quoted in Joseph Bragdon, "Cadwallader Colden, 2d, an Ulster County Tory," *New York History,* XIV (Oct. 1933), 418.

112. See also "Letter of David Colden, Loyalist, 1783," ed. E. Alfred Jones, *American Historical Review,* XXV (Oct. 1919), 79–86.

113. Thomas Jones, *History of New York During the Revolutionary War . . .* (New York, 1879), I, 41–42; Henry C. Van Schaack, *The Life of Peter Van Schaack . . . Embracing Selections from His Correspondence and Other Writings During the American Revolution* (New York, 1842), esp. pp. 48–94. See also William A. Benton, "Peter Van Schaack: The Conscience of a Loyalist," in East and Judd, *The Loyalist Americans,* pp. 44–55.

114. Article XXXVIII in the Constitution of 1777 concerned religious toleration. It ordained that "the free exercise and enjoyment of religious profession and worship, without discrimination or preference, shall forever hereafter be allowed within this state to all mankind: *Provided,* That the liberty of conscience hereby granted shall not be so construed as to excuse acts of licentiousness, or justify practices inconsistent with the peace or safety of this state." See Lincoln, *Constitutional History of New York,* I, 185–86.

115. Van Schaack, *Life of Peter Van Schaack,* pp. 103, 121–25. For an excellent account of the Van Schaacks throughout the revolutionary era, see R. J. Ashton, "The Loyalist Experience: New York, 1763–1789" (Ph.D. dissertation, Northwestern University, 1973), pp. 99–115, 135–36, 185–92.

116. *Minutes of the First Commission for Detecting Conspiracies, 1776–1778,* pp. 275, 279, 280–81, 315.

117. Henry Cruger Van Schaack, *Memoirs of the Life of Henry Van Schaack, Embracing Selections from His Correspondence during the American Revolution* (Chicago, 1892), pp. 63–64.

118. *Ibid.*, pp. 79–80, 82–83. On pp. 80–81 of this important compilation, the editor includes a lengthy letter from Goldsbrow Banyar, of Albany, to James Duane, dated Sept. 16, 1778. Here are two brief excerpts: "My views are yet what you always supposed them to be, but I never expected to be driven to the present alternative of sacrificing them or violating my conscience. . . . It must appear I think, to anyone, a matter of great difficulty to swear a country of **RIGHT INDEPENDENT** while the contest exists, the event of which can only determine whether it shall be so or not. But if he can even digest this, must not his conscience revolt when he is called to swear also that the state or country comprehends places never in their possession, and that no authority can be exercised of right in those places but what is derived from the people of the state, when the fact is, that there is an authority exercised there not by them, and whether of right cannot be doubted, as it may be the same that existed there before the state was formed, or an authority exerted in right of conquest."

119. *Ibid.*, pp. 92–93. See also the immensely interesting retrospective letter written from London by Peter Van Schaack to William Laight, Aug. 16, 1784, *ibid.*, 116–17.

120. *Ibid.*, 108–9. On p. 218 the descendant who compiled these memoirs summarized Van Schaack's principles and attendant behavior: "before the revolution he was a loyal subject of the British crown, and therefore through the struggle, although a warm friend to his country, for his oath's sake, he could not for conscience's sake take any active part in defense of the colonies, for which he severely suffered in person and purse."

121. *Minute Book of the Committee of Safety of Tryon County*, p. 84.

122. *Minutes of the First Commission for Detecting Conspiracies, 1776–1778*, p. 69.

123. Sullivan, *Minutes of the Albany Committee of Correspondence, 1775–1778*, pp. 413, 665; Paltsits, *Minutes of the Commissioners, Albany Sessions*, pp. 177–78, 542. See also "Proceedings in New-York in Relation to Disaffected Persons, 1776," in Force, *American Archives,* ser. 4, VI, 1152–83.

124. Jay to Van Schaack, Sept. 17, 1782, Jay Papers, Columbia University.

125. Extract of a letter received in London, dated Oct. 20, 1776, printed in Force, *American Archives*, ser. 5, II, 1136.

126. See Oscar T. Barck, *New York City during the War for Independence with Special Reference to the Period of British Occupation* (New York, 1931), pp. 49–50; Frederick Bernays Wiener, *Civilians under Military Justice. The British Practice since 1689, Especially in North America* (Chicago, 1967), pp. 98, 102.

127. Force, *American Archives*, ser. 5, II, 1200–1201; Morris, *John Jay: Unpublished Papers, 1745–1780*, p. 354. "Occupation of New York City by the British, 1776. Extracts from the Diary of the Moravian Congregation," *Pennsylvania Magazine of History & Biography*, X (1886), 421.

128. Sullivan, *Minutes of the Albany Committee of Correspondence, 1775–1778*, p. 672.

129. Quoted in Webb Garrison, *Sidelights on the American Revolution* (Nashville, 1974), p. 102. See also Doris Begor Morton, *Philip Skene of Skenesborough* (Granville, N.Y., 1959), pp. 55–56. On July 12, 1777, General Burgoyne appointed Skene to administer the oath of allegiance in his area and to grant certificates of protection to those inhabitants who wished to remain loyal to the Crown.

130. *Minutes of the First Commission for Detecting Conspiracies, 1776–1778*, pp. 192–94, 211–12.

131. See Hyman, *To Try Men's Souls*, pp. 91, 94.

132. Quoted in Richard B. Morris, "The American Revolution Comes to John Jay," in *Aspects of Early New York Society and Politics*, ed. Jacob Judd and Irwin H. Polishook (Tarrytown, 1974), p. 115.

133. See John R. Alden, *General Charles Lee: Traitor or Patriot?* (Baton Rouge, 1951), pp. 100–101; Lee to Provincial Congress, March 6, 1776, "The Lee Papers," in *Collections of the New-York Historical Society for the Year 1871* (New York, 1872), I, 351.

134. *Ibid.*, p. 352.

135. See Bliven, *Under the Guns: New York, 1775–1776*, pp. 88–90, 109–10, 113–14. The oath Lee concocted was a lulu: "I, ——, here, in the presence of Almighty God, as I hope for ease, honor and comfort in this world, and happiness in the world to come, most earnestly, devoutly, and religiously do swear. . . ." (*ibid.*, p. 180).

136. *Letters of Members of the Continental Congress*, ed. Edmund C. Burnett (Washington, D.C., 1921–36), I, 389–90; *Journals of the Continental Congress, 1774–1789*, ed. Worthington C. Ford et al. (Washington, D.C., 1906), IV, 195.

137. *Journals of the Provincial Congress*, II, 461–62.

138. *The Writings of George Washington . . . 1745–1799*, ed. John C. Fitzpatrick (Washington, D.C., 1934), XI, 410–11.

139. Paltsits, *Minutes of the Commissioners, Albany Sessions*, pp. 112, 204, 213.

140. We have, for example, this delightful interrogation of Major Isaac Reeve in Suffolk County, Long Island, during 1778. The Tory troops seized him, brought him before Governor Tryon, and coerced him into taking an oath of allegiance to George III (they threatened to hang him from a large tree if he refused). Reeve's dialogue with another prisoner went this way: John Benjamin said to Mr. Reeve, "Are you going to take the oath?" "Yes." "I wont." "You must." "No, I wont." When Benjamin's turn came, he was asked his occupation. "A Presbyterian." "I mean, what is your business?" "A Presbyterian." "What do you bring this fool here for?" said Tryon. "Take him away." See Henry Onderdonk, Jr., *Revolutionary Incidents of Suffolk and Kings Counties; with an Account of the Battle of Long Island, and the British Prisons and Prison-Ships at New-York* (New York, 1849), pp. 76–77.

141. See Peter Brock, *Pacifism in the United States, from the Colonial Era to the First World War* (Princeton, 1968), pp. 198, 221–22, 224–27, 229, 232; Bliss Forbush, *Elias Hicks: Quaker Liberal* (New York, 1956), pp. 37, 41, 49–50; *Journal of the Life and Religious Labours of Elias Hicks. Written by Himself*, 5th ed. (New York, 1832), p. 17; John Cox, Jr., *Quakerism in the City of New York, 1657–1930* (New York, 1930), pp. 75–80; and *A Journal of the Life and Gospel Labors of That Devoted Servant and Minister of Christ Joseph Hoag* (Sherwoods, N.Y., 1860), pp. 12–13, 17–18, 21. In 1777 a band of patriotic rangers commanded Hoag's father to join them in pursuit of some drafted men who had disappeared. The father refused to comply and, when his life was threatened, replied: "that thou mayest do, for I shall not put my life against my conscience" (*ibid.*, p. 18).

142. Brock, *Pacifism in the United States*, pp. 222, 241; Hyman, *To Try Men's Souls*, p. 91.

143. See *Minutes of the First Commission for Detecting Conspiracies, 1776–1778*, pp. 85, 197, 225, 308, 328.

144. "New York Quakers in the American Revolution," ed. Arthur J. Mekeel, *Bulletin of Friends Historical Association*, XXIX (1940), 52.

145. *Ibid.*, p. 55. See also A. Day Bradley, "New York Friends and the Loyalty Oath of 1778," *Quaker History*, LVII (Autumn 1968), 112–114.

146. Brock, *Pacifism in the United States*, p. 247.

147. See Wiener, *Civilians under Military Justice*, p. 96.

148. See Brock, *Pacifism in the United States*, p. 274, and especially p. 275 for the testimony of Samuel Johnson, a Presbyterian convert to Shakerism who insisted that "*the followers of Christ could have nothing to do with wars and fightings*" (Johnson's italics).

149. See *Minutes of the First Commission for Detecting Conspiracies, 1776–1778*, p. 400; and Ralph T. Pastore, "The Board of Commissioners for Indian Affairs in the Northern Department and the Iroquois Indians, 1775–1778" (Ph.D. dissertation, Notre Dame, 1972).

150. [Winthrop Sargent, ed.], *The Loyalist Poetry of the Revolution* (Philadelphia, 1857), p. 98.

151. Force, *American Archives*, 4th ser., VI, 781–82.

152. From Passy, France, June 26, 1785, in *The Writings of Benjamin Franklin*, ed. Albert H. Smyth (New York, 1906), IX, 348.

153. From Paris, Sept. 17, 1782, in William Jay, *The Life of John Jay: With Selections from His Correspondence and Miscellaneous Papers* (New York, 1833), I, 161. For Jay's reservations about nonjuring Anglican clergymen, however, see his letter to John Adams from New York, Nov. 1, 1785, in *The Works of John Adams . . . ,* ed. Charles Francis Adams (Boston, 1853), VIII, 335.

154. Oct. 15, in Jay, *Life of John Jay*, I, 163–64.

155. See Goffman, *Stigma: Notes on the Management of Spoiled Identity* (Englewood Cliffs, 1963); and Oscar Zeichner, "The Loyalist Problem in New York after the Revolution," *New York History*, XXI (July 1940), 284–302. For various oaths required by law, and still on the books after the war, see *Laws of the Legislature of the State of New York, in Force Against the Loyalists, and Affecting the Trade of Great Britain, and British Merchants, and Others Having Property in That State* (London, 1786), pp. 89, 90, 100–101, 106–7.

156. From Canajohary, Feb. 26, 1823, Ayer Ms. 944A, f. 315, The Newberry Library, Chicago. For the contextual developments, see James H. Kettner, "The Development of American Citizenship in the Revolutionary Era: The Idea of Volitional Allegiance," *American Journal of Legal History*, XVIII (July 1974), 208–42.

157. *Minutes of the First Commission for Detecting Conspiracies, 1776–1778*, pp. 232–33.

158. Dated April 30, 1777; in Crary, *The Price of Loyalty*, pp. 151–52.

159. To cite a few examples, see the John Peters Papers in the New-York Historical Society and the New York State Library in Albany; *Minutes of the Council of Safety of the State of New Jersey* (Jersey City, 1872); N. P. Waldenmaier, *Some of the Earliest Oaths of Allegiance to the United States of America* (Lancaster, Pa., 1944), pp. 1–12; the bound volume of oaths of allegiance signed in 1781 by South Carolina Loyalists (New York Public Library, Manuscript Room); Max Savelle, "Nationalism and Other Loyalties in the American Revolution," *American Historical Review*, LXVII (July 1962), 915; Bruce G. Merritt, "Loyalism and Social Conflict in Revolutionary Deerfield, Massachusetts," *Journal of American History*, LVII (Sept. 1970), 277–89; and G. N. D. Evans, ed., *Allegiance in America: The Case of the Loyalists* (Reading, Mass., 1969).

160. In *The Fear of Conspiracy: Images of Un-American Subversion from the Revolution to the Present*, ed. David Brion Davis (Ithaca, 1971), the documents jump from 1774 to 1795. Richard J. Regan's *Private Conscience and Public Law. The American Experience* (New York, 1972) ranges broadly through various aspects of recent American history and includes a twenty-seven-page appendix on "Western Traditions of Conscience," yet omits any discussion of the American Revolution.

Index

Adams, John, 4, 5, 87–88, 90–91, 92–97, 103, 107, 109, 111, 112, 118, 121, 123–24, 128
Adams, Samuel, 78, 87, 91, 121
Addison, Joseph, 44, 54
Aix-la-Chapelle, Treaty of (1748), 110
Albany County Committee of Safety, 148, 159
allegiance, oaths of, *see* oaths, oath-taking
Allestree, Richard, 44
American history, tragedy in, 188–89
American Revolution
  as *crise de conscience*, 12, 125–89
  French Revolution and, 21
  ideological vs. political economist views of, 126–28, 130
  renewed interest in, 5–6
  shifting views on, 3–5, 126–28
Ames, John, 77
Ames, William, 133, 135
Andros, Edmund, 10, 83, 86, 105, 106–8, 109, 119
Anglicans, 36, 37, 75, 136, 163, 181
"aristocrat," label of, 124
Aristotle, 142

Bailyn, Bernard, 11, 126–27, 128
Baker, Benjamin, 172
Baker, Jonathan, 152
Banishing Act (1778), 167, 171
banks, Massachusetts
  currency debate and, 113–17
  private, petitions for, 117–18, 120

Baptist dissenters, 19, 36–37
Beard, Charles, 128
Beardsley, John, 162–63
Becker, Carl L., 126, 128, 129, 131, 132
Beekman, John, 146
Belcher, Jonathan, 117
Bemus, Thomas, 158
Benson, Egbert, 153–55, 162, 164
Benton, Thomas Hart, 124
Berkeley, Norbone, 42
Bernard, Sir Francis, 90–91, 92
Bicentennial celebration, 5–6
Blackstone, Sir William, 44
Blair, James, 75
Bland, Richard, 8, 20, 33, 44, 45, 46–47, 49, 53, 56, 61, 62–63
Bliven, Bruce, 138
Board of Trade, 117
Body of Liberties (1641), 101
Bolingbroke, Henry St. John, 44, 134
Boston
  Anglican episcopate proposed for, 10–11, 86–87
  as crucible for rebellion, 9, 79, 120–21
  currency shortage in, 117
  opposition to Parliamentary taxation in, 120–21
  rural links with, 81
  uprising in (1689), 106–7
Boston Committee of Correspondence, 78, 79, 80, 81, 91, 117, 122
Boston Gazette, 78, 80, 90–91, 93, 97
Boston Massacre orations, 79, 90

Index

Massachusetts
  activist network in, 81
  boundary disputes of, 109–11,
      118, 119
  break with feudalism in, 101–4,
      123–24
  currency problems in (1720–
      50), 113–18, 119
  landholdings restricted in, 124
  land monopolization in, 111–13,
      119
  land titles challenged in, 104–11,
      119
  loss of charter by (1684), 104,
      133–34
  oath-taking in, compared to
      New York, 171–72
  rural communities of, 9–10, 77–
      124; *see also* farmers, Mas-
      sachusetts
  town meetings in, 81
  "vernacular sociology" of, 10,
      84
Massachusetts Bay charter, 101,
      104, 107, 133–34
Massachusetts Gazette, 89
Massachusetts General Court, 101
Massachusetts in Agony, 115, 117
Mather, Cotton, 83, 84, 95
Mather, Increase, 134
Mathews, David, 174–75
Mayhew, Jonathan, 87, 92
*Melancholy State of the Province,
      The*, 115
Mercer, James, 71
Mercer, John, 64
merchants, British
  planters' indebtedness to, 69
  Virginia currency and, 66
Midagh, Jacob, 165–66
Miller, Perry, 156
Miller, Peter, 172
Milton, John, 44
Moravians, 181, 183
Morgan, Edmund S., 156
Morgan, Joseph, 112
Morris, Gouverneur, 146
Munford, Robert, 26–27, 28, 29

Nash, Daniel, 152
Nash, Gary, 130
Navigation Acts, 104
neo-Progressives, 126–28, 130
neutrality, 140–44
  "equivocal," 140
  loyalty oaths and, *see* oaths,
      oath-taking
  in Western thought, 142–43
New England (*see also* Massachu-
      setts)
  boundary disputes of, 109–11,
      118, 119
  feudal tyranny in, 10, 83–84, 93–
      98
  resistance to lordships seen as
      tradition in, 90–93, 97–98,
      100–4, 123
  tenancies sought in, 100
New Hampshire, 103
  Massachusetts boundary and,
      109–10, 111, 119
New Haven Colony, 102
*New News from Robinson
      Cruso's Island*, 115
New York, 125–89
  class conflict seen in, 129, 130
  Commission for Detecting and
      Defeating Conspiracies of,
      145–46, 154–55, 161, 170, 183
  Committee for Detecting Con-
      spiracies of, 140, 145–46, 153,
      157–58, 162, 175–76, 182
  Constitutional Convention of,
      139–40
  detecting conspiracies in, 144–
      55
  in historiographical context,
      126–31
  Massachusetts boundary and,
      109–11, 118, 119
  neutrality in, 12, 140–42, 154,
      167–73, 183–84, 185–86
  oath-taking in, 137–86; *see also*
      oaths, oath-taking
  Provincial Congress of, 150, 152,
      177

[229]